Icebergs & Belugas

Webber's Northern Lodges
A Fourth Batch of Our Most Requested Recipes

By
Helen Webber
&
Marie Woolsey

Includes Comprehensive Index for
Blueberries & Polar Bears, *Cranberries & Canada Geese*
and *Black Currants & Caribou*

Icebergs & Belugas

by
Helen Webber & Marie Woolsey

First Printing — November 2002

Copyright © 2002 by
Helen Webber & Marie Woolsey

Published by
Blueberries & Polar Bears Publishing
P.O. Box 304
Churchill, Manitoba
Canada   R0B 0E0

All rights reserved. Except for reviews, no part of this book may be reproduced without permission from the publisher.

Canadian Cataloguing in Publication Data

Webber, Helen, 1947 -

   Icebergs & belugas : Webber's northern lodges : a fourth batch of our most requested recipes / Helen Webber, Marie Woolsey.

   Includes index.
   ISBN 1-894022-81-5

   1. Cookery. I. Woolsey, Marie, 1942-   II. Title.
TX751.W423 2002   641.5   C2002-911362-8

Cover Painting by: Barbara Stone
Longmont, Colorado, U.S.A.

Photography on site at Seal River, north of Churchill, Manitoba by:
Ross (Hutch) Hutchinson, Hutchinson and Company, Chemainus, B.C.

Inuit Carvings compliments of: Northern Images
Churchill, Manitoba

Dinnerware from The Bay, Pier 1, Mikasa

Page formatting and index by Iona Glabus

Designed, Printed and Produced in Canada by:
Centax Books, a Division of PW Group
Publishing Director, Photo Designer & Food Stylist: Margo Embury
1150 Eighth Avenue, Regina, Saskatchewan, Canada S4R 1C9
(306) 525-2304   FAX: (306) 757-2439
E-mail: centax@printwest. com   www.centaxbooks.com

   *Introduction*

Table of Contents

From Marie & Helen 4

Introduction 6

Moose, Goose & Things That Swim 7

Bread & Breakfast 29

Midday Madness (Lunches & Soups) 57

Stop & Snack Awhile 71

Taste Teasers 91

Simply Salads 107

Vegging Out 119

Tame Meats To Make You Wild 141

Final Temptations 165

Icebergs & Belugas Index 207

Comprehensive Recipe Index 212

Comprehensive Story Index 221

Recipes have been tested in U.S. Standard measurements. Common metric measurements are given as a convenience for those who are more familiar with metric. Recipes have not been tested in metric.

DYMOND LAKE SEASONING (DLS) is our own unique blend of herbs and spices. It combines a wide range of flavors that enhance many different recipes. The flavor emphasis varies from recipe to recipe. Appropriate alternatives range from plain or seasoned salt and/or pepper to a combination of oregano, basil, parsley, thyme, celery salt, onion salt, paprika, pepper, salt and garlic powder. DLS CONTAINS NO MSG. Ask for DLS in your favorite grocery or food specialty store or order it directly, see page 223.

From Helen & Marie

(MARIE) As I write this, I am sitting in the dining room at Dymond Lake Hunting Lodge, near Churchill, Manitoba. It is September and one group of hunters is just leaving, another will be arriving later this evening. The Beaver on floats has just landed, flown by Helen's son-in-law Nelson – newly involved in the family business. Another son-in-law, David, is keeping the customers entertained with his quick wit and easy-going manner. When the plane lands in Churchill it will be met by my husband, Gary, now retired from full-time ministry. He will expedite customers to and from one of five lodges to hunt goose, moose or caribou; to fish or to observe wildlife. Webber's Lodges now involves Helen's whole family, including a nephew, Jeff, whom I am introducing here for a special reason. Jeff is a "chef extraordinaire" and it is our pleasure to include 10 of his personal recipes in this collection. You'll know them by the stick-man graphic beside them.

(HELEN) No one is more surprised than I am to have the three girls and their husbands involved in our Lodge business. It is another example of the Lord's wisdom surpassing ours! It is very exciting for a number of reasons, one being that it will give me more time to pursue our cookbook business with Marie, who will also have more flexibility now that Gary is retired.

(MARIE) Our cookbook business continues to grow, operating out of Calgary, Alberta, which Gary and I call home. *Icebergs & Belugas* has been 3 years in the making. Once the title was chosen, it was obvious to us that we had to do the pictures at Seal River Heritage Lodge, owned and operated by Helen's daughter Jeannie and her husband, Mike. This lodge is located on the coast of Hudson Bay, 25 minutes by air from Churchill. (See the map on the next page.) We were there in late August when the cloudberries were in full fruit, bringing the tundra alive with translucent dots of orange. The summer's fireweed also brightened the landscape, affording a great backdrop for one picture. What we couldn't show were the swarms of blackflies that challenged us whenever the wind subsided. Two of our pictures could only be taken when the tide was out; the rocks were totally submerged at high tide. As always, we had to wait for the sun to shine!

(HELEN) Seal River's scenery is phenomenal in its stark simplicity, as the pictures will attest. The food pictures are outstanding again thanks to the beautiful setting, the weather's co-operation, plus Margo, Hutch and Lynda's expertise. Near the lodge, beluga whales abound in the waters of Hudson Bay, just a short trip away by Zodiak. The belugas are very gentle, curious animals, so gentle that Mike was not at all concerned about towing Rebecca and Karli amongst them for the picture on page 70. One actually nudged Rebecca's leg. We hope these pictures will give you some idea of the unique and exciting environments that we are privileged to enjoy while indulging our love of cooking.

Introduction

Our thanks to Betty, at Northern Images in Churchill, who so generously lent us the carvings for the pictures. Then, when I called her five minutes before heading to the airplane en route to Seal River – on her day off, she graciously went to the shop and chose some ivory beluga earrings for our "author shot". The joys of living in a small town!

We can't forget to thank our husbands, Gary and Doug, who support us in all that we do, sometimes with a raised eyebrow or two. They have not only provided good material for some of our stories, but are willing to take on new roles as they come up. This fall they'll be serving guests and telling stories as we embark on our "Pioneers of Churchill" dinners. Who knows where they may escort us in our ever-expanding marketing adventures!

A very special thank you to all of you, our loyal customers. Thank you for the recipes you share with us as well as your feedback. We appreciate your support and look forward to hearing from you again in the future.

Bye for now from Helen and Marie, or as we are known in the radio lingo of the Lodges   – **Sweet Marie and Mother Goose.**

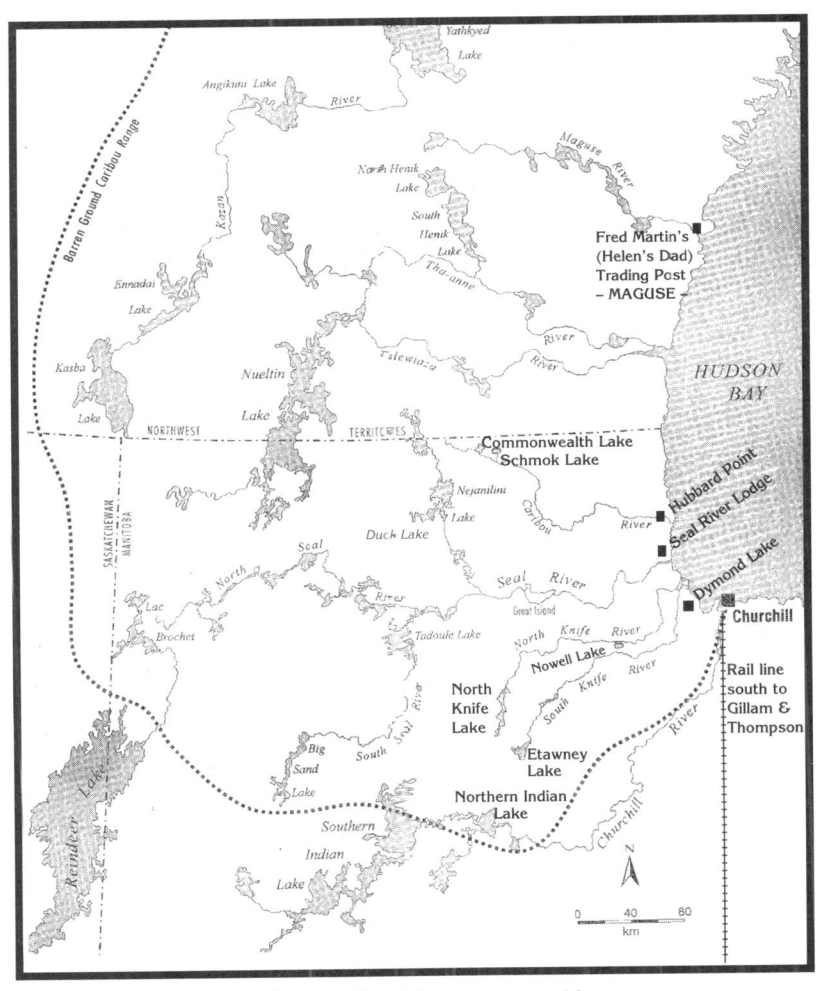

Churchill Area Map

Introduction

Introduction

"ANOTHER COOKBOOK" you say! Marie and I are just having so much fun we don't want to quit. Collecting, creating, gathering, testing and adapting recipes; eating and subjecting friends, family and strangers to tasting our experiments has just become a way of life. Lillian Vilborg, managing editor of the *Logberg-Heimskringla* – Manitoba's Icelandic weekly paper, whom we had never met, thought she was dropping in just to do an interview in Calgary – little did she know we had five wild rice recipes to test. We insisted she and her husband, Lorne, stay for lunch. Even dessert was "Creamy Wild Rice Pudding".

Coming up with a name for this fourth book presented quite a challenge. We had all kinds of help from family and friends, always followed by a good chuckle! *Muskox & Mushrooms, Sea Lettuce & Seals, Ptarmigan & Tundra* – anyway, you get the idea. Marie and I knew that when the time was right the name would come.

In keeping with the majesty of our arctic animals, we had pretty well decided we wanted to use the beluga whale, but what to go with it? We were tossing things back and forth, laughing and carrying on as we are wont to do at times, when all of a sudden Marie said *Icebergs & Belugas*. It just seemed to fit. Just in case we weren't sure, the next day a young friend, Shannon Neumann, who used to live in Churchill, dropped in as we were having dinner. She was quizzing us about when we were bringing out a new book. We said that we were thinking about doing one soon. Shannon blew us away when she responded with, "What are you going to call it? Icebergs and what . . . ? We looked at her in amazement and said, "What do you think we should put with it?" With no hesitation she said, *Icebergs & Belugas*! Marie and I looked at each other in absolute disbelief – well not really – once again we had confirmation that we were indeed on the right track. We hope that you all agree.

Moose, Goose & Things That Swim

We are constantly on the search for tastier and more interesting recipes to add to our wild meat repertoire. Our Crusty Caribou Tenderloin with Mushroom and Red Wine Reduction is nothing short of outstanding; our Brined Wild Goose had the hunters awed by its tenderness and moistness, so unusual in a roasted wild bird; Soused Trout regularly received accolades at the fishing lodge. We have also been introduced this year to the wonderful taste of bison and, though it is not named specifically, we have used it freely in appropriate wild game and beef recipes. Please use whatever is available to you and enjoy the rich flavors of these healthy choices.

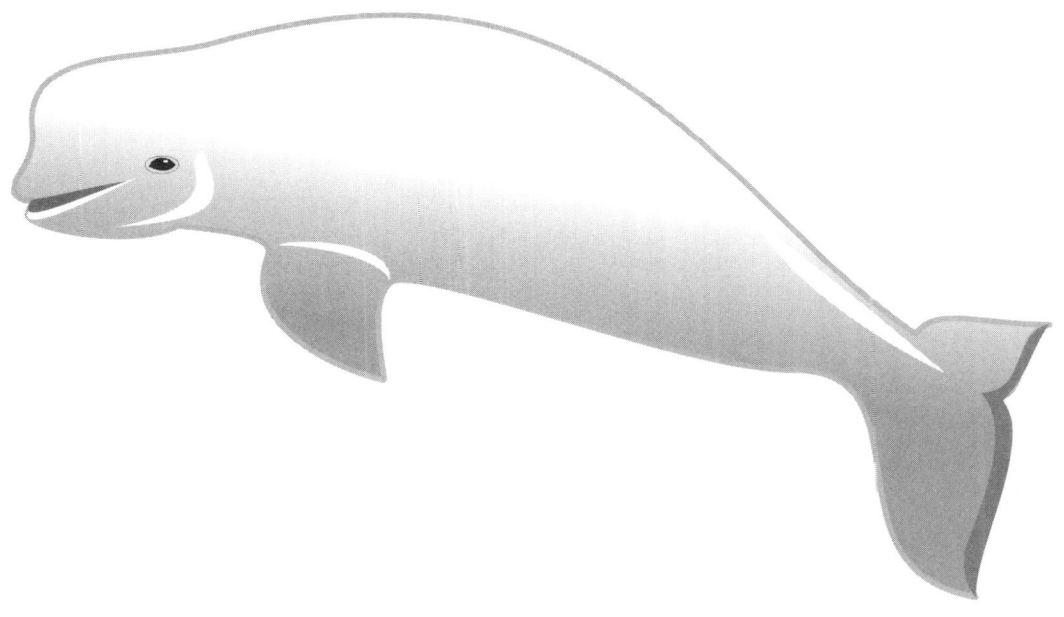

Marinated BBQ Moose Roast

(HELEN) As I have mentioned before, I am fortunate to have a family that is always looking for new culinary delights. This recipe came to us through Garry and Merelyn, my Calgary in-laws. Moose is called for here but, as always, we urge you to try caribou, deer, elk, beef or any other red meat! You have to start this dish one day before you want to eat it as it marinates for at least 24 hours.

Ginger Garlic Marinade:

1½ cups	vegetable oil	375 mL
¾ cup	soy sauce	175 mL
¼ cup	Worcestershire sauce	60 mL
½ cup	lemon juice	125 mL
2 tbsp.	dry mustard	30 mL
2 tbsp.	crushed fresh garlic	30 mL
2 tsp.	salt*	10 mL
1 tbsp.	pepper	15 mL
1 tbsp.	minced fresh ginger	15 mL
½ cup	red OR white wine vinegar	125 mL
1½ tsp.	parsley flakes	7 mL
3"	boneless top round moose steak OR 4-5 lb. (1.8-2.3 kg) boneless moose roast	8 cm

1. Combine all of the marinade ingredients in a large glass or stainless steel bowl (not aluminum), mixing well. Remove 1 cup (250 mL) of the marinade, put it in a covered container and refrigerate until ready to cook the roast.
2. Poke the meat well with a fork. Place the meat in a strong plastic bag, with no holes, and pour the remaining marinade over it. Refrigerate for 24-48 hours.
3. Cook over medium heat on a barbecue**, brushing occasionally with the reserved marinade, until done to your liking.

Serves 12-14.

* If you have Dymond Lake Seasoning on hand, you can substitute 1 tsp. (5 mL) salt and 1 tbsp. (15 mL) of Dymond Lake Seasoning for the 2 tsp. (10 mL) of salt.

** The broiler also works well for cooking this steak, and I have done the roast in the oven with very good results.

Moose, Goose & Things That Swim

Schmock Lake Caribou Liver

Schmock Lake is one of the caribou hunting lodges owned by Webber's Lodges. Helen isn't normally there (it's where Jeff cooks!) but in late September she got stranded at Schmock Lake en route to North Knife Lake by high winds and snow. Jeff was serving this wonderful liver dish and we had to have the recipe!

Garlic, Ginger and Soy Marinade:

½ cup	soy sauce	125 mL
¼ cup	brown sugar	60 mL
3-4	cloves garlic, crushed	3-4
1 tbsp.	chopped, fresh ginger	15 mL
1	caribou (deer, moose, elk, bison) liver, sliced to ¼" (1 cm) thickness, approximately 1½-2 lbs. (750 g-1 kg)	1
	bacon drippings	
2 cups	sliced onions	500 mL

1. In a small bowl, combine the soy sauce, brown sugar, garlic and ginger. Marinate the liver in the marinade for 4-8 hours.
2. Remove the liver from the marinade. In a large frying pan, melt the bacon drippings and sauté the liver quickly over medium-high heat. Place the liver on a plate and keep warm in a 200°F (93°C) oven.
3. Add more drippings to the pan; add onions and sauté, de-glazing the pan as you cook them. Cook until soft.
4. Serve the onions over the liver.

Serves 4.

VARIATION: If game liver is not available, try this delicious marinade with chicken livers. They can be sautéed and served with sautéed sliced green onions as a main dish or served without the onions as an appetizer.

Moose, Goose & Things That Swim

Crusted Caribou Tenderloin with Mushroom and Red Wine Reduction

Two thumbs up is what the guests we invited to our testing gave this dish. Use any tenderloin available, moose, elk, deer, beef or pork – but DO plan ahead, and DON'T let the long name put you off. This is definitely a company pleaser!

1 tbsp.	coriander OR mustard seeds	15 mL
1 tbsp.	black peppercorns	15 mL
3 tbsp.	Dijon mustard	45 mL
2 tbsp.	minced fresh thyme leaves OR 1 tbsp. (15 mL) dried	30 mL
3 lb.	caribou tenderloin OR back strip	1.5 kg
2 cups	soft white bread crumbs	500 mL
½ cup	finely chopped fresh parsley OR 2 tbsp. (30 mL) dried	125 mL
2-3 tbsp.	olive oil	30-45 mL
1 tsp.	salt	5 mL

Mushroom and Red Wine Reduction:

1 cup	chopped shiitake OR portobello OR white button mushrooms	250 mL
2	garlic cloves, minced or chopped	2
½ cup	finely chopped onion	125 mL
1 tbsp.	olive oil	15 mL
2 cups	dry red wine (Merlot OR Beaujolais)	500 mL
2 cups	beef broth	500 mL
1 tbsp.	minced, fresh thyme leaves OR 1 tsp. (5 mL) dried	15 mL
1 tbsp.	sugar	15 mL
2 tsp.	DLS* OR ½ tsp. (2 mL) salt and ½ tsp. (2 mL) pepper	10 mL
¼ cup	soft butter	60 mL

1. Crush the coriander seeds and black peppercorns. Add to the mustard and thyme leaves in small bowl. Mix well.
2. Pat tenderloin dry and place it on a sheet of plastic wrap. Coat it completely with the mustard mixture. Roll the plastic wrap around the tenderloin and place in a plastic bag in the refrigerator for up to 24 hours. (You don't have to let your guests see this part because, so far, it doesn't look very appetizing!)

Moose, Goose & Things That Swim

Crusted Caribou Tenderloin (continued)

3. Stir together the bread crumbs and parsley. Stir in 2 tbsp. (30 mL) of olive oil to moisten. Add a bit more olive oil if it seems too dry. Completely coat caribou with crumb mixture, pressing it into the meat. (At this point it may be refrigerated for up to 8 hours) Let sit, uncovered, at room temperature, for at least an hour before roasting.
4. **To make the reduction**, sauté mushrooms, garlic and onion in olive oil for 5-8 minutes, or until onions are softened. Add remaining ingredients, except butter. Bring to a boil and simmer until liquid has reduced to 2 cups (500 mL), about 30 minutes. Stir in the butter. Keep warm until ready to serve.
5. Preheat oven to 450°F (230°C). Sprinkle the tenderloin evenly on all sides with salt, patting the salt into the bread crumbs. Place on an oiled rack over a shallow roasting pan. Roast for 20-25 minutes, until done to your likeness: 140°F (60°C) for rare; 150°F (65°C) for medium-rare. Let the tenderloin sit, loosely covered with foil, for 10 minutes before carving. Cut into 1½" (4 cm) slices and arrange on a platter.
6. Either spoon the Mushroom and Red Wine Reduction over the sliced tenderloin or pass the reduction in a gravy boat.

Serves 8.

* Dymond Lake Seasoning, see page 3

NOTE: The cooking time may vary with the size of the tenderloin

See photograph on page 17.

A BEAR IN THE WOODPILE

as told by Rebecca Reimer (Helen's 12-year-old granddaughter)

As my mom, dad, sisters, my cousin Keely and I were walking to the runway one summer day, our two trusted dogs took off on us, barking like crazy. My dad told us to stay put and he ran after the dogs. About two minutes later he came running back. "Everyone start walking back," exclaimed my dad to the worried group.

We had a very good reason to be worried. Dad explained to us that there was a black bear right beside the woodpile.

Dad told Keely and me to run ahead and fetch Grandpa and the guns. We ran. When we reached the lodge Gramps needed someone to help him carry the guns. Keely was out of breath so I went along. We met dad and the others on the way to the lodge. I handed dad my gun while the others continued on their way to the lodge. As we made our way up the trail to the woodpile we saw a cloud of dust in front of us. We all realized that the bear had been in front of us and what danger our group had been in!! Dad and Grandpa sped off after the bear and told me to wait right where I was. After awhile, we could hear them returning with a loud chorus of barks from the dogs.

Later, everyone went back to see the trophy, and we have 10 black bear claws to remind us of the day.

Braised Caribou Meatballs in Red Wine Sauce

Team this with a spicy wild rice dish, tossed salad and crusty rolls for a meal fit for company! We have called for caribou but it lends itself well to moose, deer or beef. Make it ahead – it sits well in the refrigerator for a few days and the freezer for months.

2 cups	1" (2.5cm) day-old French bread cubes	500 mL
½ cup	milk	125 mL
2 lbs.	ground caribou	1 kg
2	eggs	2
½ cup	chopped onion	125 mL
½ cup	chopped fresh parsley OR 2 tbsp. (30 mL) dried	125 mL
1	large garlic clove, crushed or minced	1
1 tbsp.	Worcestershire sauce	15 mL
2 tsp.	salt	10 mL
1 tbsp.	DLS* OR 1 tsp. (5 mL) pepper	15 mL
1 tsp.	dried summer savory	5 mL
½ tsp.	dried thyme	2 mL
½ cup	flour	125 mL
2 tbsp.	butter	30 mL
2 tbsp.	olive oil	30 mL

Red Wine Sauce:

2 cups	dry red wine	500 mL
¼ cup	tomato paste	60 mL
3 cups	beef broth	750 mL
1 tsp.	Worcestershire sauce	5 mL
1 tsp.	dried thyme	5 mL
2 tbsp.	chopped fresh parsley	30 mL

1. Combine the bread cubes and milk in a large bowl; mix with an electric mixer.
2. To the bread, add the ground caribou, eggs, onion, parsley, garlic, Worcestershire sauce, salt, DLS, summer savory and thyme.
3. With an electric mixer, combine the caribou mixture until it looks pasty rather than shiny. Form into 1¾" (4.5 cm) meatballs; roll in the flour and place on a greased baking sheet. Bake at 350°F (180°C) for 30 minutes, turning once, until browned on all sides.

Moose, Goose & Things That Swim

Caribou Meatballs (continued)

4. Heat the butter and olive oil in a large Dutch oven over medium-high heat. Add the meatballs.
5. Whisk together the red wine and tomato paste and pour over the meatballs. Bring to a boil and continue cooking at a good simmer – bubbles should be breaking the surface – for about 8-10 minutes, stirring frequently. The sauce should reduce down a bit.
6. Stir in the beef broth, Worcestershire sauce and thyme. Reduce the heat to medium and simmer for another 25-30 minutes, stirring frequently. Season to taste with salt and pepper and garnish with 2 tbsp. (30 mL) chopped fresh parsley before serving.

Serves 8-10.

* *Dymond Lake Seasoning, see page 3.*

Curried Caribou

Derek Diorio was the director of the Great Canadian Food Show, which we filmed at Dymond Lake Hunting Lodge in September 2001. We have him to thank for sharing this curry recipe. He made it with caribou and we've tried it with deer; any ground red meat would be terrific!

2 tbsp.	olive oil	30 mL
1 lb.	ground caribou	500 g
1 cup	chopped onion	250 mL
3 cups	caribou (OR beef) stock	750 mL
2	apples, peeled and chopped	2
½ cup	crushed or chopped pineapple with juice	125 mL
½ cup	currants	125 mL
½ cup	raisins	125 mL
1	large banana, chopped	1
1	bay leaf	1
¼ cup	curry powder	60 mL

1. Heat olive oil in a large pot. Add the caribou and onion and sauté until well browned.
2. Add the stock and all remaining ingredients.
3. Simmer, uncovered, until the liquid is reduced and the curry is thickened. Serve over rice.

Serves 4.

Moose, Goose & Things That Swim

Ginger Caribou Salad

We love the opportunity to show off the goodness of our country foods. This is a winner.

Apricot Ginger Sauce:

½ cup	apricot jam	125 mL
2 tbsp.	chopped fresh ginger root	30 mL
2	large garlic cloves, crushed or minced	2
2 tbsp.	hoisin OR soy sauce	30 mL

Caribou Salad:

¼ cup	cornstarch	60 mL
1 tsp.	DLS* OR seasoned pepper	5 mL
1 tsp.	salt	5 mL
1 tsp.	cumin	5 mL
½ tsp.	cayenne	2 mL
1 lb.	caribou, cut into strips, (we usually cut it off the hip)	500 g
¼ cup	vegetable oil, approximately	60 mL
8 cups	mixed salad greens	2 L

1. In a small saucepan, over low heat, melt the jam and stir in the ginger, garlic and hoisin sauce.
2. Mix the cornstarch, DLS*, salt, cumin and cayenne in a baggie or a bowl. Dredge the caribou strips in the coating.
3. Heat the oil in a skillet over medium-high heat and stir-fry the caribou strips, adding more oil as necessary. Fry the strips in 2 or 3 batches so that the pan is not crowded.
4. Return the strips to the pan and pour the Apricot Ginger Sauce over, stirring for 2-3 minutes to coat the strips.
5. Serve immediately over mixed greens.

Serves 4.

VARIATIONS: We have featured this as a salad over greens but, for variety, serve it over cold rice or pasta. We have even stir-fried a mixture of veggies and served the caribou strips and sauce as a stir-fry!

* Dymond Lake Seasoning, see page 3.

Crisped Brined Wild Goose

(Helen) I have been cooking and serving exceptional wild goose dishes for over 30 years but a whole roasted wild goose was not among my successes until I tried this recipe. Moist, delicious and good flavor were the comments we received when we served this at Dymond Lake. We find Canada geese and Snow geese equally good in this recipe.

1. Choose a nice plump, plucked goose.
2. Follow steps 1 to 3 for a Brined Turkey on page 148.
3. Roast the goose for 30 minutes at 400°F (200°C), turn the goose breast side up and continue to roast for another 30 minutes, or until a thermometer inserted in the thickest part of the thigh registers 165°F (74°C).

NOTE: I still use the old pull-off-the-drumstick trick. If the drumstick pulls off easily, and the juices run clear, the bird is ready. Be sure not to overcook, you want the meat to be nice and juicy.

"That's Not Funny, Shari!"

(HELEN) Churchill was experiencing one of the warmest springs I can remember. It was only the end of April and we had already had a lot of above-zero temperatures. Doug and Gil, the pilot we had hired, had some work to do out at the lodge. It would mean flying in and landing on the ice on wheels. There wasn't any runway in those days, or satellite phones either, just a noisy on-again off-again radio! As it was going to be a warm, sunny weekend, Doug decided to take our youngest daughter Shari (8 years) and niece Trish (9 years). They flew off Friday afternoon and called to say they had arrived, everything was just great and they would talk to us on the radio the next morning.

I called in the morning and Shari answered. I said, "Good morning and how are you on this beautiful day?" She responded with, "I am kind of sad, the airplane fell through the ice last night." I said "Shari, that is not funny," thinking she was teasing me. Alas, she was not kidding.

Doug and Gil had checked the ice thickness in a couple of spots when they landed, but not where one of the tires was sitting. Later in the evening they had noticed that the airplane seemed to be listing to one side a bit. When they investigated, they realized the tire was sitting on a rather thin spot and they had better get it out of there fast! Doug hopped in, started up the plane and prepared to do a quick taxi out of there. The next thing he knew, he was standing beside the plane, soaking wet, and the plane was going through the ice! He says he really does not consciously remember bailing out when he realized it was going under! They managed to get a boat under each wing to keep the plane afloat until it could be salvaged.

Shari and Trish had their first helicopter ride back to Churchill.

Moose, Goose & Things That Swim

Wild Rice and Goose Casserole in Mushroom Wine Sauce

(MARIE) This delectable dish is a new all-time favorite. A "must try" with wild goose, it would be equally good with any red meat.

6-8	young, tender goose breasts	6-8
	flour	
¼ tsp.	salt	1 mL
	vegetable oil for frying	
1 cup	chopped onion	250 mL
¼ cup	Worcestershire sauce	60 mL
4 cups	cooked wild rice, see page 138	1 L
6	slices bread, buttered	6

Mushroom Wine Sauce:

¼ cup	butter	60 mL
2	garlic cloves, crushed	2
½ cup	flour	125 mL
4 cups	milk	1 L
2 tsp.	onion salt	10 mL
2 tsp.	dried oregano	10 mL
1 tsp.	pepper	5 mL
2 cups	sliced fresh mushrooms	500 mL
1 cup	white wine	250 mL

1. Cut the goose breasts in bite-sized pieces. Dredge in flour and fry in oil, with the onions, until browned. Stir in Worcestershire and set aside.
2. **To make the Mushroom Wine Sauce,** melt butter in a saucepan; add crushed garlic and saute for 1 minute. Add flour and stir until smooth. Gradually whisk in 2 cups (500 mL) of milk and stir until thickened Add onion salt, oregano, pepper, mushrooms, remaining milk and wine, stirring to make a thick, creamy sauce.
3. Grease or spray a 9 x 13" (23 x 33 cm) casserole. Spoon goose mixture into casserole. Cover with cooked wild rice. Pour sauce over.
4. Butter bread on 1 side. Remove crusts and cut each slice in quarters. Cover the sauce with the bread, buttered side up.
5. Bake, uncovered, at 350°F (180°C) for 45 minutes, or until browned.

Serves 6-8.

Crusted Caribou Tenderloin, page 10
Baked Potato Cakes, page 133
Shredded Beets and Red Cabbage with
Cranberries, page 127

 *Moose, Goose & Things That Swim*

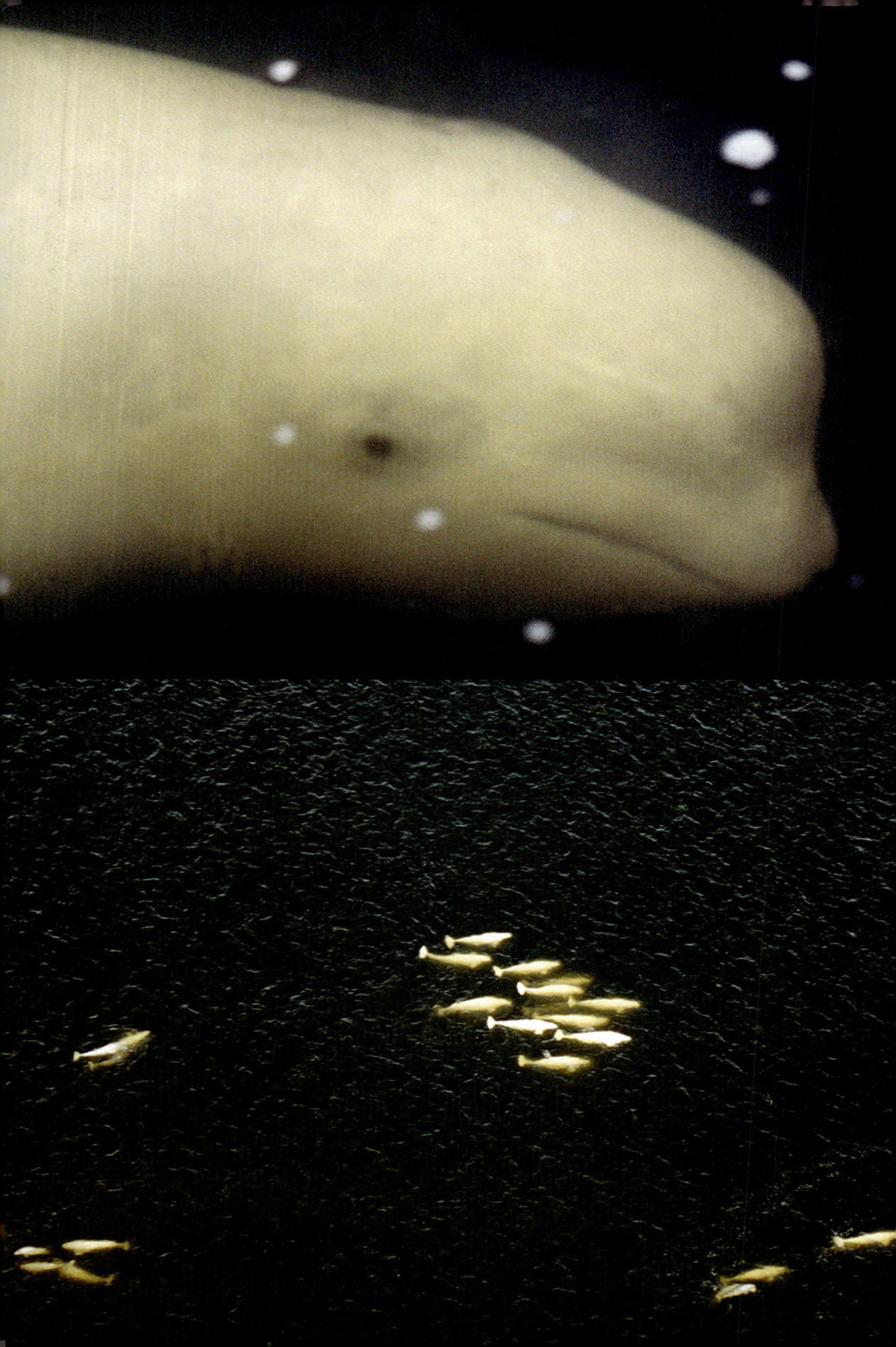

Honey-Glazed Salmon

(HELEN) *We apologize for sounding like a broken record but this recipe is simple and delicious. It came to us on a very roundabout route. My brother-in-law, Lennie, (a published recording artist – look for "I Love the Rain" by Len Osland) got this recipe from his friend Dan Price of Whitehorse. Our thanks to Dan, who gave him permission to share it with us. Be sure to try it with Lake Trout or Arctic Char if you are fortunate enough to find some.*

5-6 lb.	whole dressed salmon, trout OR char	2.2-2.5 kg
	salt and pepper	

Honey Glaze:

2 cups	mayonnaise	500 mL
3	garlic cloves, crushed or minced	3
¾ cup	chopped fresh tarragon OR 2 tbsp. (30 mL) dried	175 mL
2 tbsp.	liquid honey*	30 mL

1. Set the barbecue to medium heat
2. Liberally salt and pepper the inside and outside of the fish.
3. Place the fish on the barbecue – you can put it directly on the barbecue, on a cooking rack or on foil. Cook 10 minutes per inch (2.5 cm) of fish at the thickest part, turning once. Skin will blacken. (Have a water bottle ready to put out flare-ups). The fish should be just barely done. Remove the fish from the barbecue and discard the skin.
4. While the fish is cooking, combine the mayonnaise, garlic, tarragon and honey. Remove ¾ cup (175 mL) of the glaze and set aside to serve as a sauce with the fish.
5. Place the skinned fish on a large piece of heavy-duty foil. Spread half of the remaining glaze on 1 side of the fish; turn over carefully and glaze the other half.
6. Return the fish (on the foil) to the barbecue. Cook 4-5 minutes; turn over and cook an additional 4-5 minutes, until the glaze is bubbly and hot on both sides.
7. Remove the fish to a platter. Garnish with fresh tarragon, if you like, and serve.

Serves 8-10.

* *If you do not have liquid honey, just melt regular honey in the microwave. Start with about 10 seconds.*

Beluga whales at Seal River Heritage Lodge.

Moose, Goose & Things That Swim

Almond-Crusted Char with Leek and Lemon Cream

This fish entrée is simply amazing!

Leek and Lemon Cream Sauce:

2	medium leeks OR 2 cups (500 mL) finely chopped onion*	2
2 tbsp.	butter	30 mL
3 tbsp.	fresh lemon juice	45 mL
1 cup	whipping cream	250 mL
	salt and pepper to taste	

Almond-Crusted Char:

1 cup	chopped sliced almonds	250 mL
1 tbsp.	chopped fresh parsley OR 1 tsp. (5 mL) dried	15 mL
1 tbsp.	grated lemon peel	15 mL
½ tsp.	salt	2 mL
⅛ tsp.	ground black pepper	0.8 mL
½ cup	flour	125 mL
6 x 6 oz.	skinless char fillets	6 x 170 g
	DLS** OR salt and pepper	
1	large egg, beaten	1
2 tbsp.	butter	30 mL
2 tbsp.	olive oil	30 mL

1. **To make the sauce**, wash leeks thoroughly. Cut in half and slice thinly (Use only the white and pale green parts.) In a heavy saucepan, sauté leeks in butter for 2 minutes over medium-high heat. Reduce heat, cover and cook until tender, about 20 minutes.
2. Reduce heat to medium. Add lemon juice and stir until the liquid evaporates, about 1 minute. Stir in cream. Simmer until slightly reduced, about 2 minutes. Cool slightly.
3. Season to taste with salt and pepper. If not using immediately, refrigerate until ready to serve; then reheat.
4. **To prepare the char**, combine the almonds, parsley, lemon peel, salt and pepper on a plate. Place the flour on another plate.
5. Sprinkle char with DLS**. Dredge the char with flour, shaking off excess. Lightly brush 1 side of each salmon fillet with beaten egg. Press brushed side of fillets into almond mixture, pressing lightly to make it adhere. Set fillets aside until all are prepared.

 Moose, Goose & Things That Swim

Almond-Crusted Char (continued)

6. Melt 1 tbsp. (15 mL) butter and 1 tbsp. (15 mL) oil in a heavy, large skillet over medium heat. Add fillets, almond-side down. Cook in 2 batches if necessary. Cook until the almond crust is brown, about 5 minutes. Turn fillets over and sauté until cooked through, about 3-5 minutes. Serve with the reserved sauce.

Serves 6.

*   *Pour boiling water over onions – let sit for 5 minutes; drain and use as above.*
** *Dymond Lake Seasoning, see page 3.*

See photograph on page 123.

Soused Salmon OR Trout Barbecue

(MARIE) This recipe was given to me while on a motorcycle outing – I talk about food every chance I get! The original was passed down without a name, so we named it appropriately. I know you'll agree that the flavor transferred to the fish from the marinating liquid is exquisite. (Sugar was used in the original recipe, but I prefer it without the sugar.)

Rye, Garlic and Soy Marinade:

¾ cup	soy sauce	175 mL
1¼ cups	vegetable oil	300 mL
1	garlic clove, crushed	1
¼ cup	rye whisky	60 mL
2 tbsp.	sugar (optional)	30 mL
2	large salmon OR lake trout fillets, skin on pepper	2

1. Combine all of the marinade ingredients in a shallow non-aluminum container.
2. Lay the cleaned fish in the marinade. Sprinkle with pepper. Marinate for 4-6 hours, turning once.
3. Preheat the barbecue to high. Lay the fillets, skin-side down, directly on the hot grill. Close the lid and barbecue for 7 minutes. There will be lots of smoke, and the skin will burn, but the fish will be moist and delicious. Serve as a meal or as an appetizer.

Serves 6-8.

Pan-Seared Salmon with Capers and Peppercorns

Very easy, quick and tasty. Don't hold back on the pepper!

¼ tsp.	salt	1 mL
4 x 6 oz.	skinless salmon fillets	4 x 170 g
½ tsp.	freshly ground black pepper OR seasoned pepper	2 mL
⅓ cup	white wine	75 mL
⅓ cup	fresh lemon juice	75 mL
2 tbsp.	capers	30 mL
1 tbsp.	peppercorns, black OR assorted	15 mL

1. Sprinkle the salt in a heavy non-stick or sprayed skillet and heat over medium heat until a drop of water sizzles when it touches the pan. Add the salmon and sear each side for 1 minute.
2. Reduce heat to low and sprinkle salmon with pepper, then pour in wine and 2 tbsp. (30 mL) lemon juice. Cover and cook for 9-11 minutes.
3. Transfer the salmon to a serving platter. Add the remaining lemon juice, capers and peppercorns to the skillet and cook about 2 minutes. Pour pan juices over salmon and serve.

Serves 4.

NOTE: For a milder flavor, use pickled green peppercorns.

Jacob Hooks A Big One!

The fishermen were out enjoying another lovely sunny day at North Knife Lake. Marie and I had a few hours to spare thanks to the help of my daughter Shari and Marie's daughter-in-law Terri. We also had some grandchildren in camp who were itching to go fishing.

Marie and Terri piled into one boat with Jordan and Alyssa. Shari and I piled into another boat with Jayne, Jacob and Joshua, aged 8, 5 and 3 respectively. We knew fishing was going to be a bit tricky with the three of them, but they were anxious to get out there. We went into a nice little bay and tried to organize the children at different spots in the boat. It was working quite well, they were getting the odd bite and we had even caught a couple, when I heard Jayne scream and turned to see a hook in her cheek. Jacob, meanwhile, couldn't figure out why his hook wouldn't reel back in, and was giving it some good tugs. I yelled at Jacob to drop his rod and quickly moved to Jayne – I didn't want Shari to get there first in case she passed out on me!

Just as I got to Jayne, she quit screaming, calmly announced, "It doesn't hurt," and sat perfectly still while I reached over and gently slipped the hook out.

Thank goodness for a "barbless only" policy!

Moose, Goose & Things That Swim

Baked Fish Fillets with Lemon Mustard Sauce

I almost passed this recipe by – it seemed so simple. Admittedly, that is what caught my attention – the simplicity of it. But the taste – now, that is something else – simply delicious! Use fillets of trout, pickerel, pike or whitefish.

bread crumbs
fish fillets to fit a 9" (23 cm) square
  OR 9 x 13" (23 x 33 cm) pan
paprika

Lemon Mustard Sauce:

2 tsp.	lemon juice	10 mL
½ cup	butter, melted	125 mL
1 tsp.	prepared mustard	5 mL
1 tsp.	salt	5 mL
½ tsp.	pepper	2 mL

1. Sprinkle bread crumbs in the bottom of the baking dish. Lay fish fillets on the bread crumbs.
2. Combine all of the sauce ingredients and pour the sauce over the fish. Sprinkle with paprika.
3. Bake, uncovered, at 450°F (230°C), for 10-15 minutes. When the fish flakes easily, it is done.

Serves 4.

Thaw frozen fish in milk. The milk draws out the frozen taste and provides a fresh-caught flavor.

To remove fish odor from your hands, rub them with vinegar or salt.

Cedar Planked Trout with Balsamic Reduction Sauce

Jeff has contributed this wonderful sauce, which we've suggested using over Cedar Planked Trout. However, the sauce is terrific over chicken or any red meat. Jeff has also taught us to use it for caramelizing onions or mushrooms – delicious!

1	cedar plank	1
1 or 2	2 lb. (1 kg) lake trout fillets	1 or 2
	salt and DLS* to taste	

1. Soak an untreated cedar plank in water for 24 hours.
2. Remove the plank from the water and lay the trout fillets on the plank. Season with salt and DLS.
3. Place the plank with the trout on a hot barbecue. Close the lid and bake until the trout is done, about 10 minutes, per inch.

* *Dymond Lake Seasoning, see page 3.*

Balsamic Reduction Sauce

1 cup	balsamic vinegar	250 mL
3 tbsp.	sugar	45 mL

1. In a small saucepan, simmer the vinegar and sugar together for 15-20 minutes, or until it is reduced by a half to a third.
2. To serve, pour the sauce over the trout or serve the sauce in a small pitcher for pouring over individual servings.

Lemon Thyme Fish

This simple marinade adds zesty flavor to any mild, white fish.

Lemon Thyme Marinade:

¼ cup	vegetable oil	60 mL
1 tbsp.	lemon juice	15 mL
½ tsp.	EACH dried thyme and salt	2 mL
pinch	pepper	pinch
1½ lbs.	skinless white fish fillets	750 g
	lemon slices and parsley for garnish	

Moose, Goose & Things That Swim

Lemon Thyme Fish (continued)

1. In a shallow dish, combine the oil, lemon juice, thyme, salt and pepper.
2. Lay the fillets in the pan and spoon the lemon mixture generously over the fish. Marinate for 1 hour.
3. Grill the fish under high heat for 5-8 minutes, or until the fish flakes easily. Baste at least once with the lemon mixture.
4. Serve with lemon slices and parsley to garnish.

Serves 6.

Rainbow Trout & Wild Rice Wine Sauce

A truly delightful and sophisticated presentation, the creamy Wild Rice Wine Sauce is a beautiful complement to the Parmesan-lemon accented trout.

2	lemons	2
4	rainbow trout*	4
¼ cup	Parmesan cheese	60 mL
2 tsp.	chopped parsley	10 mL

Wild Rice Wine Sauce:

8 oz.	cream cheese	250 mL
¼ cup	Worcestershire sauce	60 mL
¼ cup	dry white wine	60 mL
1 cup	cooked wild rice, see page 138	250 mL
½ cup	chopped fresh mushrooms	125 mL
¼ cup	EACH chopped onion, red pepper	60 mL
¼ tsp.	freshly ground black pepper	1 mL
½ tsp.	freshly grated lemon zest	2 mL

1. Lay the fish on a baking tray and squeeze the juice of 1 lemon over the fish. Cover the fish with foil and bake at 400°F (200°C) for 20 minutes.
2. **For the sauce**, combine the cream cheese, Worcestershire sauce and wine in a saucepan. Stir until creamy, and add all of the remaining ingredients. Simmer for 5-10 minutes.
3. Place the fillets side by side on a broiler tray. Spread the sauce over the fillets; sprinkle with Parmesan cheese and broil for 5 minutes.
4. To serve, garnish with lemon wedges and parsley.

Serves 4.

* *You may substitute a 3-4 lb. (1.5-1.8 kg) whole dressed trout, char or salmon for the smaller fish. Increase the baking time to 30 minutes.*

Moose, Goose & Things That Swim

Tarragon-Tomato Pike and Eggplant

(HELEN) I developed this recipe when my friend Bonnie (of "North Knife Where Are You?" fame, Blueberries & Polar Bears, page 138, was staying with me while she was doing a bird count. It is always fun having Bonnie around – she learns a few more things about cooking and I learn a few more things about birding.

3 tbsp.	olive oil	45 mL
½ cup	finely chopped red onion OR shallot	125 mL
2	garlic cloves, minced	2
2 tsp.	DLS* OR ½ tsp. (5 mL) salt and 1 tsp. (5 mL) seasoned pepper	10 mL
28 oz.	can diced plum tomatoes	796 mL
2 tbsp.	chopped fresh tarragon OR 2 tsp. (10 mL) dried	30 mL
¼ cup	dry white wine	60 mL
½ cup	chicken stock	125 mL
2 tbsp.	olive oil	30 mL
1	eggplant, sliced in ¼" (1 cm) rounds	1
1	egg, slightly beaten	1
1 cup	bread crumbs**	250 mL
2 tbsp.	olive oil	30 mL
4 x 6 oz.	fish fillets	4 x 170 mL

1. In a medium-sized saucepan, heat 3 tbsp. (45 mL) of oil over medium-high heat. Add the onions, garlic and DLS. Sauté until the onion is softened and just beginning to brown, about 5 minutes.
2. Add the tomatoes and 1 tbsp. (15 mL) of tarragon and simmer for about 10 minutes. Add the wine and cook, uncovered, over medium-high heat until reduced by half, about 7 minutes. Add the stock, reduce the heat to low and simmer while you prepare the eggplant.
3. In a large non-stick frying pan, heat 2 tbsp. (30 mL) of oil over medium-high heat.
4. Dip sliced eggplant into beaten egg; then coat both sides with bread crumbs.** Sauté breaded eggplant until crisp and brown on both sides and soft in the center. Set aside in a single layer on a cooling rack while you cook the fish.

Tarragon-Tomato Pike (continued)

5. Add 2 tbsp. (30 mL) of oil to the frying pan and heat over medium-high heat. Add the fish and cook until well browned. Turn it over and pour half of the tomato mixture over and around the fish. Top with the eggplant and cover with the remaining tomato sauce. Simmer for 5 minutes, until the fish is cooked and the eggplant is reheated.
6. Spoon into a large bowl and sprinkle with remaining tarragon.

Serves 4.

* *Dymond Lake Seasoning, see page 3.*
** *Start with just ½ cup (125 mL) of the bread crumbs and add the rest as needed. This prevents them from getting too soggy from the egg wash.*

Baked Creamed Fish

One pre-season day at Dymond Lake, when we were all too busy to spend time on lunch, Elaine Friesen created this dish. We think it is good enough to share.

1½ lbs.	fresh fish fillets	750 g
	salt and pepper	
1 tbsp.	fresh lemon juice	15 mL
½ cup	butter	60 mL
½ cup	chopped onion	125 mL
½ cup	bread crumbs	125 mL
1¼ cups	white sauce, see page 138, *Cranberries & Canada Geese*	300 mL
2 tsp.	dry mustard	10 mL
⅓ cup	grated Cheddar cheese	75 mL

1. Cut the fish fillets in chunks and place in a greased, shallow baking pan. Sprinkle with salt, pepper and lemon juice.
2. Melt the butter in a frying pan and sauté the onions until translucent. Spoon the onions over the fish. Fry the bread crumbs in the remaining butter. Set aside.
3. Prepare the white sauce and stir in the dry mustard. Pour over the fish. Top with buttered crumbs and grated Cheddar.
4. Bake, uncovered, at 350°F (180°C) for 35 minutes.

Serves 4-6.

Moose, Goose & Things That Swim

Two Fires and a Flood
and I have only been here a Week!

(HELEN) It was a blistering hot Sunday in early June. We had the whole crew in at North Knife getting ready for opening. Stewart had assigned one of the new fellows to burn garbage near the garage, and the rest of us were going about our assigned tasks which included anything from working on the condo siding, getting boats and motors in the water, cleaning the interior of the lodge or making lunch! I was doing some outside cleanup when all of a sudden I heard Stewart yell, "FIRE". Everyone came running, including Stewart's pregnant wife, Barb. A spark had gotten away on our garbage burner and ignited one of the trees. The fire was moving quickly!

One task that hadn't been done yet was setting up the fire pumps! Rolly ran to get the water pump and move it into position. The women grabbed pails and shovels and starting throwing sand on the flames. The guys got involved with knocking down the tree. It was a very scary half hour or so until everything was out. The water pump was moved back to its usual position, and the next assignment of the day was getting the fire pumps and hoses into position and hooked up.

All is well that ends well – right! By the next day, Monday, temperatures had plummeted from near 30°C the day before, to about 5°C and rainy. I happened to be working just outside the back door of the lodge when Barb rushed out yelling, "A flood, a flood, there is water pouring into the storage room." I knew immediately what had happened, whoever had hooked up the water pump had forgotten to rehook the automatic shutoff – the water had overflowed the water tank at the top of the tower, flooded the top storage room, and then run through to the bottom storage room. A fine mess to clean up when time was already at a premium.

Tuesday passed quite uneventfully, and by Wednesday I was feeling that we had things pretty well under control. Once again my chores took me past the lodge and I happened to meet up with Stewart. He commented on the fact that the fireplace seemed to be smoking, but that he had opened up the patio doors and windows and it seemed to be clearing out. I expressed surprise as we had never had problems with the fireplace smoking. When I went in for lunch, I wandered into the lounge, just to check out the situation, and was quite alarmed to find little wisps of smoke wafting up from between the stones on the face of the fireplace. I quickly ran back to the staff dining room to tell Stewart. He was up and out and under the lodge like a shot.

Sure enough, the fireplace, which we had been burning day and night since the hot Sunday, had started the timbers smoldering! The fire pumps were quickly put into action and things were under control within minutes! It was the last fire in the fireplace until it had been pulled apart and rebuilt underneath!

Lying in bed that night, reflecting on the events of the past few days, I realized that not only did I have another story for the new book I kept saying I was going to write, but I had the title as well – Two Fires and a Flood and I have only been here a Week!

Bread & Breakfast

Since Helen and I both love working with dough, this is one of our favorite sections, You have no idea how excited we get when we find recipes like Cranberry Orange Coffee Cake and Cornmeal Jam Buster Muffins. Hashbrown Breakfast Casserole has already become a regular at the camps and nothing pleases us more than finding a new twist to an old favorite, like Feather-Crisp Waffles with some wonderful new sauces.

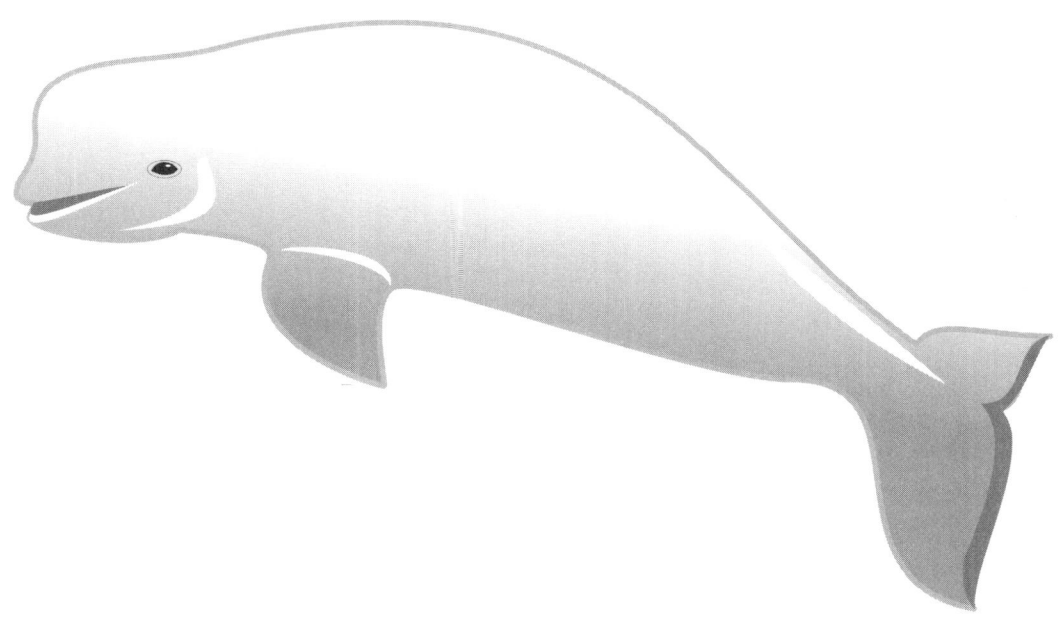

Baking With Yeast

Most, though not all, of the recipes in this section use yeast. Therefore, we would like to share some of the things we have learned, through experience, about baking with yeast.

Water Temperature: When using tap water in a bread recipe, the water should feel quite warm when tested on the inside of your wrist, but not hot! For experienced bread makers this will sound very elementary, but the rest of you can learn from two who learned to make bread by trial and error on their own – it is important to the success of the product. Hot water destroys yeast.

Rising Techniques: When setting the dough in a warm place to rise, cover it with a cloth or tea towel. Helen also puts a piece of plastic over the dry cloth. She finds that it keeps the top of the dough from drying out and creates more warmth in the dough.

For Evenly Baked Breads: When using 2 oven racks at the same time, switch the pans from top to bottom, and visa versa, halfway through the baking time.

Milk vs. Water: You may replace milk with water in all bread recipes.

Oven Temperature: Always use a preheated oven.

Oil vs. Butter or Margarine: When making bread & buns, we use oil instead of butter or margarine. We do this for convenience and find that it works just as well.

Quality of Flour: Over the years, we have tried many kinds of flour. We have found no difference in the taste and quality of our breads, whether we used a name brand or a no-name brand. Occasionally, there was a slight difference in the degree of whiteness.

Types of Yeast: Our recipes are all written for the use of INSTANT YEAST, but quick-rising yeast works just as well. For QUICK-RISING YEAST, follow package directions using some of the water called for in the recipe. Put it in a small bowl with 1 tsp. (5 mL) sugar. Sprinkle the yeast over the water, letting it fall from a distance of at least 6" (15 cm). This forces the yeast to go beneath the surface of the water where it dissolves more easily. Do not stir. Put in a warm place to sit until yeast mixture has become bubbly, about 5 minutes. Add to recipe as directed.

Freezing and Thawing Tips: Break buns apart and slice bread before freezing. This way, you thaw only what you want to use immediately. Frozen slices of bread can be toasted without thawing first. To thaw a frozen loaf of bread, put it in the microwave, uncovered, on high heat for 2 minutes. 1 bun takes 30 seconds.

Greasing Pans or Working Surfaces: When the recipe calls for greased pans or surfaces, we use a nonstick cooking spray that is environmentally safe.

Shaping Buns: Spread your fingers, palm side down, into the shape of a spider; place your curved fingers over the dough and move your hand in circular motions on the greased surface, putting a little pressure on the dough. With practice, you will quickly shape the dough into a smooth ball. With more practice, you will be doing it with both hands at once!

Light Rye Bread

Light in color, taste and texture, with or without the caraway seeds this rye bread is a winner.

2½ cups	warm water	625 mL
¼ cup	honey	60 mL
¼ cup	vegetable oil	60 mL
1 tbsp.	lemon juice	15 mL
1 tbsp.	salt	15 mL
2 cups	rye flour, dark OR light	500 mL
5 cups	all-purpose flour	1.25 L
2 tbsp.	instant yeast	30 mL
2 tbsp.	caraway seeds	30 mL
1	egg white	1
1 tbsp.	water	15 mL

1. In a large mixing bowl, combine water, honey, oil, lemon juice and salt. Add rye flour, 1 cup (250 mL) white flour, yeast and caraway seeds. Mix well.
2. Switch to a dough hook, if you have one, and add the rest of the flour gradually. Knead until the dough is no longer sticky. If kneading by hand, add as much flour as you can in the bowl, then turn out onto a FLOURED surface, and work in the rest of the flour by hand, using a kneading motion. It may take a little MORE or a little LESS flour. Just knead until the dough is not sticky, and bounces back when pressed, 8-10 minutes.
3. Shape dough into a ball, place in a well-greased or sprayed bowl, turning dough to grease the surface. Cover with a cloth; put in a warm place and let rise until doubled in size, at least 1 hour.
4. Punch dough down, turn out onto a GREASED or SPRAYED surface and cut into 2 equal halves. Shape each half into a long loaf, about 15" (38 cm) long. If desired, use a rolling pin to roll each half into a 10 x 15" (25 x 38 cm) rectangle. Beginning at a 15" (38 cm) side, roll up tightly, like a jelly roll. Seal edges well. Taper ends by rolling them gently back and forth.
5. Place loaves on a greased or sprayed baking sheet. Let rise, covered, in a warm place until doubled in size, about 1 hour. It is really important that these loaves do not over-rise! They will continue to rise a little in the oven as they bake.
6. Just before baking, brush tops of loaves with an egg white/water mixture. Bake in a preheated 375°F (190°C) oven for 30 minutes.
7. Remove baked loaves from pan and cool on racks.

Makes 2 long loaves.

* *See notes on YEAST and rising techniques on page 30.*

Russian Black Bread

You have to be into firm bread to really appreciate this flavorful loaf. We like it toasted for breakfast with honey or jam.

2½ cups	warm coffee	625 mL
2 tbsp.	EACH cider vinegar and lemon juice	30 mL
¼ cup	EACH vegetable oil and molasses	60 mL
2 tbsp.	brown sugar	30 mL
1 tbsp.	salt	15 mL
¼ cup	cocoa powder	60 mL
1 tbsp.	caraway seed	15 mL
1 tsp.	fennel seed	5 mL
2 cups	whole-wheat flour	500 mL
3 cups	rye flour	750 mL
3 tbsp.	instant yeast*	45 mL
2 cups	all-purpose flour	500 mL

1. In a large mixing bowl, combine coffee, vinegar, lemon juice, oil, molasses, sugar and salt.
2. Add cocoa powder, seeds, **2 cups (500 mL) whole-wheat flour, 1 cup (250 mL) rye flour** and instant yeast. Mix well.
3. Switch to a dough hook, if you have one, and add the rest of the flour gradually – first the rye and then the white. Knead until the dough is no longer sticky. If kneading by hand, add as much flour as you can in the bowl, then turn out onto a FLOURED surface, and work in the rest of the flour by hand, using a kneading motion. It may take a little MORE or a little LESS flour. Knead until the dough is not sticky, and bounces back when pressed, 8-10 minutes. It is fairly dense and heavy.
4. Shape dough into a ball, place in a well-greased or sprayed bowl, turning dough to grease the surface. Cover with a cloth, put in a warm place and let rise until doubled in size, at least an hour.
5. Punch dough down, turn out onto a GREASED or SPRAYED surface and cut into 2 equal halves. Shape each half into a loaf, using a kneading motion. Again, this dough is dense, but don't panic – it will rise!
6. Place loaves in well greased or sprayed 3 x 4 x 8" (7 x 10 x 20 cm) bread pans. Cover with a cloth. Let rise in a warm place until bread has just come over the top of the pans, at least an hour. (It won't rise as high as a regular loaf.)
7. Remove cloth and bake loaves at 375°F (190°C) for 30 minutes.
8. Remove from oven; immediately turn out of pans onto a cooling rack.

Makes 2 loaves.

* *See notes on YEAST and rising techniques on page 30.*

Kalamata Olive Bread

As an appetizer or a complement to lunch, this pleasantly salty bread is a winner. Serve it with a shallow dish of olive oil and balsamic vinegar.

2¼ cups	warm water	530 mL
¼ cup	Kalamata olive juice (from the jar or container)	60 mL
1 tbsp.	sugar	15 mL
1 tbsp.	olive oil	15 mL
1½ tsp.	salt	7 mL
1½ cups	pitted, chopped Kalamata olives	375 mL
2 tbsp.	chopped capers	30 mL
6-7 cups	flour	1.5-1.75 L
1 tbsp.	instant yeast*	15 mL
1	egg white, beaten with	1
1 tbsp.	water	15 mL

1. In a medium-sized mixing bowl, combine the water, olive juice, sugar, oil, salt, olives and capers. Add 3 cups (750 mL) of flour and the yeast. Mix well or beat with an electric mixer.
2. Switch to a dough hook, if you have one, and gradually add the rest of the flour, as needed, to make a stiff dough. If kneading by hand, add as much flour as you can in the bowl, then turn out onto a floured surface and work in the rest of the flour by hand, using a kneading motion. It may take a little more or less flour.
3. Shape the dough into a ball and place in a greased bowl to rise. Cover with a cloth and set in a warm place until it doubles in bulk, about an hour.
4. Punch down the dough and cut it into 4 equal parts. Shape each quarter into a 12" (30 cm) to 15" (38 cm) loaf.
5. Place the loaves on greased baking sheets, 2 loaves to a sheet. Let rise, uncovered, in a warm place until doubled in size, about an hour.
6. Just before baking, make 3 diagonal cuts on top of each loaf. Brush the tops of the loaves with the egg white/water mixture.
7. Bake at 375°F (190°C) for 25 minutes. Remove the baked loaves from the baking sheets and cool on racks.

Makes 4 thin loaves (French-loaf style)

* *See notes on YEAST and rising techniques on page 30.*

Bread & Breakfast

Cranberry Citrus Cream Cheese Pull-Apart Buns

(**HELEN**) My daughter Toni put a couple of recipe ideas together to come up with this and we thank her for sharing it with us. We like the fact that there are some options for baking. You can make them and serve them the same day or prepare them one day and bake and serve them fresh for breakfast. If you don't have time to make the dough, frozen bread dough or rolls work well.

Dough:

1 cup	warm water	250 mL
¼ cup	sugar	60 mL
1 tsp.	salt	5 mL
2 tbsp.	butter, melted	30 mL
¼ cup	mashed potato, (optional but it makes a nice light dough)	60 mL
1	egg	1
¼ cup	sour cream	60 mL
3½-4 cups	all-purpose flour	825 mL-1 L
2 tsp.	instant yeast	10 mL

Fillings:

2 tbsp.	butter OR margarine, melted	30 mL
½ cup	cranberries, dried, frozen or fresh	250 g
8 oz.	cream cheese	250 mL
½ cup	sugar	125 mL
3 tbsp.	orange juice	45 mL
1	egg	1
½ cup	sugar	125 mL
1 tbsp.	grated lemon rind	15 mL
1 tbsp.	grated orange rind	15 mL

Lemon Icing:

1 cup	icing sugar	250 mL
4-5 tsp.	lemon juice	20-25 mL

1. **To make the dough**, in a medium mixing bowl, combine water, sugar, salt, melted butter, potato, egg, sour cream, **2 cups (500 mL) flour** and yeast. Beat well.

Bread & Breakfast

Pull-Apart Buns (continued)

2. Gradually add enough of the remaining flour to make a smooth soft dough that is no longer sticky. Knead on a greased surface for 8-10 minutes, adding a little additional flour if needed. If you have a dough hook, follow manufacturer's instructions.
3. Shape the dough into a ball and place in a greased bowl, turning over to grease the top of the dough. Cover with a cloth and let rise in a warm place until doubled in bulk, about 1 hour.
4. Punch down the dough and turn out onto a greased surface. Cut into 28 pieces and form into 1" (2.5 cm) balls. (If you have extra dough, form it into balls, place on a cookie tray and freeze. When frozen, place in a plastic freezer bag and keep frozen until you need them.*)
5. To assemble: Place 14 balls in each of two 9" (23 cm) springform pans and brush with the melted butter. Sprinkle ¼ cup of cranberries over each pan.
6. Beat the cream cheese until fluffy. Add the ½ cup (125 mL) of sugar, orange juice and egg. Pour evenly over the two pans.
7. Combine ½ cup (125 mL) of sugar with the lemon and orange rind. Divide evenly over the buns. Cover and let rise. At this point, you can either let rise until doubled and then bake at 350°F (180°C) for 30-35 minutes OR refrigerate overnight** and bake in the morning.
8. Allow to set up in the pan for five minutes before removing from pans. Place the buns on a serving platter, leaving them on the pan bottom.
9. Mix the icing sugar and lemon juice into a thin icing and drizzle over the buns

Serves 12-16.
* See notes on YEAST and rising techniques on page 30.
** If using frozen dough balls, allow a little more time for rising.
*** If you are going to refrigerate them overnight, make them late in the day and cut the yeast back by about ½ tsp. (2 mL) so they don't over rise.

Bread & Breakfast

Butterhorns

If someone told you that you could make bread without kneading, would you believe it? Well, here it is – no kneading, no rising time – just 5 minutes to mix it up before bed, a cool night in the refrigerator, and a little cut and roll time in the morning. Then – hot breakfast rolls fresh from the oven!

1 cup	butter, softened	250 mL
3 tbsp	sugar	45 mL
1 tsp.	salt	5 mL
1¼ cups	warm milk	300 mL
2	egg yolks	2
3 cups	all-purpose flour	750 mL
1 tbsp	instant yeast*	15 mL

1. In a large bowl, with an electric mixer, mix together all the ingredients, adding the yeast with **2 cups (500 mL) flour**. Beat until well combined. Add the remaining flour and beat well. (Dough will be very soft and sticky.) Cover and refrigerate overnight.
2. In the morning, divide the batter into 3 parts. On a floured surface, roll each part into a 12-14" (30-36 cm) circle. Cut each circle into 10 wedges. Roll up each wedge, starting at the wide end. Place the rolls on greased or sprayed baking sheets and bake at 350°F (180°C) for 15 minutes. They will rise in the oven.

Makes 30 butterhorn rolls.

* See notes on YEAST and rising techniques on page 30.

See photograph on page 69.

To make your own self-rising flour, add 2 tsp. (10 mL) baking powder to 1 cup (250 mL) plain flour.

 *Bread & Breakfast*

Cornmeal Rolls

*(**MARIE**) I thought I had tasted every kind of dinner roll in existence until my daughter-in-law, Terri, sent me this recipe. The method is a little different, the taste is a little sweeter – but this moist and tasty roll has already become a favorite. An added bonus is that it seems to keep its freshness a little longer.*

⅓ cup	cornmeal	75 mL
½ cup	sugar	125 mL
1 tsp.	salt	5 mL
2½ cups	milk	625 mL
½ cup	shortening	125 mL
2	eggs, beaten	2
3-4 cups	all-purpose flour	750 mL-1 L
2 tbsp.	instant yeast*	30 mL

1. In a saucepan, combine cornmeal, sugar, salt, milk and shortening. Cook, stirring constantly, until thick. Set aside to cool almost completely. (It has to be cool enough not to kill the yeast you are about to add to it.)
2. Add eggs to the cooled mixture.
3. Using a dough hook, if you have one, gradually add **2 cups (500 mL) flour**, yeast, then remaining flour. (It may take a little MORE or LESS flour.) The dough mixture will be a little softer than ordinary dough, and will not totally come away from the sides of the bowl, but, when it is no longer sticky it is ready. Turn into a greased or sprayed bowl. Cover and let rise until doubled in bulk.
4. Punch down the dough and turn it onto a greased surface. Cut into 24 pieces and shape into balls; place on a 12 x 17" (30 x 43 cm) greased pan; cover and let rise for 1 hour.
5. Bake at 375°F (190°C) for 20 minutes.

Makes 2 dozen rolls.

* *See notes on YEAST and rising techniques on page 30.*

Whole-Wheat Soda Bread

(MARIE) I received this recipe from my friend Nellie a few years ago, but only tried it at the hunting Lodge this past September. I'm sorry I didn't try it sooner. Almost a cross between bread, cake and biscuit, you'll enjoy Soda Bread hot from the oven. Serve it with soup or a salad.

2 cups	all-purpose flour	500 mL
1 cup	whole-wheat flour	250 mL
1 cup	wheat bran	250 mL
2 tbsp.	flax OR sesame seeds	30 mL
2 tbsp.	sugar	30 mL
1 tsp.	baking soda	5 mL
1 tsp.	salt	5 mL
2 cups	buttermilk, yogurt OR diluted sour cream	500 mL
¼ cup	vegetable oil	60 mL
1 tbsp.	flour (for topping)	15 mL

1. In a large bowl, whisk together flours, bran, seeds, sugar, baking soda and salt.
2. In a small bowl, whisk together buttermilk and oil. Add to dry ingredients all at once. Stir with a fork until a soft dough forms.
3. Turn dough out onto a lightly floured surface and shape into a ball. With floured hands, knead lightly 10 times. Place on a greased or sprayed baking sheet. Gently pat dough out into a 6" (15 cm) circle.
4. Sprinkle flour over loaf. With a sharp knife, score a large X on top of the loaf.
5. Bake at 350°F (190°C) for 45 minutes.

Makes 1 loaf.

Restoring honey or liquifying – place the jar in a pot of warm water and gently heat until the honey is melted. Do not try this with a plastic container of honey.

Date Nut Loaf

(MARIE) From a quick visit to my sister in Dundas, Ontario, comes this loaf from the past. It was so nostalgic for both of us that Helen and I single-handedly finished off a whole loaf in two days

1 tsp.	baking soda	5 mL
1 cup	chopped dates	250 mL
1 cup	boiling water	250 mL
1	egg	1
1 cup	white sugar	250 mL
pinch	salt	pinch
1½ cups	flour	375 mL
½ cup	chopped walnuts	125 mL
½ tsp.	vanilla	2 mL
1 tbsp.	melted butter	15 mL

1. In a small bowl, sprinkle baking soda over the dates. Pour boiling water over the dates and allow them to cool.
2. In a larger bowl, mix the cooled date mixture with the remaining ingredients, adding the butter last.
3. Spoon the batter into a greased 3 x 4 x 8" (7 x 10 x 20 cm) loaf pan. Bake at 325°F (160°C) for 1 hour and 10 minutes, or until a toothpick inserted into the center of the loaf comes out clean. Allow to cool for 10 minutes in the pan, then turn out onto a rack to cool.

Makes 1 loaf.

If you double a recipe you only need to use 1½ times as much salt.

Maple Pumpkin Brunch Cake

This may be called brunch cake but it is wonderful any time of the day. The hint of maple with the pumpkin is a real taste tickler.

Maple Pecan Topping:

¾ cup	sugar	175 mL
½ cup	chopped pecans	125 mL
2 tsp.	cinnamon	10 mL
1 tsp.	maple extract	5 mL
2¼ cups	flour	550 mL
1 cup	packed brown sugar	250 mL
1 tbsp.	baking powder	15 mL
½ tsp.	salt	2 mL
½ tsp.	baking soda	2 mL
1 cup	buttermilk OR sour milk (see page 42)	250 mL
¾ cup	canned pumpkin or puréed, cooked, fresh pumpkin	175 mL
½ cup	vegetable oil	125 mL
3	eggs, beaten	3
1 tsp.	maple extract	5 mL

1. Combine the topping ingredients, mixing well. Set aside.
2. Combine the flour, brown sugar, baking powder, salt and baking soda in a large bowl.
3. In a separate bowl, beat together the sour milk, pumpkin, vegetable oil, eggs and maple extract. Add to the dry ingredients, stirring just until mixed.
4. Spread half of the batter in a greased 9 x 13" (23 x 33 cm) cake pan. Sprinkle with half of the topping ingredients. Repeat the layers.
5. Bake at 350°F (180°C) for 40-45 minutes, or until a toothpick inserted in the center comes out clean.
6. Allow to cool for 10 minutes, then serve warm. The cake may also be warmed slightly in the microwave.

Serves 15-18.

NOTE: *This cake freezes well.*

Bread & Breakfast

Sunshine Muffins

*(**HELEN**) These tasty little bursts of sunshine were introduced to us by my mother-in-law, Jeanne, (who just happens to be one of my best friends). They are just one of the tempting little morsels she usually has on hand to try and fatten us up whenever we come to visit!*

1	whole orange, including peel	1
½ cup	orange juice	125 mL
1	egg	1
¼ cup	vegetable oil	60 mL
1½ cups	all-purpose flour	375 mL
¾ cup	sugar	175 mL
1 tsp.	baking powder	5 mL
1 tsp.	baking soda	5 mL
1 tsp.	salt	5 mL
½ cup	raisins	125 mL
½ cup	chopped pecans OR walnuts	125 mL

1. Cut the whole orange into small pieces and remove the seeds. Place the orange, orange juice, egg and oil into a blender. Blend until smooth.
2. In a medium-sized bowl, combine the flour, sugar, baking powder, baking soda, salt, raisins and nuts.
3. Add the orange mixture to the dry ingredients and mix just until all the dry ingredients are moistened.
4. Spoon batter into greased or sprayed muffin tins and bake at 325°F (160°C) for 15-20 minutes.

Makes 12 medium-sized muffins.

See photograph on page 51.

If muffins are sticking to the pan, place the hot pan, right side up, on a wet towel for a few minutes. The muffins will slide right out.

Cranberry Walnut Muffins

Lemon adds an unexpected tang to this nutritious fruit and nut muffin.

1¼ cups	quick-cooking rolled oats	300 mL
1¼ cups	buttermilk OR sour milk*	300 mL
1	medium apple, peeled and grated	1
¼ cup	brown sugar	60 mL
¼ cup	vegetable oil OR melted butter	60 mL
1	egg, lightly beaten	1
1	lemon, grated rind of, OR 1½ tsp. (7 mL) dried	1
1 cup	dried cranberries	250 mL
½ cup	chopped walnuts	125 mL
1¼ cups	all-purpose flour	300 mL
¼ cup	sugar	60 mL
1 tbsp.	baking powder	15 mL
1 tsp.	salt	5 mL
½ tsp.	baking soda	2 mL

1. In a large bowl, soak rolled oats in buttermilk for 10 minutes.
2. Add grated apple, brown sugar, oil, egg, lemon rind, dried cranberries and walnuts to the oat mixture. Stir to combine.
3. In a separate bowl, combine flour, sugar, baking powder, salt and baking soda. Stir into batter, just until moistened.
4. Spoon batter into greased or sprayed muffin pans. Bake at 400°F (200°C) for 20-25 minutes, or until tops are firm to the touch.

Makes large 12 muffins.

* **To sour milk,** pour 1 tbsp. (15 mL) lemon juice OR vinegar into a measuring cup. Add milk to make 1 cup (250 mL). Let stand for 5 minutes, then stir.

Jeff's Banana Nut Muffins

(MARIE) When we first saw Jeff's recipe, which has neither eggs nor noticeable liquid, we were skeptical – but, it works! We add nuts and/or chocolate.

2 cups	mashed banana	500 mL
½ cup	butter, melted	125 mL
2 cups	flour	500 mL
½ cup	sugar	125 mL
1½ tsp.	baking powder	7 mL
1 tsp.	baking soda	5 mL
½ tsp.	salt	2 mL
1 cup	chopped pecans OR chocolate chips	250 mL

 *Bread & Breakfast*

Banana Nut Muffins (continued)

1. In a large bowl, mix the banana and butter together.
2. In a separate bowl, combine the dry ingredients and nuts. Fold into the banana mixture until just combined.
3. Fill 12 greased muffin cups. Bake at 400°F (200°C) for 20 minutes. Turn out onto a rack to cool.

Makes 12 large muffins.

Rhubarb Muffins

Light and moist, these muffins have just the right amount of sweet and sour to please the palate.

1	egg	1
1¼ cups	brown sugar	300 mL
½ cup	vegetable oil	125 mL
2 tsp.	vanilla	10 mL
1 cup	buttermilk OR sour milk, see page 42	250 mL
2½ cups	flour	625 mL
1 tsp.	baking powder	5 mL
1 tsp.	baking soda	5 mL
½ tsp.	salt	2 mL
2½ cups	diced rhubarb	625 mL
½ cup	raisins OR chopped walnuts	125 mL

Cinnamon Topping:

1 tbsp.	melted butter	15 mL
⅓ cup	brown sugar	75 mL
½ tsp.	cinnamon	2 mL

1. In a large mixing bowl, combine egg, sugar, oil, vanilla and buttermilk.
2. In a separate bowl, combine flour with baking powder, baking soda and salt. Add rhubarb and raisins. Fold into liquid mixture.
3. Spoon batter into greased muffin tins. Cups will be quite full.
4. Combine all ingredients for Cinnamon Topping and sprinkle on unbaked muffins.
5. Bake at 375°F (190°C) for 20 minutes. Let sit for 5 minutes, then lift out onto a rack to cool.

Makes 12-18 large muffins.

Apple Streusel Muffins

Use fairly tart apples for best results! This makes large muffins that overflow the edges of the cup. If you want them smaller, make more than 12!

¾ cup	brown sugar	175 mL
½ cup	vegetable oil	125 mL
1	egg	1
1 tsp.	vanilla	5 mL
1 cup	buttermilk OR sour milk, see page 42	250 mL
2½ cups	flour	625 mL
1 tsp.	baking powder	5 mL
1 tsp.	baking soda	5 mL
½ tsp.	salt	2 mL
1 tsp.	cinnamon	5 mL
2 cups	peeled, diced apples	500 mL
½ cup	chopped walnuts (optional)	125 mL

Streusel Topping:

1 tbsp.	melted butter	15 mL
⅓ cup	brown sugar	75 mL
½ tsp.	cinnamon	2 mL

1. In a large mixing bowl, combine sugar, oil, egg, vanilla and buttermilk.
2. In a smaller bowl, combine flour, baking powder, baking soda, salt and cinnamon. Add apples and nuts to the flour mixture. Fold into the liquid mixture, just until blended.
3. Spoon batter into sprayed or greased muffin tins. Cups will be quite full.
4. Combine all streusel topping ingredients and sprinkle on the unbaked muffins. Bake at 375°F (190°C) for 20 minutes. Let sit in pan for 5 minutes, then lift out onto a rack to cool.

Makes 12 large muffins.

To separate glasses that are stuck together, put the bottom glass in hot water and run cold water into the top glass.

Bread & Breakfast

Cornmeal Jambuster Muffins

Ever wonder how the jam got into the doughnut? OK, so this isn't a doughnut, but it's a lot easier than you think with this tasty muffin.

1½ cups	cornmeal	375 mL
1½ cups	buttermilk*	375 mL
¾ cup	butter OR margarine, melted	175 mL
3	eggs, slightly beaten	3
2¼ cups	all-purpose flour	550 mL
1 cup	sugar	250 mL
1½ tsp.	baking powder	7 mL
¾ tsp.	baking soda	3 mL
½ tsp.	salt	2 mL
	jam (your favorite)	

1. In a medium bowl, soak the cornmeal in buttermilk for 10 minutes. The cornmeal will absorb the liquid.
2. Add the melted butter and eggs to the cornmeal mixture.
3. In a large bowl, combine flour, sugar, baking powder, baking soda and salt.
4. Add liquid mixture to the dry ingredients. Gently fold until just combined.
5. Spray muffin tins. Spoon batter into tins, filling ¾ full. (They will rise quite a bit.)
6. Make a hollow in the center of each muffin with a spoon and slide 1 tsp. (5 mL) of jam into the hollow.
7. Bake at 400°F (200°C) for 15 minutes. As the muffin bakes, the batter will close in over the jam. Voila! – a jambuster muffin!

Makes 18 large muffins.

* Or use **sour milk** – *pour 2 tbsp. (30 mL) vinegar or lemon juice into a large measuring cup; fill with milk to 1½ cups (375 mL).*

To freshen the air in your kitchen, burn some dried rosemary leaves directly on your electric burner.

Chew parsley to get rid of garlic breath.

Bread & Breakfast

Cranberry Orange Coffee Cake

Cranberry, orange and cream cheese are a wonderful combination in our Cranberry Citrus Cream Cheese Pull-Apart Buns, page 34 and in this scrumptious coffee cake. They are both a hit when we are bed and breakfasting!

Crumb Topping:
¾ cup	flour	175 mL
½ cup	sugar	125 mL
½ cup	butter	125 mL

Cream Cheese Layer:
8 oz.	cream cheese	250 g
⅓ cup	sugar	75 mL
1	egg	1
1 tsp.	vanilla	5 mL

Cranberry Cake:
2 cups	flour	500 mL
1 cup	sugar	250 mL
1½ tsp.	baking powder	7 mL
½ tsp.	baking soda	2 mL
½ tsp.	salt	2 mL
¾ cup	orange juice	175 mL
¼ cup	butter, room temperature	60 mL
1 tsp.	vanilla extract	5 mL
1	egg, beaten	1
2 cups	cranberries, fresh or frozen*	500 mL
2 tbsp.	grated orange rind	30 mL

1. In a small bowl, stir together the flour, sugar and butter; set aside
2. In a small bowl, beat the cream cheese and sugar until light and fluffy. Beat in the egg and vanilla and set aside.
3. In a large bowl, combine the flour, sugar, baking powder, baking soda and salt. Stir in the orange juice, butter, vanilla, and egg, mixing well. Fold in the cranberries and orange rind just until mixed.
4. Pour batter into a 9" (23 cm) springform pan. Spread the cream cheese mixture evenly over the cake batter. Sprinkle with crumb topping.
5. Bake at 350°F (180°C) for 70-80 minutes, or until top springs back when lightly touched.
6. Cool on a rack for 15 minutes; remove the ring and cool completely.

Serves 12.

* *Chop commercial berries into smaller pieces; wild berries are smaller.*

Feather-Crisp Waffles

(HELEN) Marie and I are always on the lookout for something that might be just a slight improvement on something we already do well. These waffles fall into that category. The substitution of cornstarch for some of the flour adds to the crispiness; beating the sugar with the egg whites adds to the lightness; the vanilla enhances the flavor. These are great served with our homemade Pancake Syrup, Cranberries and Canada Geese, page 201. When I serve them to my grandchildren, mixed fruit and whipped cream are a must!

1½ cups	flour	375 mL
½ cup	cornstarch	125 mL
½ tsp.	salt	2 mL
1 tsp.	baking powder	5 mL
½ tsp.	baking soda	2 mL
2 cups	buttermilk OR sour milk, see page 42	500 mL
½ cup	vegetable oil	125 mL
2	eggs, separated (use 3 if they are not large)	2
2 tbsp.	sugar	30 mL
1 tsp.	vanilla	5 mL

1. Heat oven to 200°F (93°C). Heat and grease or spray the waffle iron.
2. In a medium-sized bowl, combine flour, cornstarch, salt, baking powder, and baking soda.
3. In a separate bowl, combine buttermilk, oil and egg yolks. Set aside.
4. In another bowl, beat egg whites until soft peaks just start to form. Sprinkle in the sugar gradually and continue to beat until peaks are firm and glossy. Beat in the vanilla.
5. Add the buttermilk mixture to the dry ingredients and whisk until just mixed. Drop the egg white mixture in mounds over the batter; fold the whites into the batter until just incorporated.
6. Scoop batter onto greased waffle iron. The amount of batter depends on the type of waffle; a Belgian waffler takes about 1½ cups (375 mL) of batter. Quickly spread the batter evenly with a spatula. Cook according to manufacturer's directions – watch the steam – it diminishes as the waffle cooks.
7. Place cooked waffles directly on an oven rack to keep warm and crisp. Repeat with the remaining batter. Waffles should have only about 5 minutes in the oven but can be held for longer.

Makes 3 Belgian Waffles.

VARIATIONS: Substitute ½ cup (125 mL) whole-wheat flour for ½ cup (125 mL) of the white; OR add ½ cup (125 mL) mini chocolate chips to batter; OR add 2 tsp. (10 mL) finely grated orange zest and ½ cup (125 mL) chopped dried cranberries.

Apple Walnut Pancakes

Elaine Friesen, while cooking at Dymond Lake before our hunting season opened, left a note on our recipe for Sour Cream Pancakes. It read, "I have modified this recipe to make one of our favorites." We are delighted when one of our recipes gives birth!

1½ cups	flour	375 mL
½ cup	whole-wheat flour	125 mL
2 tsp.	baking powder	10 mL
1 tsp.	baking soda	5 mL
2 tsp.	sugar	10 mL
½ tsp.	salt	2 mL
2	eggs, slightly beaten	2
½ cup	sour cream	125 mL
2 cups	milk	500 mL
2	apples, peeled and sliced	2
¼ cup	chopped walnuts	60 mL

1. In a large mixing bowl, mix together the flours, baking powder, baking soda, sugar and salt.
2. In a separate bowl, whisk together the eggs, sour cream and milk.
3. Pour the milk mixture into the dry ingredients and beat with a wire whisk until the batter is fairly smooth.
4. Fold in the apples and walnuts.
5. Pour the batter on a hot, greased griddle and cook until the tops of the pancakes are bubbly and the edges are slightly dry. Flip the pancakes and cook on the other side until just golden brown.

Makes about 20, 5" (13 cm) pancakes

VARIATION: Helen's nephew Jeff adds ½ cup (125 mL) mozzarella cheese, too!

Poached eggs – add a few drops of white vinegar to the water to stop poached eggs from losing their shape.

Bread & Breakfast

Grunt Cake

We're not sure where the name came from but this pancake hails from a good customer from Chicago – well he used to be a good customer, now he is really a good friend! This is a favorite of his grandson Mike who taught us to sprinkle it with cinnamon and sugar. Maple syrup or fruit and whipped cream are delicious, too.

2 tbsp.	butter, melted	30 mL
3	eggs	3
½ cup	milk	125 mL
½ cup	flour	125 mL

1. Melt the butter in an 9" (23 cm) ovenproof dish or frying pan.
2. Beat eggs in a medium bowl. Add milk and flour; whisk until smooth.
3. Pour the batter into the sizzling butter in the pan and bake at 400°F (200°C) for 20 minutes.

Serves 4.

Vanilla Waffle Topping

(HELEN) My son-in-law Mike introduced our family to this taste treat – delicious on waffles or pancakes. It was a Sunday morning staple at his house. Our waffles were served with strawberries and whipped cream.

2 tbsp.	cornstarch	30 mL
¼ cup	sugar	60 mL
	pinch of salt	
2 cups	milk	500 mL
1 tsp.	vanilla	5 mL
	fresh or thawed frozen raspberries OR fruit of your choice	

1. In a small saucepan, combine cornstarch, sugar and salt. Add milk, stirring to dissolve the solids.
2. Heat, stirring constantly, until the sauce comes to a simmer and thickens slightly. This is a thin sauce although it will thicken a bit as it cools
3. Remove from the heat and add the vanilla.
4. Serve warm with fruit over waffles or pancakes.

Makes about 2 cups (500 mL).

NOTE: If you like a sweeter sauce, increase the sugar by 2 tbsp. (30 mL).

Bread & Breakfast

Peach Blueberry Compote

(HELEN) This peach liqueur blueberry sauce has replaced the raspberry sauce on White Chocolate Cheesecake wrapped in Phyllo (Black Currants & Caribou, page 162). Try it on waffles, ice cream and the custard on page 174!

3 cups	blueberries, fresh or frozen, divided	750 mL
1½ cups	sugar	375 mL
¼ cup	peach schnapps	60 mL

1. Combine **1 cup (250 mL)** of blueberries and the sugar in a saucepan. Heat to boiling; simmer until juices thicken slightly, 8-10 minutes.
2. Stir in the remaining blueberries and the peach schnapps. Bring to a boil and remove from the heat.
3. Pour into a jar, cover and store in the refrigerator.

Makes 3 cups (750 mL).

Fruit Sauces

At the Lodges we turn whatever fruit we have on hand into sauces for waffles or pancakes. Most fruits need no thickening as long as very little water is used.

Mango Nectarine Sauce

1-2	mangos, peeled, pitted and chopped	1-2
2-3	nectarines, peeled, pitted and chopped	2-3
	water	
	sugar	

1. Simmer the fruit in a saucepan with very little water until tender, 5-10 minutes stir occasionally. Add sugar to taste and it's ready.

Cherry Blueberry Sauce

14 oz.	can cherries, undrained	398 mL
2 tbsp.	kirsch (optional)	30 mL
¼ tsp.	EACH, cinnamon and nutmeg	1 mL
½ cup	sugar	125 mL
1 tbsp.	lemon juice	15 mL
2 cups	blueberries, fresh or frozen	500 mL
2 tbsp.	butter	30 mL

1. In a medium saucepan, combine all ingredients, except blueberries and butter. Bring to a boil; simmer for 10 minutes, until liquid is reduced.
2. Add the blueberries; simmer for 10 minutes and add butter.

Hash Brown Breakfast Casserole, page 55
Sunshine Muffins, page 41

Breakfast Bites

These crunchy individual breakfast quiche are easy to serve and can be started ahead of time (or the night before). Plan for more than 1 per person. Serve with fruit and toast.

12 slices	whole-wheat bread	12
	butter	
4	eggs	4
¾ cup	milk OR cream	175 mL
4 slices	bacon, diced	4
4	green onions, chopped	4
⅔ cup	shredded Cheddar cheese	150 mL

1. Remove crusts from bread and spread 1 side with butter. Press bread, buttered side down, into tart or muffin tins. Bake at 325°F (160°C) for 10 minutes.
2. Combine eggs and milk in a large measuring cup. Set aside.
3. Sauté bacon in a small frying pan. When bacon is almost crisp, add onion and sauté for 2 minutes more. Drain off fat.
4. Divide the bacon and onion evenly between the 12 toast cups. You may stop here, cover the muffin pan, and refrigerate to be continued later.
5. Pour some of the egg mixture into the toast cups, allowing it to be partially absorbed, then add the rest. Sprinkle with cheese.
6. Bake at 325°F (160°C) for 16-18 minutes, or until golden and puffed.

Serves 4-6.

VARIATION: Substitute jalapeño jack cheese for the Cheddar cheese.

Bacon for a crowd.
For easy cleanup, line a baking sheet with aluminum foil. Lay out bacon strips on the foil and bake at 350°F (180°C) for 30 minutes. When bacon is done, throw the aluminum foil away.

Rainbow over Hudson Bay, at Seal River Heritage Lodge.

Bread & Breakfast

Weekender Special

Helen's mother-in-law, Jeanne, is a source of many fine recipes. We took a peek at her collection one day and couldn't resist this tempting breakfast special.

10 slices	bacon	10 slices
½	green pepper, chopped	½
½	red pepper, chopped	½
8	green onions, chopped	8
4 cups	sliced fresh mushrooms	1 L
3 tbsp.	sherry	45 mL
12	eggs	12
1½ cups	milk	375 mL
1½ tsp.	DLS* OR 1 tsp. (5 mL) seasoned salt	7 mL
1 tsp.	dry mustard	5 mL
½ tsp.	dried thyme	2 mL
4 cups	grated Gruyère OR mozzarella cheese	1 L

1. In a large frying pan, fry bacon until crisp; drain and chop. In the same frying pan, sauté green and red peppers, onions and mushrooms until limp. Add sherry and heat until sherry evaporates.
2. In a bowl, beat together eggs, milk, salt, mustard and thyme. Add bacon, vegetables and 3 cups (750 mL) of cheese.
3. Pour the egg mixture into a greased 9 x 13" (23 x 33 cm) baking pan. Cover and refrigerate overnight.
4. Bake, uncovered, at 350°F (180°C) for 40 minutes. Sprinkle with the remaining 1 cup (250 mL) of cheese. Return to the oven and bake until the cheese melts, about 2 minutes. Let stand for 10 minutes before serving.

Serves 8.

Ripen tomatoes by storing them in a dark drawer or cupboard.

Bread & Breakfast

Hash Brown Breakfast Casserole

The preparation is all done ahead, and in the morning you produce an egg, ham and potato breakfast with no fuss, all in 1 dish. We love to use this recipe at the lodges. Serve with muffins, toast or coffeecake.

3 tbsp.	vegetable oil	45 mL
2 lbs.	frozen hash-brown potatoes	1 kg
1 cup	chopped onion	250 mL
1	EACH green and red pepper, chopped	1
2 cups	cubed ham OR fried farmer's sausage	500 mL
10	eggs, beaten	10
1⅓ cups	milk	325 mL
2 tsp.	salt	10 mL
½ tsp.	pepper OR 1 tsp. (5 mL) DLS*	2 mL
1½ cups	grated Cheddar cheese	375 mL

1. Heat the oil in a large skillet. Add the hash browns, onions and peppers. Cook until the potatoes begin to brown.
2. Spray a 9 x 13" (23 x 33 cm) baking pan and spread the potato mixture in the pan. Top with ham.
3. In a medium bowl, beat together the eggs and milk. Add salt and pepper or DLS*.
4. Pour the egg mixture over the potatoes and gently stir to coat all of the ingredients with egg. Sprinkle with the cheese.
5. Cover and refrigerate overnight.
6. Bake, uncovered, at 375°F (190°C) for 50-60 minutes

Serves 8-10.

*   *Dymond Lake Seasoning, see page 3.*

See photograph on page 51.

Beluga Whales

The beluga is a mammal belonging to the Order, Cetacea, along with 80 species of whales, dolphins and porpoises. Also known as the "white whale", their color distinguishes them from all the others – though they are only white in maturity. They are also unique in the fact that they molt every summer, sloughing off the old yellowed skin to reveal fresh white skin, which is soft and smooth to the touch.

An adult beluga measures from 10-18 ft. (3-5.5 m) and weighs from 900 lbs.-2 tons (400-1000 kg). Its lifespan may be about 30 years.

Belugas are found exclusively in the northern hemisphere in the icy waters off the coasts of Norway, Russia, Alaska, Greenland and Canada, though they migrate just far enough south in the winter to avoid being totally closed in by ice packs. In the summer, they eagerly follow the receding ice north again. They are the only mammal that is equally comfortable in salt or fresh water, deep or shallow water, spending much of their time in the mouths of rivers.

Females give birth to one calf every 2-4 years, which they nurse for more than a year. At the birth, a group of adult "helpers" lifts the baby to the surface for its first breath. This calf may continue to travel with its mom even after the next calf is born, making for a close family group.

Belugas are very social, traveling in groups called pods, but individuals move freely between pods, and are often in pods of the same makeup – i.e., all males, or all females with calves.

Belugas are the most vocal of all cetaceans, using a bewildering mixture of groans, buzzes, clicks, whistles, screams, pops and "raspberries", some of which are used both above and below the water; for this reason they are sometimes called "sea canaries".

Belugas use sound to communicate and to gather information. This is called echolocation. It allows them to capture fish for food in complete darkness, and also to avoid the fishermen's nets.

Though the beluga needs air to breathe, it also feeds partially on the sea floor, holding its breath for 12-20 minutes each time it dives. Worms and sandeels are picked up from the bottom, but capelin, halibut, lantern fish, redfish and arctic cod are the main diet and are more accessible in open water.

At Churchill, whales were once killed for meat and oil, first by the Inuit and then for commercial use; the whaling factory only closed in 1968. Almost all whales captured for public viewing were taken from the shallow waters of the Churchill River. Helen and I both witnessed one of those captures around 1980, but the holding and transporting process proved to be too stressful for the animal. (Now newcomers are born in captivity and live in improved facilities.) Today, Churchill is an ideal place for viewing belugas in the wild, both in the Churchill River and in Hudson Bay.

Information gathered from **Beluga Whales** *– WorldLife Library – by Tony Martin*

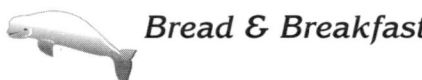

Midday Madness

Soups, hot or cold, are the mainstay of our lunches at the hunting camp. Collected from friends and family, or reproduced from memorable lunches eaten out, nothing satisfies more or is healthier fare. Some of our favorites here are Orange Carrot Soup and Black Bean Soup, but don't overlook the more unusual flavors of Spinach or Cucumber soup. For a more traditional meal, the down-home goodness of Creamy Tomato Macaroni and Cheese really can't be beat. For the more adventuresome, our Stuffed Pizza will satisfy hearty appetites.

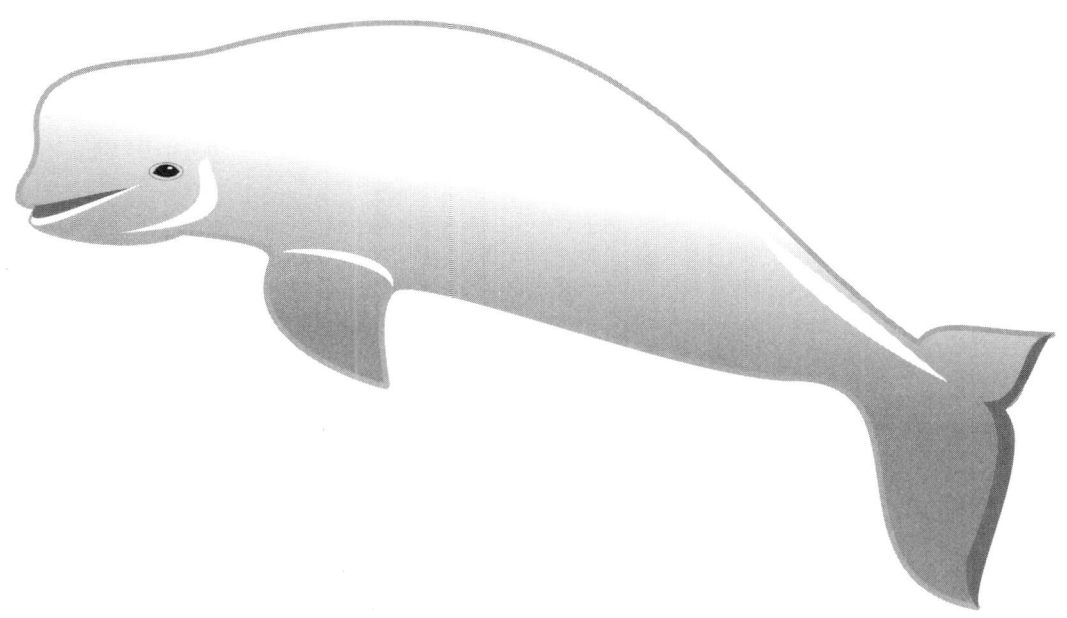

Chilled Cucumber Soup

Cold soups are so refreshing. On hot summer days this makes a great starter, or serve it for lunch with crusty rolls and Cheesy Broccoli Salad, page 114, or a tossed green salad.

3	cucumbers*	3
4 tsp.	butter	20 mL
1	medium onion, chopped	1
1	bay leaf	1
1 tbsp.	flour	15 mL
3 cups	chicken stock	750 mL
1 tsp.	salt	5 mL
1 cup	cream	250 mL
½	lemon, juice of	½
	chopped chives	

1. Peel 2 cucumbers; cut them lengthwise; remove and discard the seeds. Dice the cucumbers.
2. Melt butter in a large saucepan. Add cucumbers, onion, and bay leaf. Sauté gently for 15 minutes.
3. Stir in the flour and cook for 1 minute. Add the chicken stock; cook, stirring, until thickened. Add salt and simmer for 20-30 minutes.
4. Remove the bay leaf. Remove the soup from the heat. Purée the soup in a blender, then chill thoroughly.
5. To serve, peel and grate the remaining cucumber. Add grated cucumber to the soup, along with the cream, lemon juice and chives. Serve icy cold.

Serves 4-6.

* *If using English cucumbers, 2 are enough and there is no need to remove the seeds. Save ½ cucumber, unpeeled, for step number 5. Do not peel the English cucumber before grating.*

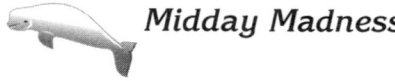

Greek Lemon Soup

Lemons are used in so many wonderful Greek dishes, Greek ribs, Greek feta-stuffed chicken, and this wonderful Avgolemono soup.

6 cups	chicken broth	1.5 L
½-¾ cups	long-grain rice	125-175 mL
3	egg yolks	3
¼ cup	lemon juice	60 mL
	salt and pepper to taste	
	fresh lemon, sliced thinly, for garnish	
½	chopped parsley OR cilantro for garnish	

1. In a large saucepan, bring the chicken broth to a boil. Add the rice; cover and reduce heat. Allow the rice to simmer for about 20 minutes.
2. Whisk egg yolks and lemon juice together until well combined.
3. When the rice is tender, remove the soup from the heat. Whisk 1 cup (250 mL) of the hot broth into the egg mixture. Whisk this back into the soup pot.
4. Return the soup to medium heat, stirring constantly. **Do not let the soup boil or it will curdle**. Add salt and pepper to taste. Garnish with lemon and parsley. Serve immediately.

Serves 6.

Onion Soup

This soup is addictive. There is nothing better on a snowy winter evening than a steaming bowl of this Onion Soup.

12 cups	very thinly sliced medium onions, in rings	3 L
¼ cup	butter	60 mL
2 x 10 oz.	cans beef consommé	2 x 284 mL
10 oz.	EACH water and red wine	284 mL
2 tbsp.	beef concentrate	30 mL
	toast, crusts cut off	
1	garlic clove	1
2 cups	grated mozzarella cheese	500 mL

1. In a large pot, sauté onions in butter until onions are translucent.
2. Add consommé, water, red wine and beef concentrate. Simmer, covered, for 2 hours. Add more broth if necessary.
3. To serve, place soup in ovenproof bowls. Rub 1 side of the toast with the garlic. Place the toast garlic side down on the soup. Top with grated mozzarella. Heat under a broiler until the cheese is bubbly.

Serves 8.

Midday Madness

Cream of Spinach Soup

A rich, creamy soup, tart with lemon, the spinach adds nutrition and color! Surprise your guests and family with this very agreeable way to serve spinach.

2 x 10 oz.	pkgs. spinach, chopped	2 x 285 g
¼ cup	butter	60 mL
¼ cup	flour	60 mL
6 cups	chicken broth	1.5 L
4	egg yolks	4
½ cup	cream	125 mL
⅛ tsp.	grated nutmeg	0.5 mL
2 tbsp.	fresh lemon OR lime juice	30 mL
¼ tsp.	salt	1 mL
dash	cayenne pepper	dash

1. Melt the butter in a large saucepan. Sauté the spinach in butter until it is soft – about 3 minutes. Stir in the flour. Gradually add the chicken broth. Simmer, stirring, for 5 minutes.
2. Blend egg yolks with cream. Remove the soup from the heat. Add a little of the broth to the egg yolks, then stir the egg mixture into the broth.
3. Return the soup to the heat and bring almost to a boil, stirring well. Add nutmeg, lemon, salt and pepper.
4. Serve hot or chilled.

Serves 6-8.

Cream of Carrot Soup

As a start to a meal, this soup is tops! It may be served hot, as suggested here, or chilled and served cold.

2 tbsp.	butter	30 mL
4 cups	peeled, sliced carrots	1 L
1 cup	chopped onion	250 mL
3 cups	chicken stock	750 mL
1 tsp.	sugar	5 mL
¼ tsp.	salt	1 mL
½ cup	orange juice	125 mL
½ cup	cream OR canned milk	125 mL
	cream, sour cream OR yogurt for garnish	
	dill for garnish	

Midday Madness

Cream of Carrot Soup (continued)

1. Melt the butter in a large saucepan and add the carrots and onions. Sauté for 5 minutes to soften the vegetables.
2. Add the chicken stock, sugar and salt. Bring to a boil. Cover and simmer for 30 minutes.
3. Remove saucepan from heat and purée the contents in a blender.
4. Return the purée to the saucepan. Add the orange juice and cream. Reheat.
5. Ladle the soup into individual bowls. Swirl some cream in the center of each bowl. Sprinkle with dill.

Serves 6.

See photograph on page 69.

Curried Squash Soup

Whenever Helen and I taste a soup we really like, we take it as a challenge to go home and duplicate it. This is one such challenge – conquered! We hope you enjoy the prize!

6 cups	peeled, chunked butternut squash	1.5 L
¾ cup	chopped onion	175 mL
2 tbsp.	chopped fresh cilantro	30 mL
1	garlic clove, crushed	1
2 cups	strong chicken stock	500 mL
½ tsp.	salt	2 mL
1 tbsp.	fresh lemon juice	15 mL
½ tsp.	cumin	2 mL
½ tsp.	curry powder	2 mL
½ tsp.	pepper	2 mL
½ cup	cream	125 mL

1. In a large saucepan, bring all of the ingredients, except the cream, to a boil. Simmer until the vegetables are very tender, about 30 minutes. Remove from the heat and purée until smooth.
2. Add the cream and reheat, but do not boil. Taste and adjust seasonings.

Serves 4.

Midday Madness

Simply Delicious Mushroom Soup

(HELEN) Marie was off to bible study and I was in charge of lunch. There were lots of mushrooms in the refrigerator and I had never made homemade mushroom soup before . . . soo, I thought, why not? I used a combination of white and shiitake mushrooms, but you should use what you have available.

¼ cup	butter	60 mL
½ cup	chopped onion, in ½" (1.3 cm) chunks	125 mL
¼ cup	chopped celery	60 mL
1	large garlic clove, chopped	1
2 tsp.	DLS*	10 mL
½ tsp.	salt	2 mL
2 cups	sliced button mushrooms	500 mL
1 cup	sliced portobello OR shiitake mushrooms, in ½" (1.3 cm) pieces	125 mL
3 tbsp.	flour	45 mL
2 cups	half-and-half cream OR evaporated milk	500 mL
2 cups	milk	500 mL

1. Melt the butter in a medium-sized saucepan. Add the onions, stirring to coat with butter. Turn the heat to low; cover and cook the onions for 5 minutes, stirring twice.
2. Add celery and garlic and cook over medium heat for 2-3 minutes. Add DLS*, salt and mushrooms. Continue to cook, stirring occasionally until the mushrooms are cooked, about 5 minutes.
3. Add 1 tbsp. (15 mL) of butter and cook until melted. Remove the saucepan from the heat. Stir in the flour until it is absorbed by the butter. Slowly add half-and-half, stirring constantly to keep the mixture smooth. Cook over medium heat until it simmers. Simmer for 2-3 minutes, stirring constantly. Stir in the milk and heat just until the soup comes to a boil.

Serves 4.

* *Dymond Lake Seasoning, see page 3, OR substitute 1 tsp. (5 mL) of seasoned pepper and adjust the salt to taste*

Midday Madness

Black Bean Soup

(MARIE) *After tasting Black Bean Soup for the first time at a conference, I was terribly excited when I came across this recipe. I was even more excited when the taste was as wonderful as the soup I remembered.*

3 tbsp.	olive oil	45 mL
½ cup	chopped onion	125 mL
2	garlic cloves, minced	2
1 tsp	ground cumin	5 mL
¾ cup	chopped celery	175 mL
¾ cup	chopped carrots	175 mL
3½ cups	chicken OR vegetable stock	975 mL
2 x 19 oz.	cans black beans, rinsed and drained	2 x 540 mL
¼ cup	chopped fresh cilantro OR 4 tsp. (20 mL) dried	60 mL
1	lime, juice of	1
1 tbsp.	tomato paste*	15 mL
	sour cream for garnish	
	salsa for garnish	
	cilantro for garnish	

1. In a large saucepan, heat the oil and add the onion and garlic, cook until tender.
2. Stir in the cumin and cook for 1 minute.
3. Add the celery, carrots, stock, beans and cilantro. Heat to boiling. Reduce the heat and simmer, covered, for 15-20 minutes.
4. Stir in the lime juice and tomato paste.
5. Purée the soup in a blender and return to the pot. Reheat; taste and add salt if necessary.
6. Serve with sour cream, salsa and cilantro as condiments.

Serves 6.

* **Tomato Paste:** *To make your own tomato paste, simmer a 28 oz. (796 mL) can of crushed tomatoes, uncovered, stirring occasionally, for 1 hour. Makes 1 cup (250 mL).*

Add salt early to soups, late to meats.

To reverse oversalting in a liquid, add a raw potato.

Midday Madness

Tomato Mushroom Pasta Sauce

From Helen's daughter Toni comes this tasty tomato mushroom sauce.

2 tbsp.	butter	30 mL
2 tbsp.	olive oil	30 mL
⅓ cup	chopped celery	75 mL
⅓ cup	chopped onion	75 mL
2	garlic cloves, crushed	2
2 cups	sliced fresh mushrooms	500 mL
1 tsp.	DLS* OR ½ tsp. (2 mL) pepper	5 mL
½ tsp.	salt	2 mL
14 oz. can	tomato sauce	398 mL
3 tbsp.	chopped fresh parsley	45 mL
2 tbsp.	sugar	30 mL
3 tbsp.	chopped fresh basil	45 mL
1 tsp.	Worcestershire sauce	5 mL

    pasta** for 4-6

1. In a large saucepan, heat the butter and olive oil. Sauté the celery, onion and garlic until softened, about 5 minutes. Add the mushrooms, DLS* and salt and sauté 5 minutes more.
2. Add the remaining ingredients, except the pasta. Simmer for 10 minutes to blend the flavors. Adjust the seasoning.
3. Cook the pasta according to the package directions and serve with the sauce.

Serves 4-6 – makes 3 cups (750 mL) of sauce.

* Dymond Lake Seasoning, see page 3.
** 1 lb. (500 g) of pasta serves 4-6, depending on the other dishes you are serving.

For tearless chopping of onions, freeze them for 20 minutes before chopping.

Creamy Tomato Macaroni and Cheese

Imagine a cold, stormy day (not hard to conjure up in September at Dymond Lake Hunting Lodge), a warm kitchen and the aroma of the ultimate comfort food? Snuggle in and enjoy this traditional fare.

3 cups	macaroni OR other small pasta	750 mL
1 tbsp.	butter	15 mL
1	small onion, finely chopped	1
¼ cup	flour	60 mL
3 cups	milk	750 mL
1 tsp.	Dijon mustard	5 mL
2 cups	shredded Cheddar cheese	500 mL
¼ cup	grated Parmesan cheese	60 mL
28 oz.	can diced tomatoes, well drained	796 mL
1 tsp.	salt	5 mL
1 tsp.	DLS* OR ½ tsp. (2 mL) pepper	5 mL

1. Cook the macaroni according to package directions. Drain well.
2. In a heavy saucepan, melt the butter over medium heat. Cook the onion until softened, about 5 minutes. Add flour and stir until smooth.
3. Gradually whisk in milk, keeping a smooth consistency. Add mustard. Cook,stirring often, until thickened, about 10 minutes. (Do not boil.)
4. Remove from heat and stir in the cheeses until melted.
5. Add the tomatoes, salt and pepper. Reheat. Pour the sauce over the macaroni and stir well.

Serves 4-6.

*   *Dymond Lake Seasoning, see page 3.*

A small amount of oil or butter added to the water when cooking pasta prevents it from boiling over or sticking together.

Stuffed Pizza

This hearty pizza has a crust on top and bottom. Every bite oozes with flavor.

Pizza Dough:
1½ cups	warm water	375 mL
2 tbsp.	vegetable oil	30 mL
1½ tsp.	salt	7 mL
3 cups	flour	750 mL
1 tbsp.	instant yeast*	15 mL
¼ cup	finely chopped green onion	60 mL

Pizza Stuffing:
½ cup	sun-dried tomatoes	125 mL
	boiling water	
1 cup	shredded Edam cheese	250 mL
¾ cup	shredded medium Cheddar cheese	175 mL
¾ cup	shredded provolone cheese	175 mL
1 cup	chopped smoked Polish sausage OR kielbasa	250 mL
½ cup	chopped green pepper	125 mL
1	beaten egg	1
2 tbsp.	grated Parmesan cheese	30 mL
¼ tsp.	coarsely ground black pepper	1 mL

1. Combine all dough ingredients, adding the flour a little at a time. Knead on a lightly floured surface until smooth and not sticky. Divide dough in half; cover and let rest for 5 minutes while you prepare the stuffing.
2. Pour boiling water over the dried tomatoes in a bowl. Let stand for 2 minutes; drain; pat dry; snip into small pieces with kitchen shears.
3. Combine Edam, Cheddar and provolone cheeses in a medium bowl.
4. Grease an 11-13" (27-33 cm) pizza pan. On a lightly floured or greased surface, roll each dough portion into a circle 1" (2.5 cm) larger in diameter than the pan.
5. Transfer 1 crust to the pan. Sprinkle with half the cheese mixture. Layer with tomato, sausage and green pepper. Sprinkle with the remaining cheese mixture.
6. Cut several slits in the remaining crust. Center over the pizza. Turn under and flute the edges. Brush with beaten egg. Sprinkle with Parmesan cheese and black pepper.
7. Bake at 375°F (190°C) for 30 to 35 minutes. Cover with foil after 20 minutes if necessary to prevent overbrowning. Cut into 12 wedges.

Serves 6-8.

* *See notes on YEAST and rising techniques on page 30.*

Spinach and Mushroom Melts

(JEFF'S) Serve on toast for lunch or on toast quarters as an appetizer.

½ cup	butter	125 mL
5	garlic cloves	5
3 cups	sliced mushrooms	750 mL
	DLS* OR salt and pepper to taste	
10 oz.	fresh baby spinach	300 g
½ loaf	French bread, toasted	½ loaf
	mozzarella OR your favorite cheese, sliced	
	sliced sun-dried tomatoes in oil (optional)	

1. In a frying pan, melt the butter and sauté the garlic and mushrooms until the mushrooms are golden brown, about 5 minutes. Add DLS* and spinach. Stir until the spinach is just wilted, about 1-2 minutes.
2. Heap the spinach mixture on toasted French bread. Top with cheese and broil until the cheese melts. Garnish with tomatoes if desired.

Serves 8-10.

* *Dymond Lake Seasoning, see page 3.*

Double Trouble

(HELEN) A group of naturalists were arriving at Dymond Lake the next day and my sister Patti and I had just been dropped off by our pilot to get the camp ready AND cook for them for four days. Ice on the lake had prevented us from getting in earlier as we were on floats. The pilot stayed around long enough to hook up the water pump for us and then he was gone. At that point Patti looked at me and said "So where is the gun for bear protection?" "Beats me, I don't think we have one; I guess we'll just have to keep our eyes and ears open!"

We proceeded to get the water pump going and I told Patti I would turn on the gas and light the pilot lights while she started making beds. I turned on the propane tanks, then went into the kitchen to light the pilots. For some reason, I turned on all the burners for the grill BEFORE I lit the match. I bent over, put the match in and "BOOM". I knew my hair was burning – I remembered seeing a towel on the counter so, with my eyes closed, I reached up, grabbed it and started rubbing my hair. I opened my eyes to see bits of hair hitting the floor. Patti walked in to find me with singed hair and eyelashes, and a slightly red face. However, I was fine.

Patti reported that the water pump was still running, so we left to find the problem. As soon as I walked into the lakefront cabin, I knew what the problem was! The water lines had all been disconnected in the fall and had not been reconnected before we started the pump. The floor was covered with at least an inch of water. Patti and I looked at one other and I said, "We do not have time to mop this up – there is only one thing to do!" We drilled about six holes in the floor and let the water run through! Thank goodness we didn't have carpets in those days. We hooked up the lines, threw around a few scatter rugs the next day, and the guests didn't guess a thing. Too bad I couldn't disguise my hair and face so easily!

"Air Born"

by Gary Woolsey

As a priest-pilot for the Anglican Church of Canada I covered an area of some 250,000 square miles in northwestern Ontario and northeastern Manitoba, visiting some 25 native villages each month. Marie and I were living in the Cree village of Big Trout Lake, approximately 250 miles northeast of Kenora, Ontario.

One beautiful summer day I decided to visit a neighboring village, Angling Lake, to see how their new handicraft business was developing. After docking the four-seater Cessna 180 float plane, I went to the little cabin to see what items were for sale. Almost immediately, a teenaged girl came in and said that I was wanted at a cabin. On entering I found the one-room log cabin packed to the door with women! They opened a path for me, and there on a mattress on the floor was a teenaged girl about to give birth to a baby.

Why had they called me? "Delivering A Baby 101" was not offered at the theological college I had attended! So I did the only thing I could do – pray! Since they did not have a Nursing Station, I asked if they had talked to the nurse at Big Trout Lake. "No," was the reply. The battery for their two-way radio was dead, so I rushed to the plane, took out the battery and, after hooking it up to their radio, made contact with the nurse. She said that she would come over to the village but there were no planes at Big Trout. I told her to be ready at the nursing station dock but it would take me about 20 minutes to get there.

I had not counted on this extra flight, and there was no time to take on extra fuel. I said a prayer and picked up the nurse. When we arrived at the village I let her proceed to the house. I went to the craft shop. Then I noticed a crowd of people heading to the dock. A messenger burst into the shop, saying that the nurse wanted the baby to be delivered at Big Trout Lake. I ran at top speed to the dock and took out the right-hand seat and the back seat. We laid the girl on the floor with her head next to my seat. The nurse squeezed in behind me.

The wind had picked up and there were whitecaps on the lake. The takeoff was quick, but bouncing off those waves made me feel for the poor girl. My gas gauges were nearing the empty mark. "Lord, help us make it safely," I murmured. I felt a tap on my shoulder and the nurse said, "I don't think we are going to make it." Then I heard it – "Waaaaaa". A baby boy was born at 500 feet above the trees, somewhere between Big Trout and Angling Lake. "Now Lord," I prayed, "give me the smoothest landing of my life.z" And He did!

Cream of Carrot Soup, page 60
Butterhorns, page 36
"Not Just Any Spinach Salad", page 10

 *Midday Madness*

Stop & Snack Awhile

We are often asked how we manage to control our weight with all the goodies we are constantly producing. We need to assure you that everything we print has been tested, tasted and enjoyed by both of us – usually more than once! When it comes to snacks, whatever is available that day is our favorite, guaranteed. It is almost impossible to single out one above the others in this new collection, but Cranberry Blondies may well become an all-time favorite. To satisfy your creative streak, have fun putting together our Sand Art Cookies – great for gift giving!

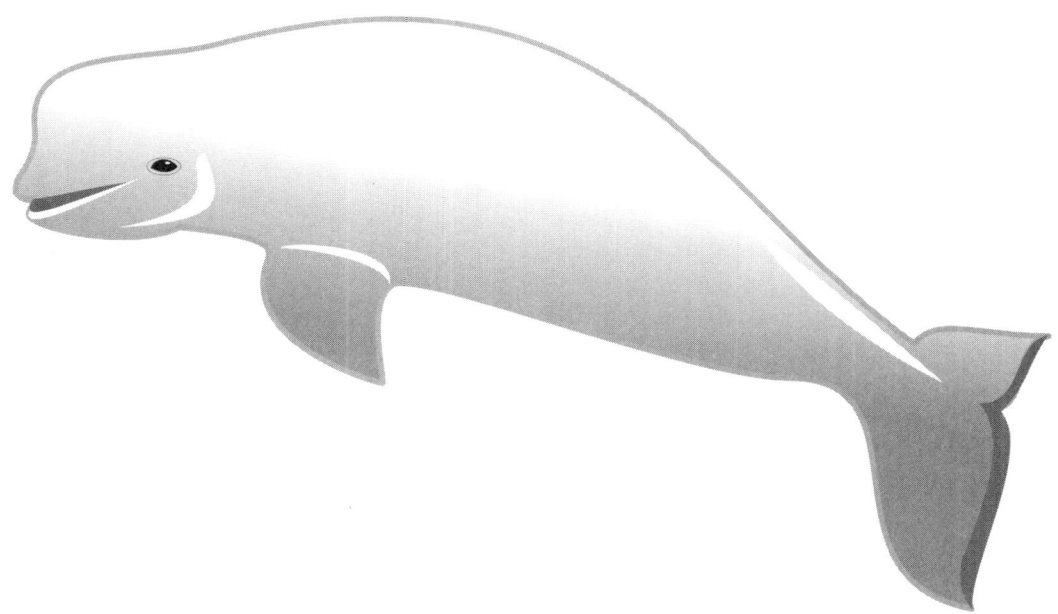

Mike, Rebecca and Karli out among the beluga whales at Seal River Heritage Lodge.

Apricot Biscotti

(MARIE) Biscotti – a word I had not heard in my youth – might be a disappointment if you're expecting a cookie. But if you're a die-hard dunker, biscotti spells heaven!

3 cups	flour	750 mL
2½ tsp.	baking powder	12 mL
1 tsp.	salt	5 mL
½ cup	butter	125 mL
1 cup	sugar	250 mL
2	large eggs	2
3 oz.	white chocolate, melted	85 g
¼ cup	orange juice	60 mL
1 tsp.	vanilla	5 mL
¾ cup	coarsely chopped almonds	175 mL
¾ cup	coarsely chopped dried apricots	175 mL

1. In a small bowl, combine the flour, baking powder and salt.
2. In a large bowl, cream butter with sugar. Add the eggs and melted chocolate.
3. Add dry ingredients, orange juice and vanilla to the butter mixture. Mix until smooth. Add almonds and apricots. The dough will be fairly sticky.
4. Grease 2 baking sheets. Divide the dough in half. Shape each half into a long flat log, 2½" (6 cm) wide. Place 1 log on each baking sheet. Bake at 325°F (160°C) for 25 minutes, switching shelves at halftime.
5. Remove the trays from the oven. Let sit for 5 minutes. Cut partially baked dough diagonally into ½" (1.3 cm) slices. Lay each slice cut side down on the same baking sheets. Reduce oven to 300°F (150°C).
6. Return the trays to the oven and bake for 15 minutes more. Remove to a cooling rack.

Makes 3 dozen.

SERVING SUGGESTION: When cool, eat with coffee or tea – a dunker's delight!

NOTE: Biscotti will harden as they cool. They may be kept in an airtight container for up to 2 weeks or frozen for longer storage.

 Stop & Snack Awhile

Pecan Espresso Biscotti

(HELEN) Espresso, biscotti – we just love these new taste sensations. This is one of my favorites – a coffee lover's dream.

2 cups	flour	500 mL
1½ tsp.	baking powder	7 mL
1 tsp.	cinnamon	5 mL
⅛ tsp.	salt	0.5 mL
½ cup	butter, softened	125 mL
¾ cup	white sugar	175 mL
¾ cup	brown sugar	175 mL
1 tbsp.	instant espresso powder OR 2 tbsp. (30 mL) instant coffee (dark roast)	15 mL
2	eggs	2
1 cup	coarsely chopped pecans OR walnuts	250 mL

Chocolate Dip (optional):

1½ cups	semi-sweet chocolate chips	375 mL
3 tbsp.	shortening	45 mL

1. In a medium-sized bowl, combine the flour, baking powder, cinnamon and salt. Set aside.
2. In a large bowl, with an electric mixer, cream the butter, sugars and espresso powder until light and fluffy. Add the eggs and beat for about 2 minutes.
3. Reduce the speed to low and add the flour mixture, mixing just until blended. Fold in the pecans.
4. Divide the dough in half and place each half on a sprayed baking sheet. Using lightly floured hands, form each half into a rectangle 2½" (6 cm) wide and ¾" (2 cm) high. Bake at 350°F (180°C) for 25 minutes, switching shelves at half time. The dough will spread during baking. Remove the baking sheets from the oven and allow the rectangles to cool on the pans for 5 minutes.
5. Cut the rectangles diagonally into ½" (1.3 cm) slices. Arrange the slices, cut side down, on the same baking sheets. Return to the oven and bake for another 10 minutes. Transfer the biscotti to cooling racks.
6. Place the chocolate chips and shortening in a microwave dish. Heat on high for 2 minutes; remove and stir. Continue to microwave and stir in 15-second intervals, until the chocolate is melted and smooth. Dip 1 end of each biscotti in melted chocolate. Place on waxed paper to cool. Store in the refrigerator.

Makes 3 dozen.

Cappuccino Flats

A perfectly round, coffee-flavored cookie, dipped in melted chocolate, it's great for afternoon tea. Your friends will think you've gone to the bakery!

2 oz.	unsweetened chocolate	55 g
2 cups	flour	500 mL
1 tsp.	cinnamon	5 mL
⅛ tsp.	salt	1 mL
½ cup	shortening, room temperature	125 mL
½ cup	butter, room temperature	125 mL
½ cup	sugar	125 mL
½ cup	packed brown sugar	125 mL
1 tbsp.	instant coffee powder, espresso OR dark roast	15 mL
1 tsp.	hot water	5 mL
1	egg	1
1½ cups	semisweet chocolate pieces	375 mL
3 tbsp.	shortening	45 mL

1. To melt unsweetened chocolate, heat for 2 minutes on medium-high in a microwave, then stir until all of the chocolate is melted OR melt in a saucepan over low heat or over boiling water, stirring until melted. Allow to cool slightly.
2. In a medium bowl, stir together flour, cinnamon and salt.
3. In a large bowl, beat shortening, butter and sugars together until light and fluffy.
4. Melt coffee powder in the warm water. Stir into the butter mixture, along with the melted chocolate and the egg.
5. Add the flour mixture to the dough.
6. Shape dough into 4, 7" (18 cm) rolls. Wrap and chill for 6-7 hours or overnight.
7. Cut rolls into ¼" (1 cm) slices. Place on a greased or sprayed baking pan. Bake at 350°F (180°C) for 10-12 minutes. When firm, remove to a rack to continue cooling.
8. Melt together the semisweet chocolate and the shortening. (See instruction #1.) Dip half of each cookie in the melted chocolate. Allow to cool on waxed paper. Store in the refrigerator and serve cold.

Makes 4 dozen cookies.

NOTE: *Add a dash or 2 of Amaretto, Grand Marnier, Kirsch or liqueur of your choice and use the leftover chocolate to dip fruit. Yummy!*

 Stop & Snack Awhile

Pecan Bites

(MARIE) My friend Aileen Shier makes these wonderful meringues to use up egg whites. They are gluten-free but, best of all, our grandchildren love them!

1	egg white	1
1 cup	packed brown sugar	250 mL
1 tsp.	vanilla	5 mL
2 cups	whole or half pecans	500 mL

1. Beat egg white until soft peaks form. Add brown sugar and beat until stiff. Mix in vanilla. Fold in nuts. Drop the batter by teaspoonfuls on greased baking sheets.
2. Bake at 300°F (150°C) for 30 minutes. Cool, then remove from the pan.

Makes 24-30 meringues (no kidding!).

Best-Ever Cookies

Also known as Church Cookies because of the frequency with which they turn up at church events, these tender cookies are chock full of fiber and goodness.

1 cup	butter	250 mL
1 cup	sugar	250 mL
1 cup	packed brown sugar	250 mL
1	egg	1
1 cup	vegetable oil	250 mL
1 tsp.	vanilla	5 mL
3½ cups	flour	825 mL
1 tsp.	baking soda	5 mL
½ tsp.	salt	2 mL
1 cup	EACH rolled oats and corn flakes	250 mL
½ cup	dried, shredded coconut	125 mL
½ cup	chopped pecans	125 mL

1. Cream the butter and sugars. Add the egg, oil and vanilla and mix well.
2. Combine the flour with baking soda and salt. Add to the creamed mixture and mix well.
3. Add the oats, corn flakes, coconut and pecans and mix until blended.
4. Drop by teaspoonfuls onto greased cookie sheets. Bake for 8-9 minutes at 350°F (180°C).

Makes 11-12 dozen small cookies.

Stop & Snack Awhile

Sand Art Cookies – Three Varieties

Arrange these ingredients in quart sealers, decorate according to the occasion and give them as gifts. They look as wonderful as they taste. Just **fill the jars in the order in which the ingredients are written.**

1. Chewy Chocolate Chip Skor-Bit Cookies

¾ cup	flour	175 mL
½ tsp.	baking powder	2 mL
¾ tsp.	baking soda	3 mL
¼ tsp.	salt	1 mL
½ cup	whole-wheat flour	125 mL
⅓ cup	skor bits	75 mL
¾ cup	rolled oats	175 mL
¾ cup	white sugar	175 mL
⅓ cup	chocolate chips	75 mL
¾ cup	brown sugar	175 mL

1. To make the cookies, combine all of the dry ingredients in a large bowl. In a separate bowl, combine ½ **cup (125 mL) melted butter, 1 egg** and ½ **tsp (2 mL) vanilla** and stir into the dry ingredients. Drop the dough by heaping teaspoonfuls (7 mL) onto greased baking sheets.
2. Bake at 350°F (180°C) for 10 minutes. Cookies will still appear moist. Allow to cool slightly before removing to a cooling rack

Makes 2½ dozen cookies

* If batter seems too dry, add 1-2 tsp. (5-10 mL) of water to batter.

2. Dad's Raisin Spice Cookies

½ cup	flour	125 mL
¼ tsp.	salt	1 mL
1½ tsp.	baking soda	7 mL
½ cup	whole-wheat flour	125 mL
1 tsp.	ginger	5 mL
1 tsp.	cinnamon	5 mL
¼ tsp.	allspice	1 mL
½ cup	dried, shredded coconut	125 mL
1 cup	rolled oats	250 mL
½ cup	white sugar	125 mL
¾ cup	raisins	175 mL
½ cup	brown sugar	125 mL

 Stop & Snack Awhile

Sand Art Cookies (continued)

1. To make the cookies, combine all of the dry ingredients in a large bowl. In a separate bowl, combine **½ cup (125 mL) melted butter** and **1 egg** and stir into the dry ingredients. Drop the dough by heaping teaspoonfuls (7 mL) onto greased baking sheets. Flatten slightly, if desired.
2. Bake at 350°F (180°C) for 12 minutes. Allow to cool slightly before removing to a cooling rack

Makes 2½ dozen cookies.

3. Double Chocolate Nut Cookies

¾ cup	flour	175 mL
1 tsp	baking soda	5 mL
⅓ cup	cocoa powder	75 mL
½ cup	whole-wheat flour	125 mL
½ cup	chopped walnuts	125 mL
½ cup	white sugar	125 mL
⅔ cup	chocolate chips	150 mL
½ cup	rolled oats	125 mL
½ cup	brown sugar	125 mL

1. To make the cookies, combine all of the dry ingredients in a large bowl. In a separate bowl, combine **½ cup (125 mL) melted butter, 2 tbsp. (30 mL) water, 1 egg, ½ tsp (2 mL) vanilla** and stir into the dry ingredients. Drop by heaping teaspoonfuls (7 mL) onto greased baking sheets.
2. Bake at 350°F (180°C) for 12 minutes. Allow to cool slightly before removing to a cooling rack.

Makes 2½ dozen cookies.

See photograph on page 87.

Honey Crisps

The first time I tasted these cookies I went back for seconds. Imagine my delight when I found out how very simple they are to make!

1 cup	butter	250 mL
1 cup	sugar	250 mL
2 tbsp.	honey	30 mL
2 cups	flour	500 mL
1 tsp.	baking soda	5 mL
2 cups	corn flakes	500 mL

1. In a large saucepan, melt the butter with sugar and honey. Remove the pan from the heat and add flour mixed with baking soda. Add the corn flakes and stir until well mixed.
2. Roll the dough into 1" (2.5 cm) balls; place on ungreased baking sheets and flatten slightly with a fork. Bake at 300°F (150°C) for 10-12 minutes. Allow to cool slightly, then remove to a cooling rack.

Makes 3 dozen.

Scottish Oat Cakes

(MARIE) I recently visited a dear friend of mine for morning coffee. Muriel is the wife of a retired clergyman and I enjoy her company as often as I can. She served me these Scottish Oat Cakes, which taste slightly sweet with a great crunch. These are wonderful served with a sharp Cheddar.

½ tsp.	baking soda	2 mL
½ cup	boiling water	125 mL
2 cups	flour	500 mL
1 tsp	baking powder	5 mL
1 tsp	salt	5 mL
1¼ cup	sugar	300 mL
2 cups	rolled oats	500 mL
2 cups	bran flakes cereal	500 mL
1¼ cups	shortening	300 mL

Scottish Oat Cakes (continued)

1. Add the water to the baking soda and let stand until cool.
2. In a large bowl, combine flour, baking powder, salt, sugar, rolled oats and bran flakes.
3. Cut in shortening. Add the water and soda mixture.
4. Roll out the dough thinly (⅛"/3 mm) on a floured surface. Rolling is the hardest part – try to keep it from breaking apart and smooth out the edges occasionally.
5. Cut the dough into squares or rectangles. (Shape isn't important.) Place on a greased or sprayed baking pan and bake at 350°F (180°C) for 13-14 minutes, until lightly browned. Remove to a cooling rack.

Makes 6 dozen (approximately).

Lemon Walnut Squares

Very lemony – with a little crunch, we love them!

1 cup	butter, softened	250 mL
2 cups	flour	500 mL
½ cup	icing (confectioner's) sugar	125 mL
4	eggs, room temperature	4
2 cups	sugar	500 mL
1	large lemon, grated rind of	1
6 tbsp.	fresh lemon juice	90 mL
1 tbsp.	flour	15 mL
½ tsp.	baking powder	2 mL
1½ cups	chopped walnuts	375 mL

1. Beat together the butter, 2 cups (500 mL) of flour and the icing sugar until well combined. Pat into a greased 9 x 13" (23 x 33 cm) pan to make a thin layer. Bake at 325°F (160°C) for 15 minutes.
2. Beat the eggs and sugar until light. Stir in the lemon rind and juice. Combine 1 tbsp. (15 mL) of flour and the baking powder and sprinkle over the lemon mixture. Add the nuts; combine well.
3. Pour the batter into baked crust and bake for another 35 minutes, or until the filling is set. Let cool slightly before cutting into squares.

Makes about 24 squares.

Stop & Snack Awhile

Classic Nanaimo Bars

Are you tired of that sickly sweet mass-produced lump of sugar commercially sold as Nanaimo Bars these days? Here are some wonderful variations – as well as the original!

Chocolate Coconut Base:

½ cup	butter	125 mL
¼ cup	sugar	50 mL
½ cup	cocoa powder	125 mL
1	egg, lightly beaten	1
1 tsp.	vanilla	5 mL
1½ cups	graham wafer crumbs	375 mL
1 cup	dried, shredded coconut	250 mL
½ cup	chopped walnuts	125 mL

Classic Butter Filling:

¼ cup	butter	60 mL
2 cups	icing (confectioner's) sugar	500 mL
1	egg	1

Chocolate Topping:

4 oz.	semisweet chocolate	113 mL
1 tbsp.	butter	15 mL

1. Melt the butter in a heavy saucepan. Stir in sugar and cocoa powder until smooth. Whisk in the egg and vanilla. Remove from the heat and stir in the crumbs, coconut and nuts.
2. Press the chocolate coconut base evenly over the bottom of a greased 9" (23 cm) square pan. Chill until set, 20-30 minutes.
3. **To make the filling**, cream the butter. Gradually beat in the sugar and egg. Spread over the base and chill for about 15 minutes.
4. **For the topping**, melt the chocolate and butter*, stirring until smooth. Spread in an even layer over the chilled filling.
5. Store in the refrigerator until the topping begins to harden. Score the topping into bars before it hardens completely. Cut the bars before they are totally solid, using a hot knife and wiping it clean between cuts.

Makes 24 bars.

NOTE: Store in the refrigerator or freezer.

See the variations on the next page.

* See the instructions on step 1, page 74.

 Stop & Snack Awhile

Nanaimo Bar Filling Variations

Peanut Butter Filling:

2 tbsp.	butter, softened	30 mL
½ cup	peanut butter, smooth	125 mL
2 cups	icing (confectioner's) sugar	500 mL
1	egg	1

Grand Marnier Filling:

¼ cup	butter, softened	60 mL
2 cups	icing (confectioner's) sugar	500 mL
2 tbsp.	Grand Marnier OR orange liqueur	30 mL
1 tbsp.	grated orange rind	15 mL

Cappuccino Filling:

3 tbsp.	butter, softened	45 mL
2 tbsp.	milk	30 mL
1 tbsp.	dark roast instant coffee OR espresso powder	15 mL
2 cups	icing (confectioner's) sugar	500 mL
½ tsp.	vanilla	2 mL

1. Follow the procedure for the filling in step number 3 in Classic Nanaimo Bars, page 80.

When making lunches on a daily basis, cut and wrap cakes and squares individually, then freeze. Pack frozen in lunch kits.

Stop & Snack Awhile

White Chocolate Nanaimo Bars

The original version of Nanaimo bars is so good who would have thought the reverse would be even better!

White Chocolate Crust:

1 oz.	white chocolate	30 mL
¼ cup	butter	60 mL
1	egg, beaten	1
½ cup	dried, shredded coconut	125 mL
1½ cups	graham wafer crumbs	375 mL

Dark Chocolate Filling:

¼ cup	butter	60 mL
⅔ cup	cocoa	150 mL
1⅓ cup	icing (confectioner's) sugar	325 mL
1	egg	1
1 tsp.	vanilla	5 mL

White Chocolate Topping:

4 tsp.	vegetable oil	20 mL
4 oz.	white chocolate, coarsely chopped	115 g
1 oz.	semisweet chocolate	30 g
½ tsp.	vegetable oil	2 mL

1. In a small heavy saucepan, over low heat, melt the white chocolate with the butter, stirring until smooth. Stir in the beaten egg and coconut. Remove from the heat and stir in the crumbs. Press evenly into the bottom of a greased 8" (20 cm) pan. Chill while preparing filling – at least 20 minutes.
2. **To make the filling**, in a heavy saucepan, melt the butter over low heat. Stir in the cocoa until smooth and then beat in the icing sugar, egg and vanilla until smooth. Spread over the bottom layer and return to the refrigerator until firm.
3. **For the topping**, in a small heavy saucepan over low heat melt the oil and white chocolate until melted and smooth. Smooth over the middle layer and refrigerate until set.
4. Melt the semisweet chocolate with the remaining ½ tsp. (2 mL) of oil and drizzle over the white chocolate.
5. Refrigerate until set and cut into squares or bars. Store in the refrigerator

Makes 24 squares.

Stop & Snack Awhile

Sweet Marie Bars

(MARIE) How could these not be included in Marie's book? These were given to me by Kathryn Tulk. They are every bit as tasty and irresistible as the commercial bar by the same name!

½ cup	peanut butter	125 mL
½ cup	corn syrup	125 mL
½ cup	brown sugar	125 mL
1 tbsp.	butter	15 mL
2 cups	rice krispies	500 mL
1 cup	red-skinned peanuts	250 mL
1 cup	chocolate chips	250 mL

1. Combine the peanut butter, corn syrup, brown sugar and butter in a saucepan; bring just to the boiling point. DO NOT BOIL!
2. Remove from heat and stir in rice krispies and peanuts.
3. Press the rice krispie mixture mixture into a greased 8 or 9" (20 or 23 cm) square pan.
4. Sprinkle chocolate chips over and place the pan under the broiler or in a 350°F (180°C) oven for 3-5 minutes, until the chips are soft (Watch carefully – it doesn't take long!) then spread the melted chocolate like icing.
5. Refrigerate until firm. Cut into bars.

NOTE: A double recipe makes a 10 x 15" (25 x 38 cm) jelly roll pan. This recipe freezes well. If you let the rice krispie mixture in step 2 cool slightly, fingers work best for pressing it into the pan.

* *Use any salted peanuts that are available.*

To remove glue or gum from hair, use peanut butter.

Stop & Snack Awhile

Brownies for a Bunch

These are great for the occasions when you get a last-minute call to contribute to a potluck, a kid's party or just to have in the freezer.

2 cups	flour	500 mL
2 cups	sugar	500 mL
1 cup	butter, melted	250 mL
1 cup	water (strong black coffee works too)	250 mL
½ cup	cocoa powder	125 mL
½ cup	buttermilk*	125 mL
2	eggs	2
1 tsp.	baking soda	5 mL
1 tsp.	vanilla	5 mL

Chocolate Butter Frosting:

½ cup	butter, melted	125 mL
2 tbsp.	cocoa powder	30 mL
¼ cup	milk	60 mL
3¼ cups	icing (confectioner's) sugar	796 mL
1 tsp.	vanilla	5 mL

1. In a large mixing bowl, combine the flour and sugar.
2. In a heavy saucepan, combine the butter, water and cocoa. Stir and heat to boiling.
3. Pour the cocoa mixture over the flour mixture; add the buttermilk, eggs, baking soda and vanilla. Mix well, using a wooden spoon or an electric mixer.
4. Spread the batter evenly in a well-greased or sprayed 11 x 17½" (28 x 44 cm) jelly-roll pan.
5. Bake at 400°F (200°C) for 20 minutes, or until brownies test done in the center.
6. **To make the frosting**, while the brownies are baking combine the butter, cocoa and milk in a saucepan. Heat to boiling, stirring constantly. Stir in the icing sugar and vanilla until the frosting is smooth.
7. Pour the warm frosting over the brownies as soon as you remove them from the oven.
8. Cool the brownies in the pan and cut into squares.

Makes 48 squares.

* *If you do not have buttermilk, pour 2 tsp. (10 mL) of vinegar or lemon juice into a measuring cup and fill to the ½ cup (125 mL) mark. Let sit for 5 minutes to sour the milk.*

 *Stop & Snack Awhile*

Outrageous Brownies

If ever a brownie threatened to melt in your mouth, this is it! Put this together by hand and do NOT over bake! Serve alone or with ice cream or whipped cream; eat with friends or as a secret midnight indulgence!

1 cup	butter	250 mL
3 oz.	unsweetened chocolate	85 g
1½ cups	semisweet chocolate chips	375 mL
4 tsp.	instant espresso powder OR 2 tbsp. (30 mL) dark roast instant coffee powder	20 mL
3	eggs	3
1 cup	sugar	250 mL
1 tbsp.	vanilla extract	15 mL
½ cup	flour	125 mL
2 tsp.	baking powder	10 mL
½ tsp.	salt	2 mL
1½ cups	semisweet chocolate chips	375 mL
1½ cups	chopped walnuts	375 mL

1. In the top of a double boiler (or over very low heat) melt together butter, unsweetened chocolate and 1½ cups (375 mL) of semisweet chocolate chips. Remove from the heat and stir in the coffee powder. Let cool.
2. In a large bowl, by hand, combine eggs, sugar and vanilla. Stir in the cooled chocolate mixture.
3. Mix together the flour, baking powder and salt. Gently mix into the batter.
4. Fold in the remaining 1½ cups (375 mL) chocolate chips and the walnuts.
5. Pour the batter into a greased or sprayed 9 x 13" (23 x 33 cm) pan. Bake at 350°F (180°C) for 30 minutes, or until a toothpick just comes out clean. Cool thoroughly in the pan. The top will sink as it cools.

Serves 12 for dessert, 24 for a snack.

Stop & Snack Awhile

Cranberry Blondies

As soon as you think you have all of the greatest cranberry recipes that exist, another one takes you by surprise. A succinctly succulent square!

1 cup	butter, softened	250 mL
4 tsp.	icing (confectioner's) sugar	20 mL
2 cups	flour	500 mL
4	eggs	4
2 cups	sugar	500 mL
⅔ cup	flour	150 mL
2 tsp.	baking powder	10 mL
½ tsp.	salt	2 mL
2 tsp.	almond extract	10 mL
½ cup	finely chopped coconut	125 mL
2 cups	whole, fresh or frozen cranberries	500 mL
½ cup	sliced almonds	125 mL

1. In a small bowl, mix the butter, icing sugar and 2 cups (500 mL) of flour together and spread evenly in a greased 9 x 13" (23 x 33 cm) pan. Bake at 350°F (180°C) for 15 minutes.
2. In a small bowl, beat together the eggs, sugar, flour, baking powder, salt, almond extract and coconut. Pour over the baked crust.
3. Distribute the cranberries and almonds evenly over the batter.
4. Bake at 350°F (180°C) for 35-40 minutes. The almonds will be browned and the center will be set. Cool on a rack.

Makes 24 squares.

To soften butter, place a warm bowl over the butter.

Cinnamon Torte, page 186
Sand Art Cookies, page 76

 **Stop & Snack Awhile**

Banana Oatmeal Cake

Really more like a banana coffee cake, serve this for an evening or afternoon snack or a dessert at lunch. Moist and delicious!

½ cup	shortening	125 mL
⅔ cup	sugar	150 mL
2	eggs	2
1 tsp.	vanilla	5 mL
1½ cups	mashed banana (about 3)	375 mL
1 cup	rolled oats	250 mL
¾ cup	flour	175 mL
1 tsp.	baking soda	5 mL

Brown Sugar Topping:

¾ cup	rolled oats	175 mL
⅓ cup	brown sugar	75 mL
2 tbsp.	butter	30 mL

1. In a large bowl, beat the shortening with the sugar. Add eggs, vanilla and banana. Beat until light and fluffy.
2. Combine the rolled oats, flour and baking soda. Mix into the banana mixture by hand.
3. Scrape the batter into a greased or sprayed 8 or 9" (20 or 23 cm) square baking pan.
4. Combine the topping ingredients. Sprinkle over the cake batter.
5. Bake at 350°F (180°C) for 35-45 minutes, or until a toothpick inserted in the center comes out clean.

Serves 9.

Overripe bananas may be frozen whole or mashed. If freezing whole, peel them first and store in sealable freezer bags.

Helen's grandchildren at Seal River and the Seal River Heritage Lodge.

Stop & Snack Awhile

Great White Bear

(MARIE) On August 28th, 1999, I arrived at Dymond Lake Hunting Lodge to cook for staff and the first guests of the season. Helen and Doug Webber, the owners of the Lodge, were entertaining guests at North Knife Lake Fishing Lodge, so I was sleeping alone in the kitchen cabin, for the first time in all the years I had been going there. At bedtime, their son-in-law David came over and placed a gun against the bedroom wall. He asked if I knew how to use it. I laughed and said, "If a polar bear comes, I'll be too scared to use a gun, I'll just yell!"

I was not the least bit nervous going to sleep on that calm, moonlit night, and was soon in dreamland. I was awakened by the two-way radio phone, which I had forgotten to turn off. It was on a party system and someone was having a late-night conversation. It ended, and I had just snuggled down again when I heard, and felt, a big thump against the building. My eyes popped wide open, my heart started thumping, and I thought, simultaneously – There is no wind blowing! AND This can't be happening! I looked at the clock – 12:34, and peered out the bedroom window. Nothing. I put on my housecoat, went into the dining room and gazed fearfully out the backdoor window. There, on the stoop, with only a door separating us, was a polar bear. I ran to the kitchen, opened a window and yelled as loudly as I could, "David! Gordon! Tommy!" There was no answer, so I shouted again. "David! Gordon! Tommy!" This time, Gordon's wife, Marie, answered. Just as I called, "There's a polar bear on the back stoop," the bear appeared around the side of the kitchen. It was now standing between Marie and me, between the two buildings. David and Gordon were easily roused. David fired off a warning shot to send the bear on its way. The bear simply turned and looked in his direction. This was not going to be easy! They had to wake Tommy who was in another building. He could come at the bear from a different angle. But Tommy would not wake up – it took another 5 minutes of calling to alert him to the danger. Meanwhile, I had climbed onto the top bunk and was actually cowering in the corner, shaking uncontrollably, praying for all I was worth.

Using a flare gun, Tommy and David finally moved the bear off. It didn't go very far, so they decided on an all-night vigil – remember that full moon? They could see where the bear had bedded down, so they took turns watching from the dining room. I quickly moved over to Marie and Gord's room and slept quite peacefully for the rest of the night.

In the morning I was wakened by the sound of tin cans rolling around. I peeked out the window and said, "Guess who's back!" Where were our mighty guardians? They had fallen asleep with the dawn! We fired off a shot to waken them and they were soon at the window, peering down their sights,. They had to put the bear down. I hate to dwell on that part because it seemed a little brutal. Normally, man and beast share the land quite well together – we simply respect each other. But when the two are competing for the same piece of land, there has to be a winner and a loser.

I have thought long and hard to find a lesson in this episode. Maybe there isn't one, but for some reason God allowed me to experience "real fear", and even though my life was probably not in danger, I don't want to take that lightly. Unlike many parts of the world, we live in a secure environment. Perhaps this was just a little reminder to say, "Thank You."

 *Stop & Snack Awhile*

Taste Teasers

(MARIE) I have been in the fortunate position of being entertained often by friends and it is not unusual for me to go home with a recipe. Two such outstanding recipes are Blue Cheese Soufflé and Baked Brie with Cranberry Ginger Chutney. Helen's nephew Jeff, on the other hand, takes great pleasure in creating his own appetizers. We are delighted to include his Spinach & Mushroom Melts and his Veggie Strudels in this section.

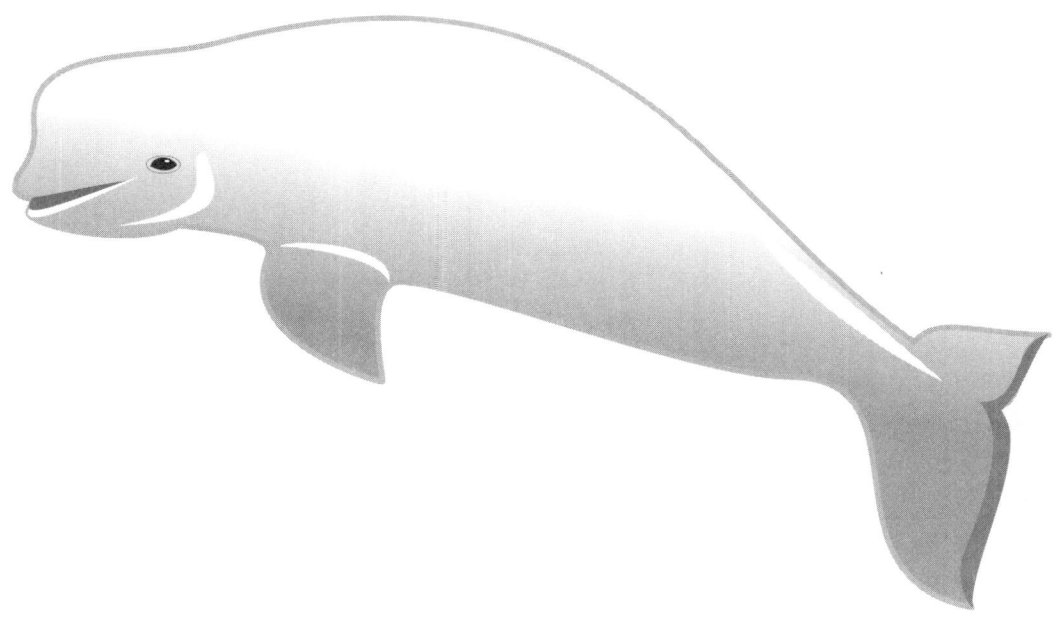

Tortillas with Hummus

A standard meal in the middle east, and now a favorite appetizer in many Canadian homes, Jeff brings us his version of this wonderful healthy and delicious treat. Of course, when you are busy, you may prefer to use commercial tortillas.

Tortillas:

3½ cups	flour	825 mL
1 tsp.	salt	5 mL
1½ tsp.	baking powder	7 mL
⅓ cup	lard	75 mL
1 cup	water, or more as needed	250 mL

1. In a medium bowl, combine the flour, salt and baking powder. Rub in the lard, using your fingers, until it is well blended and grainy. Add 1 cup (250 mL) of water, mixing with a wooden spoon until the mixture cleans the sides of the bowl. Add additional water, 1 tbsp. (15 mL) at a time, until all of the flour is incorporated. Turn onto a lightly floured board and knead until elastic and smooth.
2. Divide into 16 equal balls; cover with a damp cloth and let rest for 15 minutes.
3. Roll each ball into 7-8" (18-20 cm) circles and stack them between sheets of waxed paper.
4. Brown each tortilla in a hot, ungreased frying pan, 1 minute on the first side, 15 seconds on the flip side, pressing down the bubbles as they form.
5. Cool the tortillas on a wire rack, then stack them, keeping them covered with a tea towel to prevent them from drying out.

Makes 16 tortillas.

Hummus

19 oz.	can chickpeas (garbanzo beans)	540 mL
½ tsp.	salt	2 mL
¼ tsp.	pepper	1 mL
3 tbsp.	fresh lemon juice	45 mL
3 tbsp.	olive oil	45 mL
3	garlic cloves, crushed	3
3 tbsp.	chopped fresh parsley	45 mL

Whir all ingredients in a food processor until smooth.

VARIATION: Tahini (sesame seed paste) is traditional in Hummus, but it is not necessary, you can even substitute peanut butter for tahini. Add 1-2 tbsp. (15-30 mL) of either if you want to try this favor variation. Add ½ tsp. (2 mL) of ground cumin and a dash or 2 of hot pepper sauce for a slightly earthier, hotter version.

Taste Teasers

Tundra Tapenade

What is pungent and flavorful on the sunny slopes of Provence is equally delicious on the shores of Hudson Bay. Accompany garlic toasts slathered with Tapenade with a full-bodied red wine. You could also try to arrange for a stormy sea and a roaring fire.

4	large garlic cloves	4
2 cups	pitted Kalamata olives	500 mL
4	anchovy fillets	4
2 tbsp.	drained capers	30 mL
1 tbsp.	dried oregano	15 mL
3 tbsp.	fresh lemon juice	45 mL
4 tbsp.	olive oil (use oil from the olives if they are packed in oil)	60 mL
½ cup	chopped fresh parsley	125 mL
	freshly ground pepper to taste	

1. In a food processor, chop garlic finely. Add olives, anchovies, capers, oregano and lemon juice. Pulse until finely chopped. Add olive oil and parsley and pulse until oil is incorporated and parsley is chopped.
2. Store the tapenade in a covered container in the refrigerator. It keeps for up to 5 days.
3. Serve tapenade on warm toasted baguette slices brushed with olive oil and minced garlic.

Makes approximately 2 cups (500 mL).

*To get the skins off garlic before chopping,
pound each clove with the flat edge of a heavy knife.
The skin will pop right off.*

Any Port in a Storm Blue Cheese Spread

(HELEN) Another winner for simplicity and taste. This taste tantalizer comes to us from my brother-in-law "Len from Canmore". (No relation to "Mike from Canmore".) He and his wife, Brenda, have been part of a gourmet club for many many years and have been very generous about sharing recipes with us!

4 oz.	cream cheese – regular or light, softened	113 g
2 oz.	blue cheese	55 g
3 tbsp.	dried currants, blueberries OR cranberries	45 mL
2 tbsp.	port*	30 mL
2 tbsp.	toasted sliced almonds	30 mL

1. Combine the cream cheese, blue cheese, currants and port and spoon into a small dish.
2. Sprinkle with toasted almonds.
3. Serve with crackers.

Makes approximately 1 cup (250 mL).

NOTE: This can be doubled or tripled depending on how many hungry people you are serving. Make up to a day ahead to allow flavors to blend.

* Port is a fortified, sweet wine from Portugal that varies greatly in quality and in price. Vintage ports can be aged for 50 years or more. Less expensive ports are often just labeled Ruby or Tawny. Generic ports are made in several different countries and are fine for use in recipes with other strong flavors.

Smoked Char or Salmon Torte

Fresh dill sprigs are essential for the spectacular presentation of this very simple appetizer.

2 tbsp.	mayonnaise	30 mL
2 x 8 oz.	cream cheese	2 x 250 g
2 tbsp.	fresh lemon juice	30 mL
2-3	green onions, chopped	2-3
8 oz.	smoked char OR salmon, very thinly sliced	250 g
1-2 tbsp.	drained capers	15-30 mL
	fresh dill sprigs	

Smoked Char (continued)

1. In a food processor, combine the mayonnaise, cream cheese, lemon juice and green onions. Process until smooth.
2. Line a shallow dish with plastic wrap and spread half of the cream cheese mixture evenly in the dish.
3. Arrange the char or salmon slices over the cream cheese and sprinkle with the capers. Arrange half of the dill sprigs over the salmon.
4. Spread the remaining cream cheese over the char or salmon layer and fold the plastic wrap over the cheese layer. Refrigerate up to a day ahead to allow flavors to develop.
5. To serve, unmold the torte and arrange the remaining dill sprigs over the cream cheese. Serve with thin baguette or bagel slices.

Serves 10-12.

VARIATION: Smoked trout could be substituted for the char or salmon.

Artichoke-Heart Dip

Marie and I use every excuse we can to use artichokes, so we were quite pleased when Marie acquired this recipe at a dinner she attended. Freshly grated Parmesan gives a smoother texture, but packaged Parmesan tastes great too. Serve with tortilla chips or raw veggies.

14 oz.	can artichoke hearts, drained, chopped	398 mL
1 cup	mayonnaise	250 mL
1 cup	grated Parmesan cheese	250 mL
½ cup	sour cream	125 mL
1	garlic clove, crushed	1
1 tbsp.	lemon juice	15 mL
½ tsp.	pepper	2 mL
	paprika (optional)	

1. In a medium-sized bowl, combine all of the ingredients until well mixed.
2. Spoon into an ovenproof serving dish and bake at 350°F (180°C) until heated through and just beginning to bubble in the center, about 20-30 minutes.
3. Sprinkle the dip with paprika and serve with tortilla chips or raw vegetables.

Makes about 4 cups (1 L).

Snowball Dip

This wonderful warm dip serves a crowd and is just right for a snowy evening!

1	round loaf bread	1
2 x 8 oz.	cream cheese	2 x 250 g
1 cup	grated old Cheddar cheese	250 mL
¼ cup	chopped green onion	60 mL
½ cup	crisp-fried, crumbled bacon	125 mL
1 cup	mayonnaise	250 mL
1 tsp.	dillweed	5 mL
1 tsp.	garlic salt	5 mL
2 tsp.	Dijon mustard	10 mL
1 tsp.	horseradish	5 mL
dash	Worcestershire sauce	dash
3 drops	Tabasco sauce	3 drops

1. Cut the top off the bread to make a lid. Scoop out the bread and cut the scooped out bread into chunks.
2. With an electric mixer, beat the cream cheese until fluffy. Beat in the remaining ingredients.
3. Spoon the cream cheese mixture into the loaf. Replace the lid and wrap in foil.
4. Bake at 350°F (180°C) for 1 hour. Unwrap and serve with the bread chunks.

Serves 12-16.

Blue Cheese Soufflé

(MARIE) I love blue cheese straight up! But for those of you who approach it more cautiously, I invite you to join the Blue Cheese Soufflé Fan Club! Warning: It may be hard to stop at one bite and may even be addictive!

1 tbsp.	unflavored gelatin (1 envelope)	15 mL
2 tbsp.	cool water	30 mL
4 tbsp.	butter, softened (no substitutes)	60 mL
4 oz.	cream cheese, softened	113 g
4 oz.	blue cheese, softened	113 g
1	egg, separated	1
1 tsp.	Dijon mustard	5 mL
½ cup	heavy cream, whipped	125 mL

 Taste Teasers

Blue Cheese Soufflé (continued)

1. In a small saucepan, stir gelatin into cool water, then gently stir over low heat to dissolve.
2. Using a food processor or electric mixer, beat together the butter and cheeses. Beat in the egg yolk, mustard and gelatin.
3. Beat the egg white until stiff but not dry and gently fold into the cheese mixture.
4. Fold in the whipped cream.
5. Prepare a 1-cup (250 mL) soufflé dish with a collar of oiled waxed paper or foil. Tie the collar to the dish with string. Spoon the soufflé mixture into the dish. It should come up over the sides, up to the top of the collar. Chill for several hours or overnight.
6. To serve, remove the collar. Serve with crackers or raw vegetables.

Serves a crowd.

Zucchini Cheese Bites

(HELEN) This recipe came originally from our friend Diane who grew up with me in Churchill. She is a super cook and is very generous about sharing.

4	eggs, slightly beaten	4
1 cup	cottage cheese	250 mL
¼ cup	melted butter	60 mL
2 cups	grated jalapeño jack cheese	500 mL
½ cup	chopped onion	125 mL
3 cups	shredded zucchini	750 mL
1½ tsp.	salt	7 mL
1 tsp.	dried oregano	5 mL
1	garlic clove, crushed	1
2 tbsp.	chopped fresh parsley or 2 tsp. (10 mL) dried	30 mL
1 cup	flour	250 mL
2 tsp.	baking powder	10 mL

1. In a medium-sized bowl, combine all ingredients.
2. Pour the batter into a greased 9 x 13" (23 x 33 cm) pan and bake for 30-40 minutes, until golden brown and set in the middle.
3. Cut into 24 squares.

NOTE: To serve as a vegetable, bake this in a 9" (23 cm) square pan and increase the cooking time to 40-45 minutes; cut it into 12 squares.

Baked Brie with Cranberry Ginger Chutney

You wouldn't think this incredible blend of flavors would be a "keeper" – but so it has been proclaimed by all who taste it. Don't skimp on the ginger – more is better than less!

Ginger Cranberry Chutney:

1 cup	fresh or frozen cranberries	250 mL
⅔ cup	sugar	150 mL
⅓ cup	cider vinegar	75 mL
2 tbsp.	water	30 mL
2 tsp.	grated fresh ginger	10 mL
¼ tsp.	cinnamon	1 mL
⅛ tsp.	cloves	0.5 mL
2 lb.	round of brie cheese	1 kg
	crackers OR sliced baguette	

1. Combine the chutney ingredients in a saucepan. Bring to a boil; reduce heat and simmer over low heat until thickened, about 15 minutes.
2. Place the brie in a baking dish that fits, with just a little room left over. Score the top of the cheese into diamond shapes.
3. Spoon the chutney over the cheese.
4. Bake at 350°F (180°C) for 15-20 minutes OR microwave for about 2-3 minutes, or until cheese is soft. Serve with crackers or a sliced baguette.

Serves approximately 20.

NOTE: The chutney may be refrigerated for up to a week, or frozen for longer storage. It may also be served with meat.

VARIATION: There is enough chutney to accommodate 4, 4½ oz. (125 g) rounds of Brie if you prefer.

See photograph on page 105.

 Taste Teasers

Tomato Cheese Tart

(MARIE) As soon as I see the words "phyllo pastry" I think, "Oh, sure it's easy – NOT!" Sometimes I like to be wrong. Phyllo isn't hard to work with if you follow the instructions – nor is this hard to serve if you use a pan with a removable bottom. Most of all, I like this appetizer because it just tastes so good. Get brave and serve this to company!

3 sheets	phyllo pastry, thawed	3 sheets
3 tbsp.	melted butter, (approximately)	45 mL
3 tbsp.	Dijon mustard (approximately)	45 mL
¾ cup	shredded mozzarella cheese	175 mL
¾ cup	shredded jalapeño jack cheese	175 mL
1	large tomato, very thinly sliced	1
1	large garlic clove, crushed	1
2 tbsp.	chopped, fresh oregano OR 2 tsp. (10 mL) dried	30 mL
2 tbsp.	olive oil	30 mL
	salt and pepper	

1. Get phyllo, butter, Dijon and cheeses ready before starting the tart assembly. Have a brush ready to use, and a damp tea towel. Grease or spray a 9" (23 cm) flan or springform pan with removable bottom, or a shallow baking dish.
2. Remove 3 sheets of phyllo from the package. Cut them in half, crosswise. Place 1 of the halves on the counter. Cover the rest with a damp cloth.
3. Brush the first sheet with 1 tbsp. (15 mL) of the butter. Lay the next sheet on top, but angled slightly. Brush with 1 tbsp. (15 mL) of the Dijon mustard. Continue to angle the sheets until they form a rough circle. Alternate brushing the sheets with butter and mustard, ending with mustard. Lift the phyllo circle into the pan.
4. Sprinkle the cheeses over the phyllo.
5. Starting at the center, make overlapping circles of tomatoes. Sprinkle the garlic, oregano, olive oil, salt and pepper over the tomatoes.
6. Fold the edges of the phyllo under (or over) to make a fluted edge for the pie.
7. Place the pan on a baking sheet and bake at 375°F (190°C) for 35-40 minutes. The phyllo will be golden and the cheese will melt and surround the tomatoes.
8. Allow to cool slightly. If using a springform pan, remove from the pan to a plate. Cut into 8 wedges. Serve with a fork.

Serves 8.

See photograph on page 105

Veggie Strudels

From Helen's nephew Jeff comes this delightful appetizer. Jeff doesn't make anything the same way twice, so feel free to vary the amounts as desired.

1 tbsp.	olive oil	15 mL
1 tbsp.	butter	15 mL
1½ cups	finely chopped, mixed green, red, yellow peppers	375 mL
½ cup	diced onions	125 mL
1½ tbsp.	finely diced garlic	22 mL
¼ cup	finely diced celery	60 mL
¼ cup	finely diced carrots	60 mL
1½ tsp.	DLS*	7 mL
1 tsp.	fresh, coarsely ground black pepper	5 mL
1 tbsp.	shredded fresh basil OR 1 tsp. (5 mL) dried	15 mL
½ cup	finely chopped zucchini	125 mL
½ cup	finely chopped sliced mushrooms	125 mL
1½ cups	crumbled feta cheese	375 mL
18 sheets	phyllo pastry	18 sheets
	melted butter	

1. Heat the olive oil and butter in a large frying pan. Add the peppers, onions, garlic, celery, carrots, DLS*, black pepper and basil. Sauté the vegetables over medium-low heat, to make them sweat, about 10 minutes. Add mushrooms and zucchini halfway through. Pour everything into a fine strainer to drain off excess liquid. Allow to cool.
2. When the mixture is cooled, stir in the feta and prepare to wrap.
3. Cut each sheet of phyllo into 4, 4 x 12" (10 x 30 cm) strips.
4. Using 3 strips per strudel, brush each strip with melted butter, placing them one on top of the other. Place a healthy amount of veggie mix on one end of the strip and fold it into triangles, keeping the corners as tight as possible.
5. Place triangle strudels on greased baking sheets. Brush the tops with melted butter. Bake at 400°F (200°C) for 15-20 minutes. Remove to a rack to cool slightly. Serve warm.

Makes about 2 dozen.

NOTE: *These freeze well.*

* Dymond Lake Seasoning, see page 3.

Kahlúa Barbecued Wings

Sweet, spicy and simple – just the way we like them, this is a great addition to a buffet or appetizer table. Every once in awhile, we have just appetizers for dinner, that way we get to eat more of them!

3 lbs.	chicken wings	1.5 kg
¾ cup	Kahlúa OR Tia Maria	175 mL
¾ cup	chili sauce	175 mL
3 tbsp.	pineapple juice	45 mL
2 tbsp	cornstarch	30 mL

1. Remove the tips from the chicken wings and discard* them. Cut the wings into wingettes and drumettes and place on a foil-covered baking sheet. Bake at 375°F (190°C) for 30 minutes. Remove the wings from the pan and drain off any juices.
2. In a saucepan over medium heat, combine the Kahlúa and chili sauce. Mix the pineapple juice and cornstarch until smooth. Add to the Kahlúa mixture and cook, stirring until sauce simmers and thickens.
3. Increase the oven temperature to 400°F (200°C). Generously brush the sauce on the wings. Bake for another 10 minutes. Turn the wings over, brush with the remaining sauce, and bake for another 10 minutes.
4. Serve hot.

Serves 12 as a taste teaser or 6 for dinner.

NOTE: To cook on the barbecue, leave the wings whole and grill over medium heat with the lid down for about 15 minutes, turning to brown at least once. Then brush generously with the sauce and grill for 10 minutes. Turn the wings, brush with the remaining sauce and continue to grill for 5-10 minutes.

* Or you can save the wing tips to use when you are making chicken stock.

Parmesan Mustard Chicken Wings

Who doesn't enjoy a crisp, savory chicken wing? These appetizers can also be turned into a great meal.

20	whole chicken wings	20
½ cup	butter, melted	125 mL
2 tbsp.	Dijon mustard	30 mL
⅛ tsp.	cayenne pepper	0.5 mL
1 cup	dry bread crumbs	250 mL
½ cup	freshly grated Parmesan cheese	125 mL
1 tsp.	ground cumin	5 mL
	DLS* OR salt and pepper	

1. Cut the wing tips off and discard** them. Cut the wings in half at the joint; you now have 40 pieces.
2. In a shallow dish, whisk together the butter, mustard and cayenne.
3. In another shallow dish, combine bread crumbs, Parmesan, cumin and DLS*.
4. Dip the chicken wings in the butter mixture, then in the crumb mixture. Arrange on a greased baking pan.
5. Bake at 425°F (220°C) for 30 minutes. For extra-crisp wings, turn after 20 minutes.

Serves 6.

* *Dymond Lake Seasoning, see page 3.*
** *OR save the wing tips to use when you are making chicken stock.*

Chicken wings used to be relegated to the stockpot, but since Buffalo Wings were created in 1964, in Buffalo, New York, they have become the star attractions of many appetizer menus.

 Taste Teasers

This Bears Repeating – Part 1

(MARIE) Sept 11, 2001, will forever be embedded in our memories – there is nothing that will ever erase that dreadful day. There is an additional reason why I will never forget it.

Helen and I were busily working in the kitchen at Dymond Lake when the call came in, informing us of the terrorist attack. We had only 8 hunters in camp, a number that I could feed on my own, so Doug and Helen had planned on heading into town later that night for some meetings the next day. However, as soon as we learned that planes were being grounded, they rounded up some of the departing guests and were gone before noon. I felt totally stricken and abandoned, but had to carry on – like everyone else. What I was equally distraught about was the knowledge that I was, for the second time in my life, facing a night alone in the kitchen cabin. (See GREAT WHITE BEAR page 90.)

Our chambermaid, Sarah, kindly offered to come and share my room, so when we went to sleep, I felt fairly calm.

You can imagine my horror and surprise when I woke to a loud crash out on the porch. Time:12:30 a.m. I had already lived this nightmare once. I woke Sarah up – yes, she was still asleep – we grabbed flashlights and shone them out of all the windows, searching for the great white bear that we knew had to be out there. Alas, the night was as dark as pitch. Then, we heard a noise at the door opposite to the kitchen. This time Sarah caught a glimpse of something at the window.

We HAD to get the generator on so that we could use the yard lights. Just weeks earlier, my son Drew had installed a switch in the kitchen which would turn on the generator – after a seven minute delay! We were finally able to search but, finding nothing, we turned the switch off again and went to sit on our beds. Sleep was out of the question.

Suddenly, from the direction of the guides' cabin, there came a noise like lumber being moved around. I found a larger flashlight and shone it out of the window nearest that building. A huge, white bear was at their door and was trying to get in. This time I found my nerve. I yelled at Tommy, who was already well aware of the bear, then I yelled with all my might to scare away the bear. Off it went into the darkness.

Once more we waited the seven minutes for the lights to kick in, then Tommy and Daryl brought their bedding over to the dining room, where they would keep watch so that Sarah and I could get some sleep.

(Continued on the next page.)

This Bears Repeating – Part II
(We've Seen the Light)

The elusive bear, in conspiracy with the darkness, was seen only one more time that night. Tommy managed to scare it off with a flare.

With all of the planes being grounded, Doug and Helen were stuck in Churchill and I wasn't spending one more night without someone on guard – SO, Tommy and Daryl once more bedded down in the dining room – just in case – armed with a powerful light and a shotgun. In the wee hours, we awoke again to some commotion. This time the men were outside and had been joined by a guest. There was a shot and the bear ran away. So ended the second night.

On the third night, Tommy, Daryl and Bob (our camp manager) decided to keep watch on the roof where they would have a clear view of the bear coming down the dirt road, should he use the same approach as the night before. Scaring off this bear was now a matter of honor. They would have a clear shot from the roof should the bear co-operate with their plans.

Doug and Helen had managed a clandestine trip into camp to return the guests, who preferred to be grounded at Dymond Lake rather than in Churchill. So Helen was now my roommate. Doug had returned to Churchill, but not before equipping us with an air horn, which was a huge step forward in my humble estimation. Feeling well protected, we opened our window and drifted into sleep. Suddenly, from somewhere out of dreamland, I woke to the bang of my window closing.

I wish I had been calm enough to grab my camera instead of that air horn. The sight of that big, white head at our window will have to live on in memory, because one push of the horn and it was gone! We ran to where we could see the men on the roof – just to make sure they were still there – which they were. They may never forgive me for pushing that horn. The men hadn't even shot off a flare, but the bear never came back! We decided that maybe the bear had been attracted to the propane lamp we had been lighting in the kitchen.

The equation was simple – no more light/no more bears – at least until October, which is right in the middle of bear season – but that's another story!

Easy Cheesy Tomato Pie, page 99
Baked Brie with Cranberry Ginger Chutney, page 98

 *Taste Teasers*

Simply Salads

No meal seems complete without a salad. Is it the raw simplicity, the healthy crunch, or the wonderful combination of fruits and vegetables that appeals to our taste buds? With a hot meal, as a light lunch or as an offering at a potluck dinner, this collection has some great new salad choices. We highly recommend the Minty Beet Salad and Marinated Five-Bean Salad as two that are easily made ahead and improve with time.

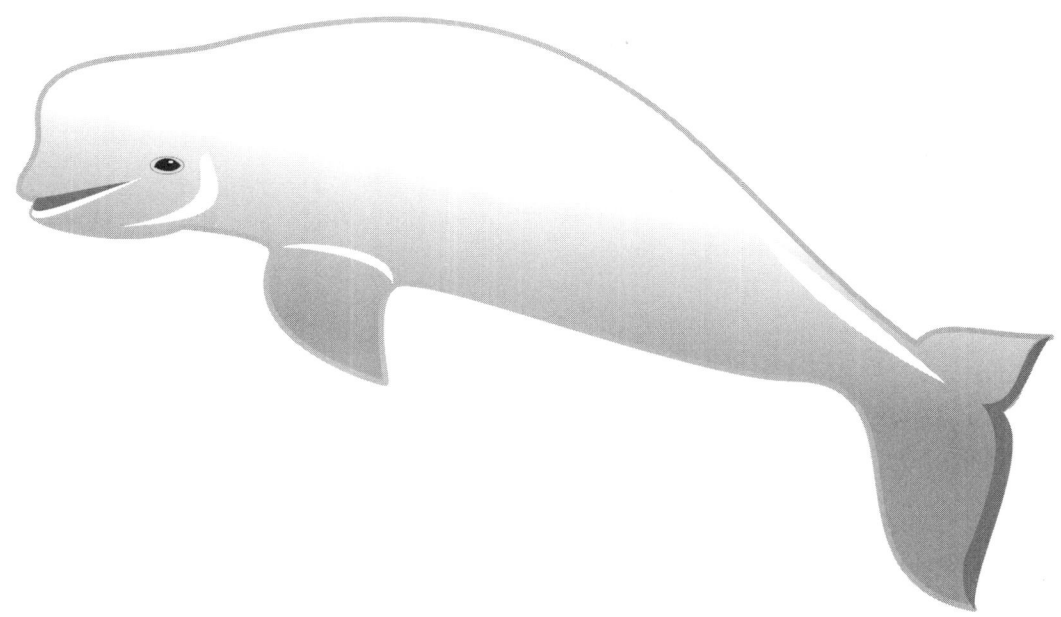

Helen and Marie's grandchildren at the airstrip at North Knife Lake Lodge.

Citrus Salad with Raspberry Wine Vinaigrette

Sometimes a salad takes you by surprise. This raspberry vinaigrette would make seaweed taste like edible greens!

10 oz.	pkg. mixed greens (8 cups/2 L)	285 g
½ cup	bean sprouts	125 mL
½ cup	chopped red onion	125 mL
1	large orange, peeled, segmented OR 10 oz. (284 mL) can mandarin oranges, drained	1
1	small pink grapefruit, peeled, segmented	1
½ cup	fresh or frozen raspberries (thawed)	125 mL
¼ cup	chopped pecans, toasted*	60 mL

Raspberry Wine Vinaigrette:

½ cup	raspberry wine OR raspberry wine vinegar**	125 mL
1 cup	frozen or fresh raspberries	250 mL
1 tbsp.	sugar	15 mL
½ cup	olive oil	125 mL
½ tsp.	salt	2 mL
1 tsp.	freshly ground pepper	5 mL

1. In a salad bowl, combine mixed greens with bean sprouts, onion, oranges, grapefruit, raspberries and pecans.
2. In a blender, blend wine, raspberries and sugar. Gradually pour in olive oil. Blend well. Season with salt and pepper.
3. Dress salad just before serving.

Serves 6.

NOTE: The onions may be marinated first in some of the dressing, if desired.

* To toast pecans: Spread pecans in an ungreased pan. Bake at 375°F (190°C) for 5-7 minutes, or until golden brown.
** Try the real thing if you can, but you may substitute cider vinegar in a pinch.

"Not Just Any Spinach Salad"

The nutty mellow flavor of Asiago is a wonderful complement to fresh pears, and this salad dressing is simply "the best".

¼ cup	pine nuts, toasted	60 mL
10 oz.	fresh spinach, washed and torn	285 g
½ cup	finely sliced red onion	125 mL
2 oz.	Asiago cheese, shredded	60 mL
2	fresh pears, cored and sliced	2

Cider Dijon Dressing:

½ cup	cider vinegar	125 mL
2 tbsp.	olive oil	30 mL
1 tsp.	sugar	5 mL
1 tsp.	Dijon mustard	5 mL

1. To toast pine nuts, place them in a nonstick skillet over high heat and stir constantly until lightly browned, about 2 minutes.
2. Prepare the remaining salad ingredients and arrange them on a large platter or in a large salad bowl.
3. Whisk or shake together the dressing ingredients. Drizzle over the salad just before serving.

Serves 4-6.

VARIATION: Substitute mozzarella cheese and sunflower seeds for the Asiago and pine nuts.

See photograph on page 69.

Spinach, Apple & Pecan Salad

René Sims shared this refreshing light salad with us and we are pleased to share it with you!

4 cups	torn spinach leaves	1 L
1	medium red apple, cored and thinly sliced	1
½ cup	pecan halves	125 mL

Honey Dijon Dressing:

3 tbsp.	olive oil	45 mL
1 tbsp.	Dijon mustard	15 mL
1 tbsp.	liquid honey, see page 19	15 mL
1 tbsp.	lemon juice	15 mL
	freshly ground black pepper, to taste	

1. Toss the spinach leaves, apple and pecan halves in a medium-sized salad bowl.
2. Mix all of the dressing ingredients in a small bowl, whisking until combined.
3. Toss the dressing with the greens.

Serves 4.

Grilled Tomato Vinaigrette

On arrival at Seal River Heritage Lodge to do the photo shoot for this book, a wonderful meal of Miner's Steak awaited us. On the side, Jeff had prepared a simple salad with this tasty vinaigrette.

2	tomatoes	2
⅓ cup	vinegar OR wine OR both	75 mL
3-4	garlic cloves	3-4
2 tbsp.	fresh basil OR 2 tsp. (10 mL) dried	30 mL
½ tsp.	salt	2 mL
½ tsp.	pepper	2 mL
¾ cup	olive oil	175 mL
2 tbsp.	sugar	30 mL

1. Blacken the tomatoes on a grill. (A smoking-hot iron skillet works too.) When cool, peel the tomatoes.
2. Combine all of the ingredients in a small bowl and mix with a hand blender until smooth.

Makes about 1½ cups (375 mL).

Simply Salads

Roasted Red Pepper Salad

Roasting red peppers is easy on a gas range, barbecue or under a broiler. Helen, wanted to try using one in a salad of her own creation. We invite you to create your own ratios of red pepper to other ingredients. The Sun-Dried Tomato Dressing will top it off beautifully.

1	red pepper, roasted and peeled	1
	green pepper, chopped	
	red onion, thinly sliced	
	sliced celery	
	chunked fresh mushrooms	
	sliced cucumber	

Sun-Dried Tomato Dressing:

2 tbsp.	finely chopped sun-dried tomatoes*	30 mL
2 tbsp.	balsamic vinegar	30 mL
¼ cup	olive oil	60 mL
1 tsp.	sugar	5 mL
1 tsp.	chopped garlic	5 mL
¼ tsp.	salt or to taste	1 mL
dash	pepper	dash

1. To roast the red pepper, set it on a gas range over a medium flame, turning it occasionally to blacken it completely. This may also be done under a broiler or on a barbecue. Place the pepper in a paper bag to allow the skin to soften for easy peeling**.
2. Peel the roasted red pepper and cut it into strips. Combine all of the salad ingredients in a large bowl.
3. Whisk all of the dressing ingredients together and pour the dressing over the salad just before serving.

Makes about ½ cup (125 mL) of dressing.

* Use the sun-dried tomatoes packed in oil – or reconstitute according to package directions

** OR place the pepper in a bowl and cover it with plastic wrap.

Zucchini, Red Onion & Tomato Salad with Balsamic Vinaigrette

One of those salads that has you coming back for more, it should marinate at least an hour, but don't be afraid to make it up a day ahead. The extra time just improves the flavor! This also doubles well for a crowd.

6 cups	thinly sliced zucchini	1.5 L
4	tomatoes, chunked	4
1	medium red onion*, thinly sliced	1
2	large stalks celery, sliced	2
½ cup	chopped fresh parsley OR 2 tbsp. (30 mL) dried	125 mL

Balsamic Vinaigrette:

¼ cup	red wine vinegar	60 mL
2 tbsp.	balsamic vinegar	30 mL
3	large garlic cloves, chopped	3
¾ tsp.	dry mustard	3 mL
¾ tsp.	salt	3 mL
¼ tsp.	pepper	1 mL
1 tbsp.	sugar	15 mL
¾ cup	olive oil	175 mL

1. In a large bowl, combine all of the salad ingredients.
2. In a food processor, mixing bowl or blender** combine the red wine vinegar, balsamic vinegar, garlic, dry mustard, salt, pepper and sugar. Add the oil slowly, whirring or whisking to incorporate the oil.
3. Pour the dressing over the salad ingredients and toss well. Cover and refrigerate for at least 1 hour or overnight.

Serves 10.

* *If the onion seems to be strong – in other words, if it brings tears to your eyes, separate it into rings in a separate bowl, pour boiling water over it and let sit for 5 minutes. Drain, add to the other vegetables and proceed with the recipe.*
** *Marie and I swear by our hand blenders for this procedure. They do a good job and are easy to clean!*

Minty Beet Salad

The sweet crunch of apples with the tart tang of beets awakens the tastebuds! If you take this salad to a potluck, be prepared to share the recipe. Our thanks to Brian, who brought it to a potluck and shared it with us.

Mint Dressing:

½ cup	chopped fresh mint leaves OR 1 tbsp. (15 mL) dried	125 mL
1 cup	pickled beet brine, drained from the pickled beets	250 mL
2 tbsp.	sugar	30 mL
2 tsp.	tarragon white wine vinegar OR 2 tsp. (10 mL) white wine vinegar and ⅛ tsp. (0.8 mL) dried tarragon	10 mL
3 cups	coarsely chopped pickled beets	750 mL
2 cups	coarsely chopped apple	500 mL
1½ cups	coarsely chopped green onions	375 mL
¾ cup	coarsely chopped celery stalks	175 mL
2 tbsp.	coarsely chopped mint leaves (optional)	30 mL

1. Combine all of the dressing ingredients in a saucepan and bring to a boil. Let simmer for 3-5 minutes, stirring occasionally.
2. Remove from the heat and strain into a bowl.
3. Place the beets, apple, onion, celery and mint in a large bowl. Toss with the dressing until well mixed. Taste for seasoning and add salt and pepper as needed.
4. Chill the salad before serving.

NOTE: All of the dressing may not be required. Add half of it at first and then add just as much as is needed to coat the ingredients well.

Serves 8-10.

Oriental Coleslaw

(MARIE) Though this salad is no longer unusual, throughout the years, at potluck suppers, it has become one of my favorites. I thought it ought to be included in our collection.

1	small head of cabbage, chopped or grated	1
4	green onions, chopped	4
½ cup	almonds	125 mL
½ cup	toasted sesame seeds*	125 mL
1 pkg.	dry soup noodles, uncooked, crushed	1 pkg.

Oriental Dressing:

1 pkg.	seasoning from noodles	1 pkg.
6 tbsp.	vinegar	90 mL
½ cup	vegetable oil	125 mL
½ cup	sugar	125 mL

1. Combine the cabbage, onions and dressing in a large bowl. Cover and refrigerate overnight.
2. Add the almonds, sesame seeds and crushed noodles just before serving.

Serves 10-12.

* To toast the sesame seeds, brown them in a small amount of oil in a frying pan, stirring constantly, for about 2 minutes.

Cheesy Broccoli Salad

(MARIE) My niece Charisse surprised me with this tasty salad on a visit to her home. She had not, heretofore, been noted for her cooking ability but the whole meal gave her a completely new reputation within the family. I think she'll be happy to share her expertise.

3	broccoli stems with florets	3
8 slices	bacon, fried crisp and crumbled	8 slices
1 cup	shredded Cheddar cheese	250 mL
½ cup	thinly sliced or chopped red onion	125 mL
½ cup	sunflower seeds OR pumpkin seeds	125 mL
1-1½ cups	red OR green seedless grapes, cut in half, if large	250-375 mL

Simply Salads

Cheesy Broccoli Salad (continued)

Mayonnaise Dressing:

1 cup	mayonnaise	250 mL
¼ cup	sugar	60 mL
1 tbsp.	vinegar	15 mL

1. Peel the broccoli stems and cut into bite-sized pieces. Place in a large bowl. Cut the florets into bite-sized pieces and add to the stems. Add the remaining salad ingredients.
2. Combine all of the dressing ingredients and toss with the salad ingredients.
3. Refrigerate the salad until ready to serve. The flavors will mellow overnight if you want to make it ahead.

Serves 10-12.

Garbanzo and Green Bean Salad

2 cups	fresh green beans, cut in 2" (5 cm) pieces	500 mL
19 oz.	can garbanzo beans (chickpeas)	540 mL
1	large tomato, chopped	1
2	green onions, chopped	2
2 tbsp.	capers	30 mL
2 tbsp.	chopped fresh parsley	30 mL

Jalapeño Dressing:

¼ cup	vegetable oil	60 mL
¼ cup	vinegar	60 mL
¼ tsp.	salt	1 mL
1	garlic clove, crushed	1
1 tsp.	finely chopped, pickled jalapeño pepper	5 mL

1. Bring the green beans to a boil in salted water. Drain immediately and let cool. Add remaining salad ingredients.
2. Combine all of the dressing ingredients and blend with a hand blender. Pour the dressing over the salad and marinate, covered, in the refrigerator for a few hours before serving.

Serves 8-10.

Marinated Five-Bean* Salad

This is also known as Emergency Salad. On those rare occasions when we find ourselves without fresh veggies at the camps, this salad can be made with just the beans.

14 oz.	can green beans, drained	398 mL
14 oz.	can yellow beans, drained	398 mL
14 oz.	can kidney beans, rinsed and drained	398 mL
14 oz.	can lima beans, drained	398 mL
14 oz.	can garbanzo beans (chickpeas), drained	398 mL
1 cup	chopped celery	250 mL
½ cup	chopped red OR green pepper	125 mL
½ cup	chopped onion	125 mL
½ cup	vinegar	125 mL
½ cup	vegetable oil	125 mL
½ cup	white sugar	125 mL
½ tsp.	salt	2 mL
	seasoned pepper to taste	

1. Combine all of the ingredients in a large bowl. Mix well, cover and refrigerate overnight. This salad lasts for days.

Serves 12 or more.

* Feel free to substitute other beans of your choice – we do.

Peel garlic cloves and place them in a bottle of olive or vegetable oil to preserve them. Store them in the coldest part of the refrigerator for no longer than 2 weeks. They may be stored in oil in the freezer for several months. Do NOT store at room temperature as there is a danger of botulism, since garlic is low in acid. Use the flavored oil to make salad dressings.

Garlic may be stored in the refrigerator, in dry red or white wine, or white or wine vinegar, for up to 4 months. Discard if any mold or yeast growth develops.

Simply Salads

Barrow Bay

Bob Barrow

Halfway into my seven-week tour as a fishing guide/maintenance person at North Knife Lake, I finally got a day off. Although I had been there on two previous occasions as a guest and weekend guide, this was my first full season guiding at the lodge.

North Knife Lake is approximately 27 miles long, running north and south, and about six miles wide. At the north end there are a series of three large bodies of water joined by a variety of channels and rivers. At the northernmost end of the lake is a bay, named on our guiding maps as "430 Bay", as well as the North Knife River, the Eagle's Nest and a camp called "North Camp". Doug and Mike made sure that all of the guides were aware that it was "not necessary" to go to the far northern end of the lake with our guests, as there were plenty of fish in the southern and middle parts.

So, on my day off I went fishing. Now, because I had never been there, and also because we had been instructed not to go there, I decided that the fishing must be even better up north. Off I ventured, with my trusty map, up through all of the various channels and rivers, straight to 430 Bay. The fishing was "fantastic"; I caught a 38" and a 39" Northern in the first half-hour. I then decided to use the rest of my time looking around this new area. I explored the North Knife River, looked for the North Camp, but couldn't find it (I later found out that it had burnt down), found the Eagle's Nest at about 3:00 p.m., then decided to head back, allowing myself two hours for the trip. I was expected back at 5.

Upon finding the first river channel heading south, off I went. On the way up I had come around a rather large island in the middle of the river, which I had passed on the east side. Going south, I had passed this island on the west side. But after about a half-hour of looking, the next channel could not be found. To verify my location, I decided to go right around the lake until I hit the Drift River. I went around the lake four times, still no river and no channel south. None of the landmarks were matching up with my guide map. Totally confused, I began doubting the map-maker.

It was now well past my scheduled ETA at the lodge so, realizing that I was lost, I started looking for a good spot to spend the night. I found a sandy beach, dug a fire pit, gathered firewood, built a windbreak and settled down for the night. Within a half-hour, I heard rustling/crackling in the bush behind me. Fearing bears, I packed up and departed the beach.

I decided to anchor in a sheltered bay and sleep in the boat where the little bit of wind would keep the mosquitoes and blackflies away. After about an hour, the wind picked up and the rains came down. Now I was faced with finding a spot to land the boat and make camp in the dark, wind and rain.

I found a point of land with a fifty-foot spruce tree and pulled the boat up on logs to keep it off the rocks. I unloaded my gear, including the floorboards, and made camp at the base of the tree. I placed one floorboard above, in the branches, to keep off some of the rain and made a tepee structure to sleep under from the other two.

Thanks to Tommy Brightnose's gift of a butane lighter and dry kindling/paper in plastic bags (shore lunch supplies), in no time I had a raging fire burning. There is nothing like the warmth of a campfire to take off the chill and provide a feeling of security. As the winds and rain increased, I spent the next two hours gathering firewood.

Fortunately, I had brought a bug-proof hat and warm gloves, which kept the clouds of mosquitoes and blackflies at bay. Lying in my makeshift shelter, wearing my waterproof floater life jacket and rain pants I finally fell fast asleep about 2 a.m.

At 6:00 a.m. I woke up, fully realizing that the folks back at the lodge had probably had a short night as well, wondering whatever had become of me. The wind was ripping up five-foot waves but, though the rains had stopped, I realized that I would still be stuck in camp as it was too dangerous to venture anywhere.

As I began to gather more wood for what I thought was going to be a long stay, I heard the unmistakable drone of Doug's Beaver, flying a search pattern at the north end. Running to the end of the point, I frantically began to wave my orange life jacket. To my relief, the aircraft turned in my direction and began approaching my location. I thought that the water and wind would be too rough to attempt a landing, and waved Doug off. However, after circling my camp a couple of times to size up what was required for a landing, Doug set her down like the experienced bush pilot that he is.

I picked up Tommy off the Beaver's float, and together we located a spot to beach my boat and the plane. I felt bad enough for getting lost in a place where I really shouldn't have been in the first place, and now I had risked lives and aircraft in the search and recovery. Upon entering the aircraft, I felt even worse when I discovered that both Doug and Gary (both experienced pilots) were extremely airsick due to the turbulent skies.

I finally had to accept the fact that the map-maker was right and I was wrong. What I had done was go all the way around the island in the river, and I wound up right back in 430 Bay. I was as far away from the lodge as I could possibly get, in a nondescript bay now known as **Barrow Bay**.

Vegging Out

Are you tired of the same old standbys? Are your veggies boring? Venture onto the wild side with Shredded Beets and Red Cabbage with Cranberries: or try the creative combination of our Orange Vegetable and Apple Casserole: delight your family with Mozzarella Mashed Potatoes. Helen and I are really pleased with this creative, yet user-friendly collection.

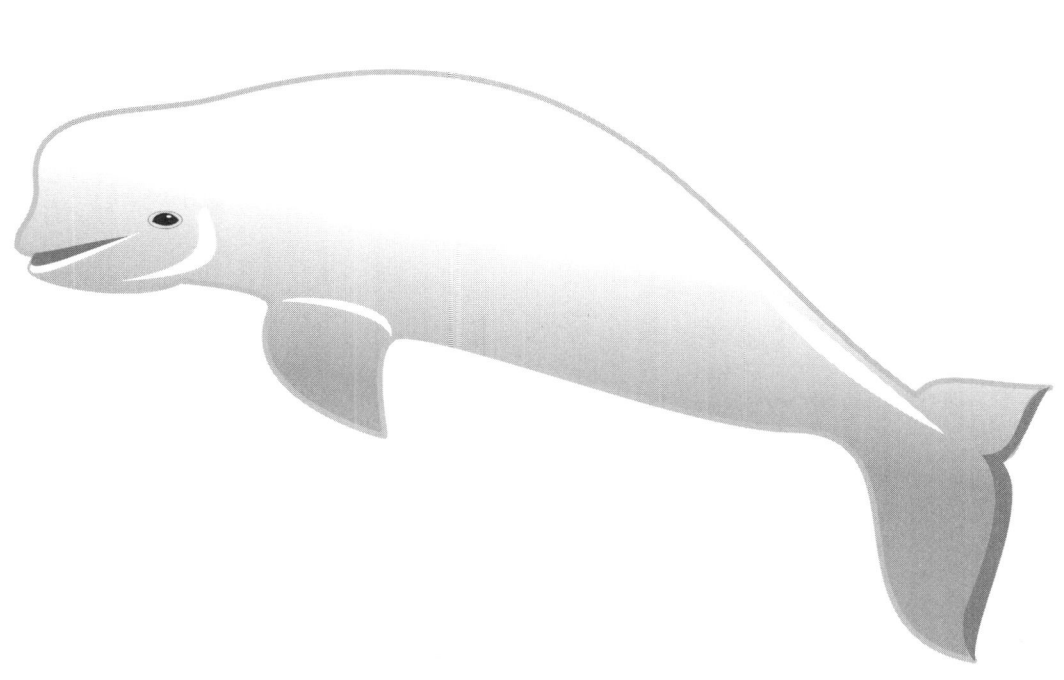

Garlic Roasted Veggies

No amounts are given for this vegetable dish. Make as much as you think you need, then make a little more, because you'll need to serve seconds!

> carrots, parsnips – in 4" (10 cm) lengths
> squash and/OR sweet potato, 2" (5 cm) cubes
> red onion, large chunks
> whole garlic cloves, peeled
> butter and olive oil
> fresh OR dried rosemary and thyme
> salt and pepper to taste

1. Place all of the prepared vegetables in a roasting pan and brush with a mixture of butter and olive oil. Season with the rosemary and thyme.
2. Roast, uncovered, at 400°F (200°C) for 45 minutes, stirring twice during baking.
3. Sprinkle with salt and pepper just before serving.

NOTE: Adding the salt before roasting will cause the vegetables to lose moisture and will affect the texture and flavor.

Corny Mexicali Vegetable Mix

The herbs we've used here are a perfect complement for the combination of vegetable flavors. Make this ahead and reheat before serving for easy meal planning.

2 cups	chopped onion	500 mL
1	red OR green pepper, diced	1
2 tbsp.	olive oil	30 mL
2	garlic cloves*, crushed	2
3 cups	chopped tomatoes	750 mL
1 tbsp.	chopped fresh marjoram leaves OR 1 tsp. (5 mL) dried	15 mL
1½ tsp.	fresh thyme leaves OR ½ tsp. (5 mL) dried	7 mL
2 cups	frozen corn kernels, thawed	500 mL
14 oz.	can baby corn (optional)	398 mL
	salt and pepper OR DLS** to taste	
¼ cup	chopped fresh parsley	60 mL

Vegging Out

Corny Mexicali (continued)

1. In a large skillet, sauté the onion and peppers in olive oil until the onions are translucent, about 5 minutes.
2. Add garlic and stir-fry for 1 minute.
3. Add the tomatoes, spices and corn. Simmer for 10 minutes, until the corn is tender.
4. Add salt and pepper to taste and stir in the chopped parsley.

Serves 12.

* Adjust the amount of garlic to suit your taste.
** Dymond Lake Seasoning, see page 3.

Mushrooms and Onion Gratin

1 lb.	mushrooms, thinly sliced	500 g
¼ cup	butter	60 mL
¼ cup	flour	60 mL
2	large onions, thinly sliced	2
	salt and pepper to taste	
6 tbsp.	whipping cream OR canned milk	90 mL
1 cup	grated Gruyère cheese	250 mL
¼ cup	fresh bread crumbs	60 mL

1. In a skillet, cook the mushrooms in 3 tbsp. (45 mL) of the butter over moderately low heat. Stir and cook until they are softened and most of the liquid they give off has evaporated. Stir in the flour and cook, stirring, for 3 minutes.
2. In a 2-quart (2 L) casserole, layer half the onions, the remaining butter – cut into bits, the mushrooms, onions, salt and pepper to taste, and the remaining onions.
3. Pour the cream over the onions. Combine the cheese and bread crumbs and sprinkle over the onions.
4. Bake at 325°F (160°C) for 50-60 minutes, or until the onions are tender and the bread crumbs are golden.

Serves 8-10.

NOTE: The gratin may be prepared in 6, 1½-cup (375 mL) ramekins. It may be prepared 2-3 hours ahead, just keep it covered and cool until ready to bake.

Vegetarian Chili

(MARIE) Chili recipes are as varied as your imagination. Holly Swift suggested this recipe when I was feeding a crowd that included some vegetarians. Everybody loved it. The chili flavor is mild, so adjust seasonings to your taste.

2 cups	dry kidney beans*	500 mL
12 cups	water	3 L
1½ cups	chopped onions	375 mL
4	garlic cloves crushed	4
2 tbsp.	olive oil	30 mL
1 cup	EACH, chopped carrots, celery and green pepper	250 mL
28 oz.	can tomatoes	796 mL
1 tsp.	salt	5 mL
½ tsp.	pepper	2 mL
1½ tsp.	cumin powder	7 mL
1 tsp.	basil	5 mL
1½ tsp.	chili powder or more to taste	7 mL
¼ tsp.	cayenne pepper	1 mL
7 oz.	can tomato paste	189 mL

1. In a large saucepan, soak** the dry kidney beans overnight in enough water to cover. Drain, rinse well, then cover with water again and cook until the beans are soft, about 1½ to 2 hours
2. In another pot, sauté the onions and garlic in olive oil for about 5 minutes. Add the vegetables, including the tomatoes, and the spices. Simmer until the vegetables are tender.
3. Add tomato paste and kidney beans. Continue to heat on the stove top, or place in a casserole and bake at 300°F (150°C) until ready to serve.

Serves 4-6.

SERVING SUGGESTION: Serve with a bowl of grated Cheddar cheese to sprinkle on the chili and with French bread.

* Substitute 2, 19 oz. (540 mL) cans kidney beans and omit instruction #1.
** A faster soaking method, preferred by many, is to cover the beans with cold water, 3 cups (750 mL) of water for every 1 cup (250 mL) of beans, in a heavy saucepan and bring them slowly to a boil. Boil for 2 minutes and remove the pan from the heat. Cover the beans and let them stand for 1 hour. Drain, rinse and proceed with the second half of step #1.

Almond-Crusted Char with Leek and Lemon Cream, page 20, nestled in a walrus-hide lariat – to the right is a Cephalopod (giant squid) fossil. Rosemary, Pepper and Potato Medley, page 134

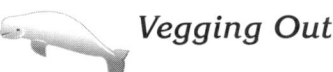

Broccoli Soufflé

This light, creamy soufflé can be partially made ahead and finished just before baking.

¼ cup	grated Parmesan cheese	60 mL
3 cups	finely chopped broccoli florets and stalks	750 mL
3 tbsp.	butter	45 mL
½ cup	chopped green onions	125 mL
¼ cup	flour	60 mL
1 cup	milk	250 mL
½ tsp.	salt	2 mL
¼ tsp.	pepper	1 mL
⅛ tsp.	EACH nutmeg and cayenne	0.5 mL
1 cup	shredded Cheddar cheese OR Gruyère	250 mL
4	egg yolks	4
6	egg whites	6
⅛ tsp.	cream of tartar	0.5 mL

1. Grease or spray a 9 x 13" (23 x 33 cm)/3-quart (3 L) casserole. Sprinkle Parmesan cheese evenly over the bottom of the dish.
2. In a saucepan with a small amount of boiling, salted water, cook broccoli for about 3 minutes. Drain, rinse with cold water, drain, set aside.
3. In a saucepan, melt butter; add onions and cook about 2 minutes. Stir in flour; cook for 2 more minutes, until lightly browned.
4. Gradually add milk, whisking until smooth. Add seasonings. Bring to a boil, reduce heat and simmer until thickened. Remove from heat. The sauce should be thick. If it forms a ball, add more milk.
5. Add the cheese and stir until smooth. (Use a little heat if necessary.) Stir in eggs yolks, 1 at a time, blending well. Pour into a large mixing bowl; stir in broccoli. Set aside. Do not proceed any further until you are ready to pop the casserole into the oven.
6. In a separate bowl, beat egg whites with cream of tartar until stiff peaks form. Stir a quarter of the egg whites into the cheese mixture; gently fold in remaining egg whites until no streaks remain.
7. Pour into prepared casserole. Bake, uncovered, at 375°F (190°C) for 30 minutes, or until puffed and golden. Serve immediately.

Serves 8.

NOTE: *To halve recipe, bake in an 8" (20 cm) square dish with 2" (5 cm) sides.*

Helen's daughter Jeanne with her husband Mike
and their children at Seal River.
Helen's granddaughters with their catch at North Knife Lake.

Breaded Eggplant with Cheese

(MARIE) Variety is the spice of life, we're told, so I urge you to venture beyond broccoli and corn and try this unappreciated vegetable. This version has a good texture and it is really easy to prepare.

1	large eggplant	1
1	egg, beaten	1
	bread crumbs	
2 tbsp.	olive oil	30 mL
	mozzarella cheese	
½-¾ cup	tomato salsa	125-175 mL

1. Wash the eggplant and slice in ¾" (2 cm) slices. Dip in egg, then in bread crumbs, coating evenly on both sides.
2. Heat the oil in a skillet over medium heat. Brown the eggplant on both sides, about 5 minutes per side.
3. Remove the eggplant to a greased baking dish large enough to hold the eggplant in a single layer. Lay slices of mozzarella cheese on top of the eggplant. Don't skimp.
4. Heat under a broiler for 1-2 minutes, until the cheese is melted.
5. Serve with salsa.

Serves 4.

Ginger Pear Braised Cabbage

Helen's nephew Jeff loves to experiment with flavor combinations. Here he has chosen just the right accents to complement the versatile cabbage.

¼ cup	butter	60 mL
1 tbsp.	chopped fresh ginger*	15 mL
1 tsp.	minced fresh garlic	5 mL
½ head	cabbage, thinly sliced	½ head
½	red onion, sliced	½
½ cup	julienned carrots	125 mL
1	apple, peeled and finely diced	1
1½	pears, halved and thinly sliced	1½
3 tbsp.	white wine OR wine vinegar	45 mL
¼ tsp.	nutmeg	1 mL
½ tsp.	salt	2 mL
¼ tsp.	pepper	1 mL

Ginger Pear Cabbage (continued)

1. Melt the butter in a large frying pan or Dutch oven. Add ginger and garlic and brown slightly.
2. Add the cabbage, onion, carrots and apple and sauté until the onion and cabbage are translucent.
3. Add all of the other ingredients and simmer for 2 minutes.

Serves 8-10.

* *Jeff has taught us that it is not necessary to peel the ginger, and that chopping is more effective than grating.*

Shredded Beets and Red Cabbage with Cranberries

We are always interested in recipes that use cranberries. We were intrigued with this unusual recipe and we were not disappointed!

2 tbsp.	olive oil	30 mL
1½ cups	shredded red cabbage	375 mL
1½ cups	coarsely grated cooked beets OR canned	375 mL
⅓ cup	whole berry cranberry sauce	75 mL
1 tbsp.	balsamic vinegar	15 mL
1 tsp.	salt	5 mL
¼ tsp.	black pepper	1 mL
⅛ tsp.	ground allspice	0.5 mL
⅛ tsp.	ground cloves	0.5 mL

1. Heat the oil in a large saucepan over medium heat. Add the cabbage and sauté, stirring for 5 minutes.
2. Stir in the remaining ingredients. Cook, covered, until tender, about 10 minutes.

Serves 4-6.

See photograph on page 17. This recipe is arranged on Hudson Bay lettuce (marsh ragwort/mastodon flower/Senecio cogestus).

Orange Vegetable and Apple Casserole

Credit for this wonderful and imaginative orange vegetable combination, based on an old favorite, goes to Pat Reinders. A deep, round casserole is recommended.

1	small turnip	1
1	sweet potato	1
6	carrots	6
2 tbsp.	butter	30 mL
	salt and pepper to taste	
4	apples, skinned and sliced	4
	brown sugar and cinnamon	

Brown Sugar Topping:

⅔ cup	brown sugar	150 mL
½ cup	flour	125 mL
2 tbsp.	butter	30 mL

1. Peel the orange vegetables and cut them into chunks. Place them in a large saucepan with salted water and boil until tender. Mash, then add the butter and salt and pepper to taste.
2. Layer half the mashed vegetables in a greased 2-quart (2 L) casserole. Arrange all of the sliced apples on top. Sprinkle with sugar and cinnamon. Cover with the remaining vegetables.
3. Combine the topping ingredients and sprinkle over the casserole.
4. Bake, uncovered, at 350°F (180°C) for 45 minutes. The top should brown slightly.

Serves 12.

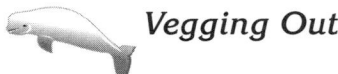

Oven-Roasted Carrots, Parsnips and Celery

Tuck this dish into the oven 45 minutes before the roast is due to come out and it will be ready to take to the table along with the meat platter. You can even prepare it in the morning, just cover it and refrigerate until it is time to bake.

6	carrots (1 lb./500 g)	6
8	parsnips (1½ lbs./750 g)	8
4	large celery stalks	4
¼ cup	butter OR margarine, melted	60 mL
¼ cup	dry sherry	60 mL
2 tbsp.	brown sugar	30 mL
1 tsp.	dry mustard	5 mL
1 tsp.	salt	5 mL
¼ tsp.	mace	1 mL
¼ tsp.	pepper	1 mL
2 tbsp.	chopped parsley (optional)	30 mL

1. Peel and chop the carrots and parsnips. We do some in 2" (5 cm) matchsticks and some in diagonal slices for interest. Cut the celery into ½" (1.3 cm) slices.
2. Combine the butter, sherry, brown sugar, dry mustard, salt, mace and pepper in a 9 x 13" (23 x 33 cm) baking dish. Add the vegetables and toss to coat.
3. Bake at 375°F (190°C) for 1 hour, or until tender. Stir every 20 minutes.
4. Remove the vegetables from the oven; stir once more and sprinkle with parsley, if desired.

Serves 8-10.

Béchamel Turnip

A little extra effort is needed to prepare this turnip dish, but it can be done ahead and kept until baking time. The first time we served it, we had to share the recipe – that's a great endorsement!

2 cups	cooked, mashed turnip	500 mL
1	egg	1
2 tbsp.	butter	30 mL
1¼ tsp.	savory	6 mL
½ tsp.	salt	2 mL
¼ tsp.	pepper	1 mL

Béchamel Sauce:

1 cup	milk	250 mL
1	small onion, peeled and quartered	1
5	whole cloves	5
4	peppercorns	4
1	small carrot, chopped	1
1	bay leaf	1
2	sprigs of parsley	2
3 tbsp.	butter	45 mL
3 tbsp.	flour	45 mL
½ cup	grated cheese for topping	125 mL

1. Mash the hot, cooked turnip with the egg, butter, savory, salt and pepper.
2. **To make the Béchamel Sauce**, in a small saucepan, bring the milk, onion, cloves, peppercorns, carrot, bay leaf and parsley to a boil. Remove from heat; cover and let sit for 15 minutes. Strain out all of the solids.
3. In a small saucepan, melt the butter over medium-low heat. Stir in the flour and heat for 1 minute. Gradually whisk in a cup (250 mL) of the strained milk, whisking to keep it smooth. Bring to a boil, reduce heat and simmer gently for about 5 minutes, to cook the flour.
4. Pour sauce over turnip. Sprinkle cheese over sauce.
5. Bake, uncovered, at 350°F (180°C) for 30 minutes, or until bubbly and heated through.

Serves 8.

Vegging Out

Sweet Potatoes and Carrots with Honey Glaze

Isn't it great when something that is good for us tastes so wonderful! Don't be afraid to throw in some onion chunks and/or parsnips.

2 lbs.	sweet potato, peeled, cut in 1½" (4 cm) pieces	1 kg
3	large carrots, peeled, cut in 1½" (4 cm) pieces	3
6 tbsp.	butter	90 mL
3 tbsp.	honey	45 mL
1 tsp.	fresh lemon juice	5 mL
	salt and pepper to taste	

1. Arrange the vegetables in a 9 x 13" (23 x 33 cm) glass baking dish.
2. In small saucepan, stir the butter, honey and lemon juice over medium heat until the butter melts.
3. Pour the butter mixture over the sweet potatoes and carrots and toss to coat. Sprinkle generously with salt and pepper.
4. Bake at 350°F (180°C), stirring occasionally, for approximately 50 minutes, until tender when pierced and the glaze is sticky.

Serves 6.

Spiced, Roasted Sweet Potatoes

The natural sweetness of sweet potatoes is enhanced by these fragrant spices. As the potatoes brown, they give the illusion of being sugar coated. Very tasty! Amounts are easily increased to serve more people. Try this recipe with squash.

1	sweet potato (1 lb./500 g)	1
1½ tbsp.	olive oil	22 mL
½ tsp.	curry powder	2 mL
¼ tsp.	ground cumin	1 mL
pinch	salt	pinch

1. Peel the sweet potato and cut it in half lengthwise. Slice each half crossways into ½" (1.3 cm) slices.
2. In a large bowl, combine the olive oil, curry powder, cumin and salt. Toss the potato slices in the oil mixture, using a brush to cover all sides.
3. Place the potato slices on a baking sheet, then brush with the remaining oil mixture. Roast at 375°F (190°C) for 30 minutes, turning once. When browned and tender, remove from pan and serve.

Serves 4.

Grilled Dijon Potatoes

(MARIE) Marinated potatoes grilled directly on the barbecue – interesting! My daughter-in-law, Terri, was the source of this incredible recipe.

| 1½ lbs. | potatoes cut to golf-ball size | 750 g |

Dijon Marinade:

2 tbsp.	Dijon mustard	30 mL
2 tbsp.	soy sauce	30 mL
2 tbsp.	olive oil	30 mL
¼ tsp.	salt	1 mL
¼ tsp.	pepper	1 mL

1. Place the potatoes in a large saucepan and cover with water. Bring to a boil and simmer until just tender, about 15 minutes. Drain.
2. Whisk together the marinade ingredients. Add the drained potatoes; toss to coat well. (This part does not look appetizing – do not be discouraged!) Cover and let stand at room temperature for 1 hour.
3. Preheat the barbecue to high. Place the potatoes on the grill and close the lid. Grill for about 10 minutes, turning the potatoes occasionally to brown all sides. Serve immediately.

Serves 4.

Crusty Baked Potatoes

(HELEN) I don't know if Mike from Canmore can cook, but Len from Canmore sure can. Every visit finds us writing out new recipes.

> baking potatoes
> hot water
> salt AND/OR DLS*

1. In the microwave or oven, bake the number of potatoes you need for your crowd, until almost done.
2. Remove the potatoes from the oven and, one at a time, run them under hot water, and sprinkle them liberally with salt. If you have DLS*, sprinkle them with that as well.
3. Bake at 375°F (190°C) until done, when a fork inserted in the middle pierces them easily.

Top with Dilled Potato Topping, see next page.

Dilled Potato Topping

1 cup	sour cream	250 mL
1 cup	mayonnaise	250 mL
2 tsp.	dried dillweed or 2 tbsp. (30 mL) fresh	10 mL
2 tsp.	DLS* OR ½ tsp. (2 mL) pepper	10 mL

1. Combine all ingredients and spoon over baked potatoes.

* *Dymond Lake Seasoning, see page 3.*

Baked Potato Cakes

An impressive accompaniment for chicken, beef, caribou. These have eye appeal and taste appeal!

3 tbsp.	olive oil, divided	45 mL
1 large	garlic clove, finely chopped	1
1 lb.	baking potatoes, peeled and sliced into ⅛" (3 mm) rounds	500 g
1 tbsp.	chopped fresh thyme OR 1 tsp. (5 mL) dried	15 mL
1 tbsp.	grated Parmesan cheese	15 mL
	DLS* OR seasoned pepper	

1. Generously brush a large baking sheet with 2 tbsp. (30 mL) of olive oil.
2. In a small skillet, heat the remaining olive oil over moderate heat. Add the garlic and sauté until just golden, about 1 minute. Remove the pan from the heat.
3. Divide the potatoes into 8 equal portions. For each cake, arrange the slices in an overlapping circular pattern about 4" (10 cm) in diameter on the baking sheet, making a total of 8 cakes. Brush the cakes with the garlic oil. Sprinkle with thyme, Parmesan and DLS*.
4. Bake the cakes until tender and lightly browned, about 20 minutes.

Serves 4.

* *Dymond Lake Seasoning, see page 3.*

See photograph on page 17.

Rosemary, Pepper and Potato Medley

We are always looking for new potato recipes that meet our criteria for simple yet delicious. This one fits the bill.

6	potatoes (2 lbs./1 kg)	6
1	red pepper	1
1	orange pepper	1
1 large	onion	1
1½ tsp.	chopped fresh rosemary OR ½ tsp. (2 mL) dried	7 mL
2 tsp.	DLS*	10 mL
½ tsp.	salt	2 mL
¼ cup	olive oil	60 mL
¼ cup	water	60 mL

1. Cut peeled or unpeeled potatoes into ¼" (1 cm) thick slices. Halve the peppers, remove the seeds and cut into ¼" (1 cm) slices. Cut the onion into large chunks.
2. In a 9 x 13" (23 x 33 cm), 3-quart (3L) baking dish, combine the rosemary, DLS*, salt and olive oil.
3. Add the potatoes, peppers and onions and toss to coat well.
4. Sprinkle with the water.
5. Cover and bake at 375°F (190°C) for 45 minutes. Uncover and bake for an additional 10 minutes, or until the potatoes are tender.
6. If you prefer a browned look, place the pan under the broiler for a couple of minutes. Watch carefully to prevent burning.

Serves 6-8.

* *Dymond Lake Seasoning, see page 3 – if you do not have DLS, substitute 1 tsp. (5 mL) seasoned pepper and another ½ tsp. (2 mL) salt.*

See photograph on page 123.

Speedy, Creamy Scalloped Potatoes

Well, speedy might not be too accurate, since you have to cook the potatoes and onions first, though you do have the option of using leftover potatoes, and you won't have to wonder if they are be soft enough. However, creamy is an understatement! We may never use another recipe for scalloped potatoes!

3 lbs.	potatoes	1.5 kg
½ cup	butter	125 mL
2 cups	sliced onions	500 mL
2 cups	whipping cream OR evaporated milk	500 mL
	salt and DLS* OR seasoned pepper	
	Parmesan cheese	
2 cups	shredded Cheddar cheese	500 mL

1. Peel, quarter and boil the potatoes until just tender. Drain; slice in ¼" (1 cm) slices and set aside.
2. Melt the butter in a skillet over medium heat. Fry the onions until translucent and set aside.
3. Lightly grease or spray a 9 x 13" (23 x 33 cm) pan. Pour ½ cup (125 mL) of cream in the bottom of the pan. Layer ⅓ of the sliced potatoes over the cream. Sprinkle with salt and DLS*. Add half the onions. Sprinkle with Parmesan.
4. Pour ½ cup (125 mL) cream over the onions. Repeat with another ⅓ of the potatoes, salt and DLS*, the remaining onions, Parmesan and the rest of the cream.
5. Add the final layer of potatoes. Season with salt and DLS*. Top with the Cheddar cheese.
6. Bake, uncovered, at 350°F (180°C) for 30-45 minutes. Let set for 5-10 minutes before serving.

Serves 10-12.

NOTE: This recipe may be made ahead and reheated. Cover with foil to reheat.

* Dymond Lake Seasoning, see page 3.

Mashed Potatoes with Spinach and Cheese

Pleasing to the eye as well as the palate, this casserole may be made ahead or served straight from the pot.

10 oz.	fresh spinach	300 mL
2 lbs.	potatoes, peeled	1 kg
¼ cup	butter	60 mL
¾ cup	whole milk OR cream	175 mL
1½ cups	grated Gruyère OR mozzarella cheese	375 mL
	salt and pepper to taste	

1. In a large pot, boil the spinach in ½" (1.3 cm) salted water for 1 minute. Drain well. Set aside.
2. Cut the potatoes into chunks. In a large saucepan, cook the potatoes in boiling, salted water until very tender, about 30 minutes. Drain well.
3. Add the butter, milk and cheese to the hot potatoes. Mash and/or beat until smooth.
4. Fold the spinach into the potatoes. Season to taste with salt and pepper.
5. Either serve immediately, or spoon into a buttered casserole to reheat later. Reheat, covered, at 350°F (180°) for about 30 minutes.

Serves 6.

Mozzarella Mashed Potatoes

Creamy mashed potatoes full of flavor, we didn't think anything would rival our Creamy Oven Mashed Potatoes in Blueberries & Polar Bears *but these are right up there. Make them the day before you need them and just pop them in the oven to heat through. Even better, double the recipe and freeze half to use another day.*

3 lbs.	potatoes, peeled and quartered	1.5 kg
8 slices	bacon, diced	8
2	garlic cloves, crushed	2
1 cup	sour cream	250 mL
¼ cup	butter, room temperature	60 mL
1 tsp.	salt	5 mL
½ tsp.	pepper	2 mL
¼ cup	chopped chives	60 mL
1 cup	grated mozzarella cheese	250 mL

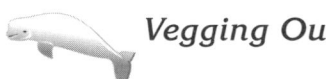

Vegging Out

Mozzarella Mashed Potatoes (continued)

1. In a large saucepan, cook potatoes in boiling salted water until tender.
2. While the potatoes are cooking, fry the diced bacon until crisp. Remove the bacon from the pan, drain off all but about 1 tbsp. (15 mL) of drippings and add the garlic. Sauté over medium-low heat for 2 minutes. Remove from the pan and add to the bacon.
3. When the potatoes are tender, drain well. Mash with a potato masher until smooth. Add the bacon, garlic, sour cream, butter, salt, pepper, chives and the cheese, mixing well.
4.. Turn the potato mixture into a greased 1½-2-quart (1.5-2L) casserole. Bake, covered, at 350°F (180°C) for 45 minutes, removing the cover for the last 15 minutes of baking time.

Serves 6-8.

NOTE: *If you make these ahead, allow them to cool, then cover and refrigerate or freeze. Let them thaw completely in the refrigerator overnight, before baking. If you forget to do this, add up to 30 minutes to the baking time.*

Len's Coconut Rice

Helen's brother-in-law Len likes to use an aromatic specialty rice like jasmine, basmati or Kokhua Rose, so that is recommended for best flavor. However, feel free to use what you have on hand and adjust the times accordingly.

1 cup	rice (see above)	250 mL
14 oz.	can coconut milk (full fat)	398 mL
1 cup	water	250 mL
½ tsp.	ground turmeric	2 mL
½ tsp.	curry powder	2 mL
¼ tsp.	ground cumin	1 mL
½ tsp.	salt	2 mL
½ cup	coarse shredded coconut	125 mL

1. In a 3-quart (3 L) heavy pan, combine the rice, coconut milk, water and spices. Heat over medium-high heat until it comes to a boil. Boil until the rice just starts to appear above the water, about 15 minutes. Immediately turn the heat to low; cover and simmer for 15 minutes.
2. Remove the pan from the heat and place it on a cold, wet tea towel. Let it sit for 10 minutes. This will release the rice from the bottom of the pan.
3. Stir in the shredded coconut and serve.

Serves 6.

Wild Rice Poultry Stuffing

Wild rice and poultry complement each other very well. The dried cranberries add a touch of sweetness and the almonds add a bit of crunch.

4 tbsp.	butter, melted	60 mL
½ cup	chopped onion	125 mL
¼ cup	chopped celery	60 mL
½ cup	chopped fresh mushrooms	125 mL
1	large garlic clove, chopped	1
1 tsp.	DLS* OR ½ tsp. (2 mL) seasoned pepper and ½ tsp. (2 mL) salt	5 mL
1 tsp.	poultry seasoning	5 mL
1 tbsp.	chopped fresh parsley OR 1 tsp. (5 mL) dried	15 mL
1½ tsp.	chopped fresh rosemary OR ½ tsp. (2 mL) dried	7 mL
2 cups	cooked wild rice**	500 mL
½ cup	dried cranberries	125 mL
½ cup	sliced almonds	125 mL

1. Melt the butter in a large skillet. Add the onion and celery and sauté, covered, over medium-low heat for 5 minutes.
2. Add the celery, mushrooms and garlic and sauté for an additional 5 minutes over medium heat.
3. Remove the pan from the heat and add the DLS*, poultry seasoning, wild rice, dried cranberries and almonds.
4. Bake in a casserole at 325°F (160°C) for 30-40 minutes or use to stuff a 4 lb. (2 kg) roasting chicken.

Serves 4-6.

* Dymond Lake Seasoning, see page 3.
** It is often useful to cook more wild rice than you need for a recipe. Refrigerate leftovers for up to 1 week. It freezes well.

TO COOK WILD RICE: Bring ½ cup (125 mL) wild rice and 2½ cups (625 mL) water to a boil. Simmer, covered, for 45 minutes, or until the rice has reached the desired consistency. For 1 cup (250 mL) of raw wild rice use 3 cups (740 mL) water. Yield is about 4 cups (1 L) cooked rice to 1 cup (250 mL) raw.

Fire at North Knife Lake

by Doug Webber

The 1994 fishing season started out innocently enough but, by the middle of July, the forests in Northern Manitoba were tinder dry from lack of rain. Lightning storms with little associated rain would come streaking across the country, leaving a line of small fires in their wake and occasionally becoming raging infernos, eating up thousands of acres of black spruce forest with no current commercial value other than for the odd lodge or outcamp nestled in its embrace.

One such innocuous strike produced a tiny fire about 20 miles southwest of our lodge on North Knife Lake. We nervously phoned the fire crews stationed in Thompson, 150 miles to the south. Why were we nervous? The high-pressure areas that had predominated our weather for most of the season produced mostly westerly to southwesterly winds that we knew from experience would eventually bring the fire to our doorstep. Our pleas fell on deaf ears, however. The "powers that be" sent a single Otter, with a crew chief, to assess the situation early one morning, about 5 days after the fire started. The fire, following its usual custom, was still in the process of becoming a blazing inferno. This oversized campfire encompassed only a couple of acres by the time they got to the area at 1,000 hours. They flew on to the lodge (for coffee and some of Helen and Marie's famous baking) to assure us that there was NO danger whatever from this puny little fire that was still 15 miles away. The wind had not picked up by the time they arrived so the fire was barely moving.

Not long after they left for Thompson, however, the wind picked up from the southwest to about 15 miles per hour, sending the fire into express-train mode (actual speed about one-half mile per hour) right toward the lodge. More frantic calls to the fire station were greeted with, "We were just there and you are just overreacting. Keep an eye on it and if it's still burning in a couple of days, we'll come and have another look."

Two days and 27 frantic phone calls later, they decided that they would send the single Otter back for another look. By the time they got there, the wind had switched to the north and the fire was burning back on itself, advancing at the leisurely speed of maybe 75 feet an hour. "No problem," we were assured as they showed up for the second time for coffee and goodies. "That fire will be out completely in a couple of days."

The next day, the wind switched back to the southwest and proceeded on its relentless drive toward the lodge. More frantic calls and more assurances by the firefighters that we were in "No danger". By this time the fire had sneaked to within 5 miles of the Lodge and our days were spent in a haze of choking smoke, as we tried to assure our guests that there was no danger of being incinerated while they were out fishing.

The morning of July 30th dawned with bright blue skies and a light breeze from the southwest. Camp manager Stewart Webber (no relation) started calling about 0600 hours, informing the firefighters that the fire had advanced to within 4 miles of the lodge. He also informed them that if they were just going to send the Otter for another coffee break, they should not bother coming. He managed to convince them of the seriousness of the situation and had a helicopter and attack crew on site by 0800 hours.

(Continued on page 140.)

Fire at North Knife Lake (continued)

As soon as they arrived on the scene, they immediately called for reinforcements as they knew if they didn't get this thing under control by 1100 hours, at the latest, we'd all be in BIG TROUBLE. By 1000 hours there were 2 CL215 Water Bombers, two more helicopters and two more attack crews on their way to North Knife Lake. The crew chief had set up a command post in the lodge and was talking directly to the fire crew who were working frantically to contain the fire.

About 1100 hours, just as we were loading the 2 helicopters with hoses and pumps, we heard the leader of the attack crew at the fire holler, "We're losing it!!!!!!" The two crews at the runway immediately scrambled aboard the choppers and headed for the fire. About the same time, the first water bomber arrived on the scene and was soon rumbling toward the fire with its first load of water.

The next three hours were tense, with more action than the busy airport at Thompson would normally experience. In all, it took 3 Water Bombers, 3 helicopters with buckets and 3 attack crews to bring the blaze under control, and it wasn't until the next day, when the wind switched to the west, that we got any relief. With the wind shift, the fire changed direction and burned itself out on the small lake just above Helen's Falls (about two miles south of the lodge and one mile south of the bottom of North Knife Lake). The cavalry had carried the day, arriving just in the nick of time to save the lodge from certain destruction.

Thank you God . . . for standing by me so far this day. With your help, I haven't been impatient, grumpy, judgmental, or lost my temper. But . . . I'll be getting out of bed soon, and I'll really be needing your help then!

Tame Meats To Make You Wild

Many people think that we only cook wild meat, but we are every bit as interested in researching and collecting interesting and tasty recipes for more available meats. From Dancing Chickens to Broiled Lamb Chops with Caper Sauce to Ginger Soy Sherry Flank Steak, we've found some delectable meals with simple preparation. For the more adventuresome, we've included Brined Turkey – guaranteed to be the most tender, moist and flavorful turkey you've ever tasted! To augment the selection of beef recipes, remember that any of the big game recipes in Moose, Goose & Things That Swim, are equally delicious using beef.

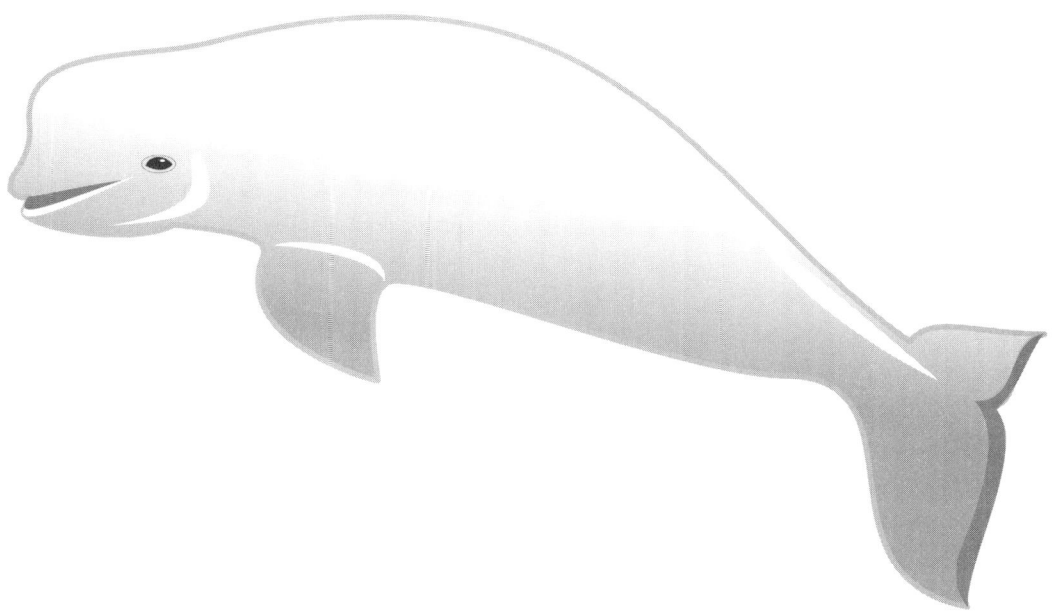

Ginger Soy Sherry Flank Steak

You needn't purchase the most expensive cut of meat to enjoy succulent flavor and tender beef. A little planning ahead is all it takes.

Ginger Soy Marinade:

½ cup	soy sauce	125 mL
½ cup	sherry OR red wine	125 mL
½ cup	vegetable oil	125 mL
2-3	garlic cloves, minced	2-3
1 tbsp.	grated fresh ginger	15 mL
1 tbsp.	grated orange peel	15 mL
1-2 tbsp.	concentrated orange juice	15-30 mL
1 tbsp.	Worcestershire sauce	15 mL
½ tsp.	Tabasco sauce	2 mL
	salt and freshly ground pepper to taste	
3 lbs.	flank steak	1.5 kg

1. In a large measuring cup, combine all of the marinade ingredients.
2. Score the steak(s) on both sides in a diamond pattern. This helps the steak absorb the marinade flavors.
3. Place the steak(s) in a large sealable plastic bag. Pour the marinade over the steak and seal the bag. Place the bag in a pan large enough to hold the steak and refrigerate. Turn the steak in the marinade every few hours. The steak should be marinated overnight, but can be marinated for 3-4 days.
4. Barbecue the steak(s) to your desired doneness, 5 minutes per side over very high heat for a medium steak. To serve, slice thinly on the diagonal.

Serves 8.

Tame Meats to Make You Wild

Jeff's Green Curry Beef

Jeff loves exotic foods and he loves them hot! When he isn't working for Doug and Helen, he is often traveling to far-off places. This recipe came from Thailand but has been adapted to include only ingredients that are readily available in North America.

Green Curry Paste:

6	green onions	6
5	medium green chilies, seeded	5
1	medium green chili with seeds	1
2	garlic cloves	2
1 tbsp.	grated fresh ginger	15 mL
1 tbsp.	coriander seeds	15 mL
1 cup	chopped fresh basil	250 mL
1½ cups	chopped fresh cilantro	375 mL
¼ cup	olive oil	60 mL
½ cup	lime juice (zest of 1 lime)	125 mL
1 tsp.	salt	5 mL
1 lb.	beef strips*	500 g
2 tbsp.	olive oil	30 mL
1½	green peppers, chopped	1½
1½	onions, chopped	1½
2	carrots, diced	2
½ cup	chopped celery	125 mL
1	apple, peeled and chopped	1
2	bananas, sliced	2
1⅔ cups	coconut milk (full fat)	400 mL

1. Put all of the paste ingredients into a food processor and purée until smooth. (Makes 2 cups [500 mL] of paste.)
2. In a large skillet, heat the olive oil and sauté the beef until browned. Add the vegetables and apples and sauté until slightly softened.
3. Add the Green Curry Paste and coconut milk. Reheat and serve over rice.

Serves 8.

NOTE: The Green Curry Paste may be frozen and used later or in smaller amounts. It is also good with chicken or fish. For a hotter paste, use more chili seeds.

* Strips of young tender wild goose breast work well too.

Bobotie (ba-boo-tie)

From Wendy Both comes this unusual curried meat loaf – a South African favorite! Team it with Len's Coconut Rice, page 131, for a sensational meal.

1	thick slice of bread	1
½ cup	milk	125 mL
1 cup	finely chopped onion	250 mL
1 tbsp.	vegetable oil	15 mL
1 tbsp.	hot curry powder*	15 mL
1 lb.	ground beef	500 g
½ tsp.	sugar	2 mL
1 tsp.	salt	5 mL
pinch	pepper	pinch
1 tbsp.	lemon juice	15 mL
1 tbsp.	mango chutney OR apricot jam	15 mL
⅓ cup	raisins	75 mL
1	egg	1
	whole or slivered almond to cover loaf	
4	bay leaves	4
½ cup	milk	125 mL
1	egg	1
	chopped parsley for garnish	

1. Soak the bread in the milk, then mash.
2. In a skillet, sauté the onions in oil until translucent; add the curry power and fry for 1 more minute.
3. In a large bowl, combine the ground beef with the bread, onions, sugar, salt, pepper, lemon juice, chutney, raisins and egg. Mix well and form into a loaf.
4. Place the loaf in a greased 3 x 5 x 9" (8 x 13 x 23 cm) loaf pan. Press almonds lightly into meat to cover the top of the loaf. Lay bay leaves on top of almonds.
5. Cover the loaf with waxed paper, shaping it around the top of the loaf. Bake at 350°F (180°C) for 45 minutes. Remove waxed paper and pour off fat.
6. Beat remaining milk and egg lightly together and pour over meat loaf. Return to the oven and bake, uncovered, for another 30-45 minutes.
7. Garnish with parsley and serve with chutney, sliced bananas, sliced tomatoes, and/or coconut.

Serves 6.

* *Curry powder comes mild, medium and hot. Adjust the amount according to your preference and to what you have*

Cheddar Wild Rice Meat Loaf

This is as good as the name suggests. A colorful tossed salad, dilled carrots, crusty rolls and they'll be back for seconds.

Wild Rice Meat Loaf:

1 lb.	lean ground beef	500 g
3	eggs, beaten	3
2 cups	cooked wild rice	500 mL
½ cup	chopped celery	125 mL
½ cup	chopped onion	125 mL
¾ cup	sliced fresh mushrooms	175 mL
1	garlic clove, chopped	1
1 tbsp.	Worcestershire sauce	15 mL
½ tsp.	salt	2 mL
2 tsp.	DLS* OR ½ tsp. (2 mL) pepper	10 mL

Cheddar Sauce:

2 tbsp.	butter OR margarine	30 mL
2 tbsp.	flour	30 mL
1 cup	milk	125 mL
1 cup	grated medium Cheddar cheese	125 mL

1. Combine all of the meat loaf ingredients, mixing well. Press firmly into a 3 x 5 x 9" (8 x 13 x 23 cm) loaf pan and bake at 350°F (180°C) for 1 hour.
2. **To make the sauce**, melt the butter in a saucepan over low heat and stir in the flour, blending until smooth. Remove from the heat and gradually add the milk, stirring until smooth. Return to medium heat and cook, stirring constantly, until the sauce comes to a boil and is thickened. Remove the pan from the heat, add the cheese and stir until smooth.
3. When the meat loaf is cooked, remove from the oven and let sit in the pan for 10 minutes. Pour off any pan liquid and turn the loaf out onto a platter. Slice and top with the Cheddar Sauce.

Serves 6.

* *Dymond Lake Seasoning, see page 3.*

Tame Meats to Make You Wild

Fennel Roast Pork

Marie's friend Ellen passed this on to us – definitely cookbook quality! Try it also with a mixture of caraway and mustard seeds.

3½ lb.	boneless pork loin roast	1.75 kg
2	large garlic cloves, slivered	2
⅓ cup	flour	75 mL
1 tsp.	salt	5 mL
½ tsp.	pepper	2 mL
1 tbsp.	fennel seeds	15 mL
1 cup	chopped onion	250 mL
3 cups	chicken broth	750 mL

1. Make deep slits in the roast and insert the garlic slivers into the slits.
2. Combine the flour, salt and pepper. Roll the roast in the seasoned flour until completely coated. Place the roast in a roaster.
3. Pat the fennel seeds and onion over the top of the roast.
4. Roast at 400°F (200°C) for 1 hour. Pour off any fat.
5. Add **1 cup (250 mL)** of chicken broth to the pan and cover lightly with foil or the pan lid. Roast for another 40 minutes, or until a thermometer inserted in the center reads 165°F (74°C). Check after 20 minutes and add more chicken broth if needed.
6. Remove the roast from the pan and cover lightly with foil. Set it in a warm place to rest for 15-20 minutes before carving.
7. While the roast rests, add the remaining chicken broth to the roasting pan and simmer until it is somewhat reduced. Serve with the roast.

Serves 8.

Breaded Pork Fillet

At the Smiths' house, this simple dinner, lovingly known as the Dreaded Pork Fillet, is served often. It's also good with caribou or beef tenderloin.

1-1½ lb.	pork tenderloin	500-750 g
2	eggs	2
¼ cup	water	60 mL
1 tsp.	salt	5 mL
½ tsp.	dried thyme	2 mL
pinch	pepper	pinch
1½ cups	dried bread crumbs	375 mL
3 tbsp.	EACH vegetable oil and butter	45 mL

Tame Meats to Make You Wild

Breaded Pork Fillet (continued)

1. Cut each tenderloin almost in half, lengthwise, taking care not to cut all the way through. Open it out and pound it with a meat mallet until it is ¼" (1 cm) thick. Cut each tenderloin into 2 or 3 pieces.
2. In a shallow bowl, whisk together the eggs, water, salt, thyme and pepper. Dip the pork fillets in the egg mixture, then in the bread crumbs. Repeat to make a double coating. Chill for 30 minutes.
3. Heat the oil and butter in a large frying pan. Add the pork and sauté for about 10 minutes, until browned and tender, turning once.
4. Serve with Mushroom Wine Sauce, page 16, use only half of the recipe.

Serves 4-6.

Broiled Lamb Chops with Lemon Caper Sauce

Lamb is rarely the first choice for North Americans when it comes to entertaining. Do we know what we are missing? These lamb chops make up in thickness, what they lack in circumference. Broiled only to medium doneness and bathed in a lemon caper sauce, here is an entrée to write home about!

8	1½-2" (4-5 cm) loin lamb chops*	8
	salt and pepper to taste	
3 tbsp.	butter	45 mL
1 tbsp.	freshly grated lemon zest	15 mL
1 tbsp.	capers	15 mL
3 tbsp.	fresh lemon juice	45 mL

1. Sprinkle the lamb chops with salt and pepper
2. Broil the chops on the rack of a broiler pan, about 4" (10 cm) from the heat, for 6 minutes. Turn the chops and broil for 4 minutes (10 cm) more. Let stand for 5 minutes.
3. While the chops are broiling, in a small saucepan, melt the butter and stir in the lemon zest, capers and lemon juice. Simmer gently for a minute.
4. Pour the sauce over the chops and serve.

Serves 4.

* *If you can't find thick lamb chops, buy the whole rack and cut between every 2 ribs.*

Tame Meats to Make You Wild

Crisped Brined Roast Turkey

The Sawyers from Texas were kind enough to share this recipe with us. The brining not only seasons the turkey throughout but it also keeps the breast nice and juicy. Combined with the crackly, crisp skin, you can't beat it. It is necessary to start this process the day before you want to eat the turkey.

2 cups	table salt OR 4 cups (1 L) kosher salt	500 mL
8 quarts	cold water	8 L
1 turkey	12-14 lbs.* (5.5-6 kg) with neck and giblets removed	1
1 cup	chunked onion	250 mL
½ cup	chunked carrot	125 mL
2	chunked celery ribs	2
6 sprigs	fresh thyme OR 1 tsp. (5 mL) dried leaves	6 sprigs
⅓-½ cup	melted butter	75-125 mL
2-4 tbsp.	DLS** OR 1 tsp. (5 mL) seasoned pepper	30-60 mL

1. Dissolve the salt in cold water in a stockpot or bucket that is large enough to completely submerge the turkey. Add the turkey and refrigerate or set in a very cool spot for 4-6 hours. You can brine the turkey overnight but in that case you would only use half the amount of salt.

2. Remove the turkey from the salt water and rinse under cool running water. Pat dry inside and out with paper towels. Place the turkey, breast side down, on a flat wire rack set over a rimmed baking pan. Refrigerate at least 8 hours or overnight.

3. **To roast the turkey**, remove it from the refrigerator and fill the cavity with onions, carrots, celery and thyme. At this point, either tie the legs together with twine, or use meat skewers to close the cavity. Place the turkey on a greased rack in a roaster. A V-shaped rack works well for this. Brush the breast of the turkey with melted butter and sprinkle liberally with DLS** or seasoned pepper. Turn the turkey breast side down on the rack. Pour **½ cup (125 mL) of water** into the pan.

4. Roast for 45 minutes at 400°F (200°C). Remove the turkey from the oven, brush the back with butter and turn over on the side. Roast for 15 minutes. Remove from the oven and brush the exposed parts of the turkey with more butter. Turn again on the other side. Roast another 15 minutes. Brush exposed areas again and turn so the turkey is now breast side up. Add ½ cup (125 mL) of water if all the liquid has evaporated. Continue roasting until an instant-read thermometer registers 165°F (74°C) at the thickest part of the breast and 170°F (77°C) to 175°F (79.4°C) at the thickest part of the thigh. This should be approximately 30-45 minutes. Let rest 20-30 minutes while you prepare the gravy***.

 Tame Meats to Make You Wild

Crisped Brined Roast Turkey (continued)

If you have stuffed the bird with your favorite stuffing, roast as follows:

1. Brush the turkey breast with butter and sprinkle with DLS**. Place the turkey breast down on the rack. Brush the back with butter and sprinkle with DLS**. Roast at 400°F (200°C) for 1 hour. Reduce the oven temperature to 250°F (120°C) and roast for 2 more hours.
2. Turn the turkey breast side up, increase the oven temperature to 400°F (200°C) and continue to roast for 1-1½ hours, or until the thermometer reads as above. Let rest 20-30 minutes while you prepare the gravy***.

* This method works for a larger turkey but cooking times would increase.

** Dymond Lake Seasoning, see page 3.

*** **To make the gravy,** to the hot drippings in the pan, add flour, whisking constantly until all the drippings are absorbed – you should see very little fat in the pan. Scrape the pan with a wooden spoon to get all the browned bits off the bottom. Add hot water, whisking constantly, until the gravy is about the consistency you like. Put over high heat and bring to a boil. Add more water or chicken broth if necessary. Season with salt and pepper. Add ½ tsp. (2 mL) each of ground thyme and savory for a richer flavor.

The average Canadian eats 139 pounds (64.5 kg) of red meat, 77 pounds (35 kg) of poultry and 22 pounds (10 kg) of fish annually.

Tame Meats to Make You Wild

New Orleans Jambalaya

A dinner invitation yielded this wonderful jambalaya which begs to be shared. The original recipe came from Peg Lombardi of Denver. We have cut it in half. Be sure to prepare this a day ahead, then serve it with French bread and a green salad.

½ lb.	smoked sausage OR kielbasa	250 g
1½ tbsp.	olive oil	22 mL
⅓ cup	chopped green pepper	75 mL
1	garlic clove, minced	1
½ cup	chopped fresh parsley	125 mL
½ cup	chopped celery	125 mL
19 oz.	can peeled, diced tomatoes	540 mL
1 cup	chicken broth	250 mL
½ cup	chopped green onion	125 mL
1 tsp.	ground thyme	5 mL
1	large bay leaf	1
1 tsp.	oregano	5 mL
½ tsp.	chili powder	2 mL
¼ tsp.	cayenne pepper	1 mL
⅛ tsp.	ground black pepper	0.5 mL
1 cup	raw, long-grain rice	250 mL
3 cups	boneless chicken breasts, cut into bite-sized pieces	750 mL
1½ lbs.	medium-sized raw shrimp, cleaned and peeled	750 g

1. In a heavy 4-quart saucepan, sauté the sausage until firm. Remove and add olive oil to the drippings. Add the green pepper, garlic, parsley and celery and sauté for 5 minutes.
2. Add the tomatoes with liquid, chicken broth, green onion, spices and herbs to the pot. Add the rice and sausage; cover and simmer for 20 minutes, stirring occasionally.
3. Add the chicken and shrimp and cook about 10 more minutes, until the shrimp curl and turn pink. Transfer to a buttered 4-quart (4 L) casserole. Cover and refrigerate overnight.
4. Bake, covered, at 350°F (180°C) for 1 hour, or until heated through.

Serves 8-10.

Chicken in Mushroom Wine Sauce

This is so easy to prepare, it can be a last-minute meal on the run.

6	skinless, boneless chicken breasts	6
¼ cup	butter, melted	60 mL
1 cup	flour	250 mL
1 tsp.	salt	5 mL
¼ tsp.	pepper	1 mL
4 cups	thickly sliced fresh mushrooms	1 L
½ cup	grated Parmesan cheese	125 mL
¾ cup	white wine*	175 mL
¾ cup	chicken broth	175 mL
	DLS** OR seasoned pepper	

1. Rinse and dry the chicken breasts. Pour butter into a small bowl. Stir together the flour, salt and pepper in another bowl.
2. Dip each chicken breast into the melted butter, then roll in the flour mixture until thoroughly coated. Place in a 9 x 13" (23 x 33 cm) baking dish.
3. Add the sliced mushrooms, tucking them around the chicken breasts. Sprinkle the whole casserole with Parmesan cheese. Pour the wine and broth around the chicken. Sprinkle with DLS**.
4. Bake at 375°F (190°C) for 30-40 minutes, basting the chicken with the liquid once or twice. The sauce should be thickened and bubbly. Serve with rice or noodles.

Serves 3-6.

*   You may omit the wine and just double the chicken broth.
** Dymond Lake Seasoning, see page 3.

Tame Meats to Make You Wild

Dancing Chickens

Dancing chickens, drunken chickens, it doesn't matter what you call them they are simple and succulent! Fun too, people always chuckle when you open the barbecue to the sight of dancing chickens.

	Dymond Lake Seasoning*	
	OR	

Seasoned Rub:

4 tsp.	paprika	20 mL
2 tsp.	salt	10 mL
2 tsp.	onion powder	10 mL
2 tsp.	pepper	10 mL
1 tsp.	garlic powder	5 mL
1 tsp.	sage	5 mL
1/2 tsp.	cayenne	2 mL
3½-4 lb.	chicken	1.75-2 kg
12 oz.	beer	341 mL

1. Use DLS* OR combine all of the ingredients for the rub.
2. Wash the chicken and pat dry with paper towels. Sprinkle DLS* OR the rub over the whole chicken, coating well. Any unused rub can be stored in a covered container for later use.
3. Open the can of beer (you can drink about a third of it) and insert the can into the cavity of the chicken, keeping it upright. Stand the chicken in a foil-covered baking pan with sides (it can make a mess). The foil is for easy cleanup.
4. Set the pan in a preheated barbecue over medium-low heat. Close the cover and cook for 1¼-1½ hours.

Serves 4.

* *Dymond Lake Seasoning, see page 3.*

 *Tame Meats to Make You Wild*

Roast Chicken and Potatoes

This is one of those recipes that is so simple that you wonder why you didn't think of it yourself. Wonderful roasted potatoes with chicken and you only dirty one pan!

6 tbsp.	vegetable oil	90 mL
8	chicken pieces OR a 4 lb. (2 kg) chicken, cut up	8
2 lbs.	potatoes, peeled and cut into wedges	1 kg
3 tbsp.	fresh lemon juice	45 mL
3	large garlic cloves, minced	3
1 tbsp.	DLS* OR dried oregano	15 mL
	salt and pepper OR DLS* to taste	

1. Brush the inside of a large roasting pan with **2 tbsp. (30 mL) oil**.
2. Place the chicken in the centre of the roaster in a single layer and surround chicken with potatoes. Drizzle the chicken with lemon juice.
3. Combine **4 tbsp. (60 mL) oil** with garlic and DLS* OR oregano. Brush most of the oil mixture over the potatoes, coating them well. Drizzle the remaining oil mixture over the chicken.
4. Sprinkle the chicken and potatoes with the desired amount of salt and pepper OR DLS*.
5. Bake, uncovered, for about 1 hour and 10 minutes. Everything should be well browned, tender and full of flavor. Baste the chicken with the pan juices and serve.

Serves 4-6.

* *Dymond Lake Seasoning, see page 3.*

Soaking a lemon in hot water for 15 minutes before squeezing it will yield almost twice the amount of juice.

Cranberry-Glazed Chicken

A soiree at the home of Sarah Marshall brought this delicious recipe home to roost.

½ cup	flour	125 mL
½ tsp.	salt	2 mL
½ tsp.	DLS* OR pepper	2 mL
4-6	chicken pieces	4-6
2 tbsp.	butter	30 mL
2 tbsp.	olive oil	30 mL

Sweet and Sour Cranberry Sauce:

1½ cups	cranberries	375 mL
1 cup	brown sugar	250 mL
¾ cup	water	175 mL
1 tbsp.	wine vinegar	15 mL
1 tbsp.	flour	15 mL
½ tsp.	cinnamon	2 mL
¼ tsp.	cloves	1 mL
¼ tsp.	allspice	1 mL
¼ tsp.	salt	1 mL

1. In a plastic bag, combine the flour, salt and DLS*. Add the chicken and shake to coat.
2. Heat the butter and oil in a large skillet. Add the chicken pieces and brown slowly, about 30 minutes. Remove the chicken from the pan. Discard all but 2 tbsp. (30 mL) of drippings.
3. To the pan, add the cranberries, brown sugar and water. Cook for 5 minutes, or until the cranberry skins pop.
4. Mix the vinegar with flour and seasonings; add to the cranberry mixture. Cook, stirring constantly, until thickened.
5. Return the chicken pieces to the sauce and simmer for 30 minutes. Alternatively, put the chicken pieces in a large casserole, pour the sauce over and bake at 350°F (180°C) for 1 hour.

Serves 4-6.

* *Dymond Lake Seasoning, page 3.*

Tame Meats to Make You Wild

Cranberry Orange Chicken

This wonderful cranberry and orange combination dresses up chicken for company.

½ cup	flour	125 mL
½ tsp.	salt	2 mL
½ tsp.	DLS* OR pepper	2 mL
3 lbs.	chicken pieces	1.5 kg
2 tbsp.	butter	30 mL
2 tbsp.	olive oil	30 mL

Cranberry Orange Sauce:

1 cup	cranberries	250 mL
¼ cup	chopped onion	60 mL
1 tsp.	freshly grated orange peel	5 mL
¼ tsp.	ground ginger	1 mL
¼ tsp.	ground cinnamon	1 mL
½ cup	sugar	125 mL
½ cup	orange juice	125 mL

1. In a plastic bag, combine the flour, salt and DLS*. Add the chicken and shake to coat. In a large skillet, heat the butter and oil. Add the chicken and brown turning once.
2. Pour and sprinkle all of the sauce ingredients over the chicken. Simmer for 30 minutes, stirring occasionally. (The chicken and sauce may also be heated in a casserole in the oven at 350°F/180°C for 40 minutes.)

Serves 4-6.

* *Dymond Lake Seasoning, page 3.*

Frying with butter:
As the butter begins to melt in the pan, add a little olive or vegetable oil. This will lower the point at which the butter would burn.

Tame Meats to Make You Wild

Lemon Greek Chicken

(Helen) We have written this recipe for 4 but I have double, tripled and quadrupled it to take to the cabin. It is one of those no-fuss recipes that allow you play outside with the grandchildren and come in just when it is time to eat!

2 tsp.	lemon zest	10 mL
¼ cup	lemon juice	60 mL
2 tbsp.	olive oil	30 mL
4	large garlic cloves, crushed or chopped	4
2 tsp.	dried oregano leaves	10 mL
½ tsp.	salt	2 mL
1 tsp.	DLS* OR ¼ tsp. (1 mL) pepper	5 mL
2	medium potatoes, each cut into 8 wedges	2
1	medium red bell pepper, cut into 1" (2.5 cm) pieces	1
1	medium green bell pepper, cut into 1" (2.5 cm) pieces	1
1	medium red onion, cut into wedges	1
2 cups	fresh whole mushrooms, halved or quartered if large	500 mL
2	whole chicken breasts, 4 halves, OR 8 thighs	2

1. In a 9 x 13" (23 x 33 cm) baking pan or casserole, combine lemon zest, lemon juice, oil, garlic, oregano, salt and DLS*.
2. Add the potatoes, peppers, onion and mushrooms, tossing to coat well.
3. Place the chicken pieces on top of the vegetables. Use a pastry brush to pick up the lemon mixture from the bottom of the pan and brush over the chicken.
4. Bake at 400°F (200°C) for 1 hour, or until the chicken is no longer pink in the center. Brush the chicken and vegetables with the pan juices after the first 30 minutes.

Serves 4.

NOTE: *For real convenience, you can assemble this dish, cover it well, refrigerate it overnight and bake it the next day.*

* Dymond Lake Seasoning, see page 3.

See photograph opposite.

Ginger Peanut Stir-Fry

Recommended by Doug's Aunt Eileen, this is definitely a keeper.

3 tbsp.	soy sauce	45 mL
2 tbsp.	peanut butter	30 mL
1 tbsp.	white wine OR rice wine vinegar	15 mL
1 tbsp.	brown sugar	15 mL
¼ cup	chopped fresh ginger	60 mL
2	garlic cloves, chopped or minced	2
½ tsp.	hot pepper sauce or more if you like more bite	1 mL
1 tbsp.	peanut oil OR vegetable oil	15 mL
¾ lb.	boneless, skinless chicken breasts, cut into bite-size pieces	340 g
2	medium carrots, thinly sliced	2
2	sweet peppers, 1 red, 1 green, cut into strips	2
1½ cups	snow peas	375 mL
¼ cup	chopped toasted peanuts for garnish	60 mL

1. In a small bowl, stir the soy sauce with peanut butter, vinegar, brown sugar, ginger, garlic and hot pepper sauce until blended. Set aside.
2. In a large skillet, heat oil over medium-high heat. Add the chicken and stir-fry until browned all over, about 3 minutes. Add the carrots and stir-fry for 2 minutes. Add the peanut sauce, peppers and snow peas. Stir-fry until vegetables are tender but still crisp and the chicken is cooked through, about 2 minutes.
3. Sprinkle with the peanuts and serve over rice or noodles.

Serves 4.

In the long run, the pessimist may be proved right, but the optimist has a better time on the trip.

Low tide and high tide (with the moon rising) at Seal River Heritage Lodge on Hudson Bay.

Tame Meats to Make You Wild

Peachy Picante Chicken

We know how many cooks love short ingredient lists. This one is super short and the recipe doesn't disappoint. Vary the amounts of salsa and peaches until the recipe is just the way your family likes it. Thank you to Heather for passing on this recipe.

4-6	boneless chicken breasts	4-6
	oil for frying	
1 cup	mango salsa OR tomato salsa (more or less)	250 mL
1 cup	canned sliced peaches (more or less), with juice	250 mL
1¼ oz.	pkg. taco seasoning	35 g
1	green pepper, chunked (optional)	1
1	tomato, chunked (optional)	1

1. Cut the chicken in strips. Brown the chicken strips in oil. Add the salsa, peaches and taco seasoning. Simmer for 20 minutes. Add the green pepper and tomato and reheat.
2. Serve with rice and a salad.

Serves 4.

Mango and Red Pepper Salsa

Fresh and tasty, this salsa complements any grilled meat or fish.

1 cup	finely diced, ripe mango	250 mL
1 cup	diced, roasted red pepper*	250 mL
¼ cup	chopped, fresh cilantro	60 mL
2 tbsp.	chopped, fresh mint OR 2 tsp. (10 mL) mint sauce	30 mL
2 tbsp.	lemon juice	30 mL

Combine all of the ingredients. Let the salsa sit to blend flavors. Store in the refrigerator.

Makes about 2 cups (500 mL).

* To roast red peppers, place them in a baking pan under the broiler. When the skin is blackened and soft, place the peppers in a bowl and cover until cooled. Peel and then chop. If you have a gas stove, set the peppers over a medium flame and turn them until the skins are blackened.

Chicken Lasagne

(MARIE) *My friends are accustomed to having me ask for recipes. If they save the best ones to impress me, it works! Margaret Cull served this at a dinner meeting. I'll never remember what we talked about, but I sure won't forget the meal!*

Creamy Hollandaise Sauce:

8	egg yolks	8
2 tbsp.	fresh lemon juice	30 mL
4 shakes	cayenne pepper	4 shakes
1 lb.	butter, melted	500 g
1 cup	cream	250 mL
3 cups	sliced mushrooms	750 mL
¾ cup	chopped onion	175 mL
	vegetable oil	
6	lasagne noodles, cooked	6
2 lbs.	cooked chicken breasts, sliced	1 kg
	DLS* OR pepper to taste	
1 tsp.	dried basil	5 mL
1 tsp.	dried oregano	5 mL
3 cups	shredded mozzarella cheese	750 mL
1 bunch	fresh asparagus**, steamed tender-crisp	1
1 cup	grated Parmesan cheese	250 mL

1. **To make the sauce,** place the egg yolks in a blender with lemon juice and cayenne. Add warm, melted butter in a slow stream, while blending. Continue to blend while adding cream. **(Makes 5 cups/1.25 L.)**
2. Sauté the mushrooms and onions in oil until the onions are translucent.
3. Spread half of the sauce in a greased 9 x 13" (23 x 33 cm) glass pan. Top with a layer of noodles, then half the sliced chicken. Sprinkle the chicken with DLS*. Add half of the mushroom mixture and sprinkle with all of the basil and oregano. Top with half the mozzarella cheese.
4. Repeat the layers of sauce, noodles, chicken, DLS* and mushroom mixture. Lay the asparagus across the top of the casserole, alternating tips. Top with the remaining mozzarella, then all of the Parmesan cheese.
5. Bake, uncovered, at 350°F (180°C) for 35-45 minutes.

Serves 8.

* Dymond Lake Seasoning, see page 3.
** OR 2 x 12 oz. (341 mL) cans asparagus tips, drained.

Tame Meats to Make You Wild

My Churchill River Swim/Tragically Wet

by Jeff

One fabulous spring day I was at Dymond Lake getting ready to come home after closing up from a spring goose hunt. It had been particularly warm that spring and the ice was well on its way to being too weak to travel on. My biggest concern was crossing the Churchill River, so I called Mike on the satellite phone. He said "There's a lot of water on the river, but come on over; it will be OK." I made my final preparations and headed out on our ancient, dependable, but "gutless" snow machine. The first section of the trip across Button Bay went smoothly. My Discman serenaded me with pleasant background noise that was mixed with the monotonous wail of the snowmobile motor.

When I arrived at Seahorse Gully, the lack of snow made me glad that I had chosen to strap a light load to the back of the snow machine rather than pull a qamatiq. I only got stuck once in the soft, heavily drifted snow. Finally free of Seahorse Gully, I was feeling more optimistic . . . until I came to the Churchill River. Mike's words of assurance rang through my head, but my heart sank when I saw WATER – ALL THE WAY ACROSS THE RIVER! However, being an obedient slave, er I mean employee, I decided that the water was not deep enough to swamp the Bravo and I continued on. I drove to the farthest point of land, which looked like a significant drift of ice and snow, but it turned out to be a pile of slush ice.

I soon found myself plowing through the slush rather than riding on top of it! With full throttle, the Bravo screaming and the Discman music maintaining my sanity, I leaned back as much as possible to keep the front of the Bravo above the water. The back edge of the track was grinding across the ice, below the deepening water, which was getting ever closer to filling my rubber boots and drowning the Bravo. Unable to turn around, I prayed to stay afloat.

However, the Bravo coughed and sputtered to an untimely death. I was less than a quarter of the way across the river and up to my chest in freezing water. My Discman wasn't waterproof, so the Tragically Hip became "tragically wet". With only the top half of the windshield showing, and the back seat level with the water, I collected the important items and started back to shore. I found myself doing the Michael Jackson "moonwalk" and was soon forced to unload, item by item, until I was left with only my backpack and was SWIMMING back to shore.

Overhead I heard a Beaver, which turned out to be Uncle Doug's bushplane searching for me, as I was now 2 to 3 hours past my ETA in Churchill. Meanwhile, on the other side of the river, Mike, in his comfortably warm, dry clothes, was checking the status of the water on the river (ha, ha). With his binoculars he could now get a good look at his FAITHFUL WET SLAVE, er EMPLOYEE, DRAGGING HIMSELF OUT OF THE BITTERLY COLD WATERS OF THE FLOODED RIVER (due to a high tide and a weir farther upriver).

 Tame Meats to Make You Wild

Having accepted the fact that I was now without music to keep me company, I tried to think logically and calmly about how to get myself out of this jam. Before I could do anything, the Beaver dropped me a note, about 200 yards away. It read, "GO BACK TO DYMOND!" They obviously didn't see the sunken Bravo! Not being able to readily relay a message back, I resorted to a graphic charade to relay my predicament. Then I stripped down to my boxer shorts and proceeded to wring the water out of my clothes and Discman while muttering some "unprintable" language.

Since it was a wonderfully warm day, I changed into dry, warm, dirty (smelly) clothes and felt a little better. I knew the trek back to Dymond would take me the better part of the evening, with arrival somewhere between midnight and two a.m., if all went well.

The Beaver was still buzzing around, like a pesky little fly, despite my "obvious" message. In a visible snowdrift at the base of a hill I stamped out my second message: GO HOME I'M OK. Then came another note: "Is the strip between that rock and that willow bush OK to land on?" Observing no area capable of allowing an airplane to land, because of the rocks, willow bushes and soft ice, I proceeded back to my snowdrift and stamped out "NO", all the while thinking, "Heck NO, you silly elbow."

The next few hours were quite pleasant because the Beaver went home and, thinking that it would be faster, I went on a hike along the ridge above Seahorse Gully, eating cranberries along the way. Yummy.

My chosen route allowed me to see Fort Prince of Wales in the distance, but I was out of sight of the Beaver, which was searching for me. After sliding along patches of frozen ice, I ran into some melt-ice which claimed my only dry footwear! By now I had developed a whole dictionary of nasty phrases and words to describe the miserable situation I was in. The Beaver spotted me and dropped another surprise package, which landed some 500 yards away (Uncle Doug's aim had not improved) on the opposite side of that large patch of melt-ice I had just crossed. The airmail care package – an 80-pound full backpack, which narrowly missed the melt-ice – contained a fresh pair of socks, hoodie, nylon army fatigue pants, a jacket, satellite phone, matches and paper, a cracker gun (to fend off wild animals) and, most importantly, a light snack (a stale doughnut, some carrot sticks, a freshly bruised apple, and a juice box that 'had humidified' some of the other items in the pack). The comforting note enclosed said, "WAIT THERE. WE'LL THINK OF SOMETHING!" Being the foolish, faithful slave, er employee, I waited.

After awhile a snow machine drove up and, like any other hitchhiker, I thumbed a ride back to Churchill. We went the long way around, the way I should have gone, the way I had thought about for a millisecond. Finally, around 11:30 p.m., I sat down to a much appreciated, reheated dinner of something similar to the food you'll find in this fine publication of culinary delights compiled by my lovely Auntie Helen and her cookbook partner, Marie.

Show Bear

Helen and I were to be the guests on The Great Canadian Food Show, being filmed in Churchill and Dymond Lake Hunting Lodge in northern Manitoba. The season's guests had departed and we had welcomed the four-man crew and the host of the show, Carlo Rota, to Dymond Lake on the shores of Hudson Bay. We would be their sole caregivers for the five-day shoot, i.e., we not only prepared everything for the show, we also cooked and shared three meals a day with them. (Actually, they could have given us cooking lessons!)

On the first day of the shoot, part of the script was to include some berry picking. Helen and I were in the habit of carrying a can of pepper spray with us – though I always wondered what would happen if we saw a bear and the wind was blowing toward US! Anyway, Carlo carried the spray and looked for bears. We were pretty sure that he was very skeptical about there being any danger. As is usually the case, we saw no bears that day.

On the third day of the shoot, we were having lunch in the dining room when one of the crew saw something white on the opposite shore of the lake. We assured him it was just a rock – a natural mistake – when the rock started to move! We were treated to a real-life action scene of a bear moving in and out of the trees – too far away to be a danger, but enough to validate our precautions when out picking berries.

On the fourth day the gods were with us. No one could have planned the action that took place. We were just preparing breakfast in the kitchen when one of the crew came over and excitedly told us that a bear was walking down the road toward the camp. The guest cabin was a little closer to the road than we were, and a big picture window gave a panoramic view of the action. Derek had set up the camera at the window and he recorded every precious moment as the bear slowly neared the cabins, then crossed right over in front of the picture window. To see a bear like that, in daylight, is a truly awesome thing.

We hope the crew got the shoot they were expecting for the Food Show; we know they got an experience of a lifetime, thanks to the "Show Bear".

Final Temptations

Well, there is absolutely no doubt that this is our favorite part of researching a new cookbook. Some recipes have been tested and reworked until we are satisfied that they are the best. Some have been adapted – like Lynne's Fruit Compote, which originally came from Ireland. We had to substitute some ingredients, but we also had to be creative with the method. At North Knife Lake, we don't have a broiler to brown the sugar topping – it's an unbaked dessert, so we didn't want to pop it into the oven; the solution? – a blow torch attached to a 10-pound (5 kg) propane cylinder – not ideal, but it worked in a pinch!

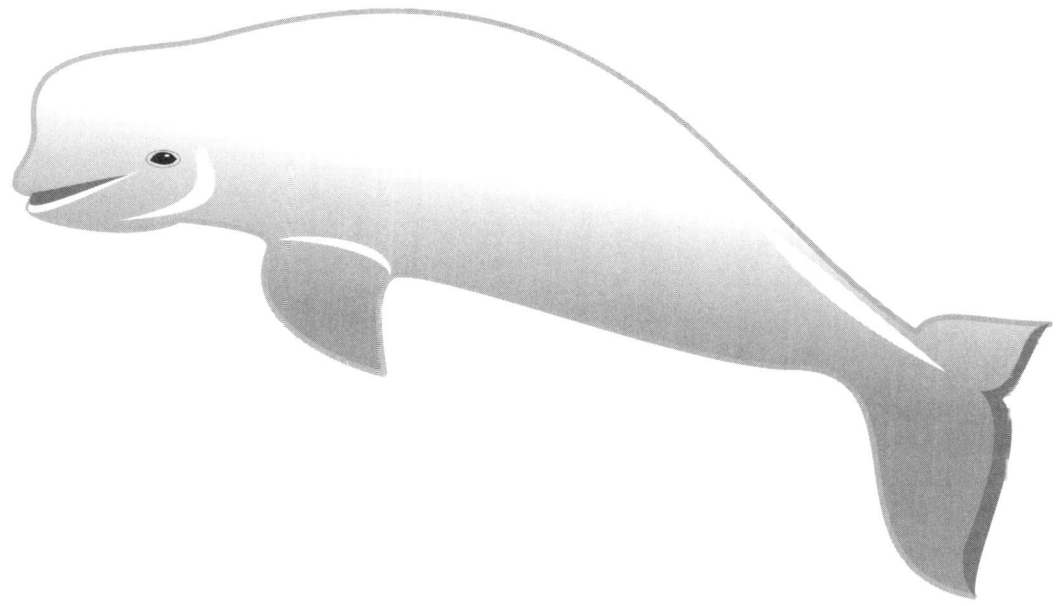

Lynne's Fruit and Cheese Compote

Originally from Ireland, and brought to Lynne Smith by her friend Rosemary Poots, this wonderful dessert is the Canadian version – we couldn't find Greek yogurt or double cream but we're very happy with our substitutions. We sure haven't had any complaints!

2 x 20 oz.	pkgs. frozen, mixed fruit	2 x 600 g
¼ cup	sugar OR 1 tbsp. (15 mL) honey	60 mL
2 tbsp.	lemon juice	30 mL
8 oz.	cream cheese OR mascarpone*	250 g
1 cup	sour cream	250 mL
2 tbsp.	sugar	30 mL
1 tsp.	lemon juice	5 mL
½ cup	demerara OR golden sugar	125 mL

1. Place the frozen fruit in a deep casserole, with a fairly small surface area – the cheese topping will be thicker – but, go with what you've got! Sprinkle the fruit with sugar and lemon juice. Allow to thaw at least partially.
2. Mix the cream cheese, sour cream, sugar and lemon juice until fairly smooth. Spread over the fruit.
3. Sprinkle the brown sugar over the cheese mixture and pat down. Place under broiler for 3 minutes, or until melted and flecked with darker spots.
4. Place in the refrigerator and chill until serving time.

Serves 6-8 people.

NOTE: If you are using a 9 x 13" (23 x 33 cm) pan, and would like a thicker topping, just double the topping ingredients.

* To make substitute mascarpone see page 179.

Keep brown sugar soft by adding a piece of fresh bread to the container.

Fresh Cloudberry Pie

This fall, while doing our photo shoot at Seal River Heritage Lodge in northern Manitoba, we were serendipitously surrounded by fields dotted with orange cloudberries (bakeapples – from the Inuit appik). This fresh berry pie was outstanding, but you could substitute raspberries, blackberries or any similar berry found in your part of the country.

1	baked 10" (25 cm) pie crust	
4 cups	fresh cloudberries	1 L
½-1 cup	apple OR crabapple OR cloudberry jelly	125-250 mL

1. Prepare the pie crust.
2. Pile the cloudberries into the baked crust.
3. Melt the jelly and thin it with a bit of water or juice to the desired consistency. Brush or spoon the glaze evenly over the berries.

Serves 8.

SERVING SUGGESTION: Serve chilled, with whipped cream.

VARIATION: **Fresh Berry Tarts** – make baked tart shells and heap cloudberries or other berries into the shells. Glaze as above.

See photograph on page 175.

Cloudberry Jelly

Helen's cousin Diane spends hours picking berries on the tundra. She makes a large variety of jams and jellies, which she sells in the shops of Churchill. Cloudberries (bakeapples) can be found in abundance on the tundra in the month of August.

5 cups	berry juice*	1.25 L
1½ oz.	pkg. powdered pectin	49 g
7 cups	sugar	1.75 L
1 tbsp.	lemon juice	15 mL

1. In a large, heavy saucepan or Dutch oven, bring the juice and pectin to a boil. Add the sugar and lemon juice; boil for 1 minute. Remove the pan from the heat.
2. Pour the jelly into sterilized jars and seal immediately.

Makes about 7 cups (7 x 250 mL).

NOTE: If the juice is cloudy, it should be filtered first.

Final Temptations

Cloudberry Meringue Pie

Cloudberries, also known as bakeapples on the east coast, are not a common berry in most of Canada, but if you happen to live someplace where you can pick your own, this pie is not to be missed! Helen's nephew Jeff created this delightfully creamy pie. It looks like butterscotch, tastes a little like lemon, but the distinctive cloudberry flavor is unique.

1	baked 10" (25 cm) pie crust	1
2 cups	cloudberry purée	500 mL
	cream, if necessary (see step #2)	
½ cup	sugar	125 mL
3 tbsp.	cornstarch	45 mL
2	egg yolks	2
1 tsp.	vanilla	5 mL
2	egg whites	2
¼ tsp.	cream of tartar	1 mL
2 tbsp.	sugar	30 mL

1. Prepare the pie crust.
2. To make the purée, simmer the cloudberries in ¼ cup (60 mL) water, until the berries are mushy. Press the berries through a sieve to remove all of the seeds. Measure the purée. If necessary, add cream to bring it to 2 cups (500 mL).
3. In a medium saucepan, mix together the sugar and cornstarch; gradually blend in the cloudberry purée. Place over medium heat; stir constantly until the purée comes to a boil and thickens.
4. Beat the egg yolks slightly; stir a little of the hot mixture into the yolks. Pour the yolks into the hot mixture in the saucepan. Cook over low heat, stirring constantly, for 2 minutes, or until thick and smooth. Remove from the heat; add vanilla and cool slightly.
5. Pour the hot filling into the prepared pie crust.
6. Beat the egg whites with cream of tartar until glossy soft peaks form. Gradually add sugar, beating until stiff peaks form.
7. Cover the cloudberry filling with the meringue, bringing the meringue right out to the edges of the pie.
8. Bake at 350°F (180°C) for about 15-20 minutes, or until lightly browned. Cool to room temperature before serving, about 4 hours. Do not refrigerate until after the pie has cooled completely.

Serves 8.

Final Temptations

Peach Praline Pie

A great treat to serve when peaches are in season, this combination of peaches and crunchy topping is a lovely contrast in flavors and texture

1	unbaked 9" (23 cm) pie crust	1
½ cup	flour	125 mL
1 cup	sugar	250 mL
6 cups	sliced peaches	1.5 L
1 tbsp.	lemon juice	15 mL
½ cup	brown sugar, firmly packed	125 mL
⅓ cup	flour	75 mL
¾ cup	chopped pecans	175 mL
¼ cup	butter OR margarine	60 mL

1. Prepare the pie crust.
2. Mix ½ cup (125 mL) flour and the sugar in a large bowl. Add the peaches and lemon juice.
3. Combine the brown sugar, ⅓ cup (75 mL) flour and the pecans in a small bowl. Mix in butter until the mixture is crumbly.
4. Sprinkle ⅓ of the pecan mixture over the bottom of the pie shell. Cover with the peach mixture and sprinkle with the remaining pecan mixture.
5. Bake at 400°F (200°C) for 40-50 minutes, until the peaches are soft and the pie is set in the middle.

Serves 8.

When making fruit pies, sprinkle the sugar under the fruit instead of on top. The juice will boil up through the fruit and not out and over the top.

Ripen peaches or pears by placing them in a closed paper bag.

Final Temptations

Lemon Pie with Blueberry Topping

Blueberries and lemon – just the thought gets my taste buds dancing! Not a traditional lemon pie, but if you're ready for a change, this is your chance.

Graham Crust:

⅓ cup	butter OR margarine	75 mL
1⅓ cups	graham cracker crumbs	325 mL
¼ cup	sugar	60 mL

Lemon Filling:

4	eggs	4
1¼ cups	sugar	300 mL
3 tbsp.	butter, melted	45 mL
2 tsp.	grated lemon peel	10 mL
3 tbsp.	flour	45 mL
½ cup	buttermilk OR sour milk*	125 mL
¼ cup	lemon juice	60 mL

Blueberry Topping:

2 cups	fresh or frozen blueberries (approx. ½ lb./250 g)	500 mL
⅓ cup	blueberry jam**	75 mL
½ cup	sugar	125 mL
¼ tsp.	freshly grated lemon rind	1 mL
½-1 tbsp.	Grand Marnier (optional)	7-15 mL

1. To make the crust, in a small bowl, melt the butter and stir in the sugar and graham crumbs.
2. Press the crumbs into the bottom and up the sides of a 9" (23 cm) pie plate.
3. Bake at 375°F (190°C) for 8 minutes. Cool.
4. **To make the filling**, separate 1 egg, putting the white in a small bowl and the yolk in a large bowl.
5. Beat the white with a fork until foamy and brush the inside of the crust with the white, several times, allowing it to dry for a couple of minutes between coats.
6. Add the sugar, butter and lemon peel to the yolk and beat until smooth. Beat in the remaining eggs 1 at a time. Beat in the flour, then the buttermilk and lemon juice.
7. Pour the filling into the prepared crust and bake at 350°F (180°C) for 30-35 minutes, or until the filling is golden brown and set at the center. Allow to cool for several hours.

Final Temptations

Lemon Pie (continued)

8. To make the topping, in a small bowl, combine the berries with the jam, sugar, lemon rind and Grand Marnier if using. If using frozen berries, allow the topping to stand until the berries thaw. Stir well.
9. Cut the pie into wedges and top each slice with the blueberry topping.

Serves 8.

* *To make ½ cup (125 mL) of sour milk, put 1 tsp. (5 mL) of vinegar or lemon juice in a measuring cup and fill to the ½ cup (125 mL) line. Let sit for 10 minutes.*

** *If you do not have any jam on hand, mix an extra cup (250 mL) of blueberries with ½ cup (125 mL) of sugar and cook over medium heat until thickened to jam-like consistency. This takes 10-15 minutes. You do not need a full jam consistency, as long as it thickens somewhat.*

Blueberry Chiffon Pie

We sometimes receive recipes by mail from our cookbook users. This one came from Darlene Schmidt in Edmonton, Alberta.

1	baked 10" (25 cm) pie crust	1
2 cups	fresh blueberries	500 mL
1 cup	sugar	250 mL
¼ cup	fresh lemon juice	60 mL
¼ tsp.	salt	1 mL
1 tbsp.	gelatin (1 envelope/7g)	15 mL
¼ cup	cold water	60 mL
2	eggs, separated	2

1. Prepare the pie crust.
2. Heat 2 cups (500 mL) of blueberries with ⅔ cup (150 mL) sugar, lemon juice and salt. Cook until sugar is dissolved. Remove from heat.
3. Soak the gelatin in the cold water, then add to the hot mixture.
4. Beat the egg yolks with ⅓ cup (75 mL) sugar. Stir into the berry mixture. Chill until partly set.
5. Beat the egg whites until stiff. Add to the chilled filling and beat well. Pour into the pie shell. Chill.
6. Serve with whipped cream and garnish with fresh berries.

Serves 8.

Sour Cream Apple Pie

I love apple pie! I love the crust and the cinnamon and the sweet/tart taste of the apples themselves. Now imagine all those good things in a creamy sauce.

1	9" (23 cm) unbaked pie crust	1
2 tbsp.	flour	30 mL
¼ tsp.	salt	1 mL
¾ cup	sugar	175 mL
1	egg	1
1 cup	sour cream	250 mL
1 tsp.	vanilla	5 mL
3 cups	pared, sliced apples	750 mL

Cinnamon Topping:

½ cup	brown sugar	125 mL
⅓ cup	flour	75 mL
1 tsp.	cinnamon	5 mL
¼ cup	butter	60 mL

1. Prepare the pie crust.
2. In a large mixing bowl, whisk together the flour, salt and sugar.
3. In another bowl, beat together the egg, sour cream and vanilla. Combine with the flour mixture.
4. Fold the prepared apples into the batter. Spoon the apple mixture into the unbaked pie shell.
5. Combine all of the topping ingredients. Spread over the apples.
6. Bake at 400°F (200°C) for 15 minutes. Turn the oven down to 350°F (180°C) and bake for 30 minutes, or until the apples are tender.

Serves 6-8.

Strawberry Shortbread Dessert

A simple, light dessert, this is also impressive to serve and to taste.

½ cup	butter, softened	125 mL
¼ cup	brown sugar	60 mL
1 cup	chopped pecans OR walnuts	250 mL
1 cup	flour	250 mL
1 cup	whipping cream	250 mL
¼ cup	brown sugar	60 mL
¼ cup	sugar	60 mL
1 tsp.	vanilla	5 mL
4 cups	sliced strawberries	1 L

Strawberry Dessert (continued)

1. Combine the butter, brown sugar, nuts and flour. Press into a 9" (23 cm) springform pan and bake at 350°F (180°C) for 25 minutes. Cool
2. In a large bowl, combine the cream, sugars and vanilla. Using an electric mixer beat until the cream holds soft peaks. Fold in the strawberries and spread over the cooled shortbread.
3. Refrigerate for several hours – overnight is best. Remove the shortbread from the springform pan and cut into wedges to serve.

Serves 12.

NOTE: This dessert may be frozen, but thaw it in the refrigerator before serving.

VARIATION: Replace half of the strawberries with sliced mango.

Blueberry Trifle

3 cups	whipping cream	750 mL
¼ cup	sugar	125 mL
1 tsp.	vanilla extract	5 mL
1 cup	sliced almonds	250 mL
2 tbsp.	sugar	30 mL
1	sponge cake, see page 194, OR 20 lady fingers, cut in half lengthwise	1
½ cup	port OR sherry	125 mL
¾ cup	strawberry jam	175 mL
6 cups	fresh or frozen blueberries (thawed and drained if frozen)	1.5 L

1. Whip the cream until soft peaks are formed. Add ¼ cup (60 mL) sugar and vanilla and whip until stiff peaks are formed.
2. Toast the almonds, sprinkled with 2 tbsp. (30 mL) sugar, in a 350°F (180°C) oven. Turn once to ensure browning and remove when golden.
3. Line the bottom of a 4-quart (4 L) glass bowl with ⅓ of the sponge cake, cut in ½" (1.3 cm) slices.
4. Layer, in order: ⅓ of port, ⅓ of strawberry jam, ⅓ of blueberries, ⅓ of whipped cream. Repeat the layers twice – 3 layers in total, beginning with ⅓ of the sponge cake.
5. Just before serving, sprinkle with the toasted almonds.

Serves 10-12.

No Ordinary Custard

(HELEN) My father-in-law, Charlie, a man of few words, tasted this luscious dessert and commented, "That was no ordinary custard!"

1½ tsp.	unflavored gelatin*	7 mL
2½ tbsp.	cold water	37 mL
2 cups	whipping cream	500 mL
1 cup	sugar	250 mL
2 cups	sour cream	500 mL
1 tsp.	vanilla	5 mL
1 tsp.	almond extract	5 mL
	raspberries, mangos, grapes OR fresh fruit of your choice	
	mint leaves (optional)	

1. In a small bowl, sprinkle the gelatin over the cold water. Allow to soften for 1 minute; do not stir.
2. Combine the cream and sugar in a small saucepan. Using a rubber spatula, blend the gelatin mixture into the cream.
3. Over medium heat, bring the cream mixture to a low simmer, stirring constantly. Remove from the heat and cool slightly.
4. Gently whisk in the sour cream, vanilla and almond flavoring until smooth. Pour into individual serving dishes and chill.
5. To serve, garnish with cut fruit and a mint leaf. (Fresh fruit is best but we have used individually frozen raspberries if fresh are not available.)

Serves 8.

* *A package of Knox's Gelatin contains 1 tbsp. (15 mL), so do not use the whole thing!*

To clean the dross from freshly picked berries, the old-fashioned method of winnowing is still the best. Choose a very windy day, then, standing in the wind, pour the fruit from one container to another. Watch the leaves fly away.

Fresh Cloudberry Pie, page 167
Chocolate Volcanoes with Warm Cinnamon Cherry Sauce, page 196

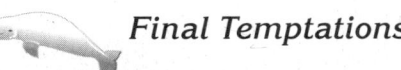

Final Temptations

Chocolate Dream Pudding

This great scratch chocolate pudding comes to us from Helen's daughter Toni.

⅓ cup	sugar	75 mL
¼ cup	cornstarch	60 mL
2 cups	milk	500 mL
1 cup	whipping cream	250 mL
2	eggs, beaten slightly	2
4 oz.	semisweet chocolate, grated	115 g
1 tsp.	vanilla	5 mL

1. Combine the sugar and cornstarch in a heavy saucepan. Gradually blend in the milk and whipping cream. Cook over medium heat, stirring constantly, until the custard comes to a boil and thickens.
2. Add a little of the hot milk mixture to the beaten eggs, then return the eggs to the saucepan and stir well. Heat to boiling, stirring vigorously.
3. Take the custard off the heat; stir in the chocolate, then the vanilla.
4. Pour into individual serving dishes to cool.

Serves 4-6.

Créme Fraîche

The velvety texture and tangy flavor of créme fraîche can be duplicated by stirring 2 tbsp. (30 mL) of buttermilk or sour cream into 1 cup (250 mL) of whipping cream. Use a glass container and cover well. Let the cream stand at room temperature, 70°F (21°C), until very thick, 8-24 hours. Stir well and refrigerate for up to a week. Serve as a sauce over fruit or fruit desserts or chocolate desserts, or add to soups or sauces as it can be boiled without curdling.

For 1 square of unsweetened cooking chocolate, substitute ¼ cup (60 mL) cocoa powder plus 1 tsp. (5 mL) butter.

Sunset over Hudson Bay at Seal River Heritage Lodge.

Final Act Raspberry Tiramisu

Whether you are in suburbia, where mascarpone cheese and ladyfingers are available, or in a remote rural setting, where all you can access is cream cheese and pound cake, you can entertain with this superb final act.

2 x 10 oz.	pkg. frozen raspberries	2 x 300 g
16 oz.	mascarpone OR 2 x 8 oz. (250 g) cream cheese	500 g
½ cup	sugar	125 mL
2	egg yolks	2
¼ cup	brandy	60 mL
1 tbsp.	lemon juice	15 mL
1½ tsp.	vanilla	7 mL
1½ cups	whipping cream	375 mL
12	small, soft ladyfingers, halved, OR 1 lb. (500 g) of pound cake, thinly sliced	12
1 tbsp.	unsweetened cocoa powder	15 mL
½ cup	fresh raspberries (optional)	125 mL
1 tbsp.	sugar	15 mL
½ tsp.	vanilla	5 mL

1. In a colander, thaw the raspberries, reserving the juice. Set aside.
2. In a large bowl, beat the mascarpone with sugar.
3. In a separate bowl, set over hot, not boiling, water, beat the egg yolks with clean beaters for 5 minutes, or until pale and thickened. (We pre-warm eggs by placing them in hot water for a few minutes before cracking them. This speeds up the beating process.) Beat the yolks into the cheese mixture.
4. Stir brandy, lemon juice and vanilla into the cheese mixture.
5. In a small bowl, using an electric mixer, whip 1 cup (250 mL) of cream until soft peaks form. Fold into the cheese mixture.
6. Line the bottom of an 8-cup (2 L) glass bowl with 12 ladyfinger halves (or pound cake slices to cover). Brush well with about 3 tbsp. (45 mL) of the reserved raspberry juice. Spread with ¼ of the cheese mixture. Sift 1 tsp. (5 mL) of the cocoa over the cheese. Sprinkle with ⅓ of the raspberries, pressing some against the glass so they show through.
7. Repeat the cheese, cocoa and raspberry layers twice – 3 layers in total.
8. Cover the final raspberry layer with the remaining 12 ladyfinger halves; brush with raspberry juice and top with the remaining cheese mixture. Cover and refrigerate for 4 hours or overnight.

Raspberry Tiramisu (continued)

9. Dust the outer rim of the tiramisu with more sifted cocoa powder. Whip the remaining ½ cup (125 mL) of whipping cream until stiff peaks form. Mound whipped cream in middle of the tiramisu, leaving the ring of cocoa powder visible. Garnish with fresh raspberries.

Serves 10-12.

*SUGGESTION: Don't throw away the remaining raspberry juice. Use it to make a delicious raspberry jelly (*Blueberries & Polar Bears, *page 201); thicken it with cornstarch and sugar for a tangy sauce (*Cranberries & Canada Geese, *page 175) or use it in a blended fruit drink.*

Mascarpone

Mascarpone is an Italian triple-cream cheese. It is very rich and buttery and delicately flavored. If you can't find it locally, try the following substitutes:

In a large bowl, place 2, 8 oz. (250 g) pkgs. cream cheese, plus ½ cup (125 mL) sour cream and 2 tbsp. butter. Beat well.

OR, blend 8 oz. softened cream cheese with 4 tbsp. (60 mL) butter and 4 tbsp. (60 mL) whipping cream.

Freeze leftover whipped cream by dropping dollops on a cookie sheet. When frozen, store in a plastic bag.

Piña Colada Cheesecake

(HELEN) Have you ever noticed that some mistakes turn into great recipes? That is what happened with this cheesecake. We had ordered coconut milk from the closest supermarket, which is 150 miles away, but they sent us coconut CREAM instead. Well, when something has already traveled 150 miles, you don't send it back, you use it. We came up with this recipe and it has become ANOTHER favorite!

Coconut Crumb Crust:

1 cup	graham wafer crumbs	250 mL
½ cup	shredded, dried coconut	125 mL
¼ cup	butter OR margarine, melted	60 mL

Coconut Pineapple Filing:

3 x 8 oz.	cream cheese, softened	3 x 250 mL
¾ cup	sugar	175 mL
4	eggs	4
1 cup	sour cream	250 mL
1 can	coconut cream	1
14 oz.	can crushed pineapple, well drained*	398 mL
2 tbsp.	cornstarch	30 mL
1 tbsp.	lemon juice	15 mL
½ cup	apricot jam	125 mL
2	kiwi, peeled and cut into thin slices	2
14 oz.	can pineapple tidbits, well drained	398 mL
1 cup	shredded, dried coconut, toasted**	250 mL

1. Combine the graham wafer crumbs, coconut and butter. Press into the bottom and slightly up the sides of a 10" (25 cm) springform pan. Bake at 350°F (180°C) for 10 minutes. Cool on a rack.
2. **To make the filling**, in a large bowl, using an electric mixer, beat cream cheese and sugar until smooth. Beat in eggs, 1 at a time, until just blended. With the mixer on low, beat in the sour cream, coconut cream, pineapple, cornstarch and lemon juice.
3. Pour the filing into the crust. Wrap the outside of the pan in foil and set the pan in a larger pan of hot water, so that it comes up about 1" (2.5 cm) around the foil. Bake at 350°F (180°C) for about 1 hour and 40 minutes, or until the center is just set.
4. Run a knife around the cake and allow to cool completely in the pan. Chill at least 6 hours or overnight.

Piña Colada Cheesecake (continued)

5. **For the topping**, melt the jam over medium heat. Sieve to remove the fruit pieces. Arrange the kiwi and pineapple tidbits on top of the cake. Brush the fruit and sides of the cake with jam. Press coconut onto the sides of the cake.

Serves 12-16.

* To drain easily, pour the pineapple into a sieve and press with a spoon to remove as much juice as possible.
** To toast coconut, spread it on a baking sheet and bake at 350°F (180°C) for 8 minutes, stirring once.

Creamy Chocolate Banana Dessert

Another of our favorite combinations – chocolate and banana, be sure to make this ahead so it can be well chilled, or better yet, have it handy in the freezer.

Chocolate Crust:
2 cups	chocolate wafer crumbs	500 mL
⅓ cup	sugar	75 mL
½ cup	butter, melted	125 mL

Chocolate Banana Filling:
8 oz.	semisweet OR bittersweet chocolate	250 g
8 oz.	cream cheese, softened	250 g
1½ cups	whipping cream	375 mL
⅓ cup	sugar	75 mL
1 tsp.	vanilla	5 mL
4-5	bananas	4-5
2 tbsp.	chocolate wafer crumbs	30 mL

1. Measure the chocolate wafer crumbs into a medium-sized bowl. Mix in the sugar and melted butter. Pat into the bottom of a 9 x 13" (23 x 33 cm) pan. Bake at 375°F (190°C) for 8 minutes. Cool.
2. Melt the chocolate in a microwave or over very low heat; watch carefully.
3. In a large bowl, beat the cream cheese until smooth. Using low speed, beat in chocolate until well combined.
4. Beat the cream until soft peaks form; beat in sugar and vanilla.
5. Stir ¼ of the cream mixture into the chocolate, until combined. Fold in the remaining cream with a rubber spatula until no streaks remain.
6. Cover the bottom of the cooled crust with a layer of thinly sliced bananas and cover with the chocolate cream mixture.
7. Sprinkle with the crumbs. Refrigerate 8 hours before serving.

Serves 12-15.

Cream Cheese Apple Custard Cake

A layered apple cake that is a cross between a cake, a pie and a cheesecake – delicious. Make ahead and allow 2 hours baking time. Serve at room temperature with ice cream or whipped cream.

2 cups	flour	500 mL
½ tsp.	baking soda	2 mL
1 tsp.	cream of tartar	5 mL
¼ tsp.	salt	1 mL
1 cup	butter	250 mL
¾ cup	sugar	175 mL
1 tsp.	vanilla	5 mL
2	eggs	2

Cream Cheese Filling:

2 x 8 oz.	cream cheese, softened	2 x 250 g
2 tsp.	vanilla	10 mL
⅓ cup	sugar	75 mL
2 tsp.	whipping cream	10 mL

Custard Topping:

1 cup-2 tbsp.	whipping cream	220 mL
2	eggs	2
½ cup	sugar	125 mL
1 tbsp.	lemon juice	15 mL
½ tsp.	cinnamon	2 mL
⅛ tsp.	nutmeg	0.5 mL

2½ lbs.	apples, peeled, in ⅛" (3 mm) slices	1.25 kg
⅓ cup	chopped pecans	75 mL

1. Tightly wrap the outside of a 10" (25 cm) springform pan with heavyweight foil to cover the bottom and sides of the pan. Spray the inside of the pan with non-stick spray.
2. In a small bowl, combine the flour, baking soda, cream of tartar and salt.
3. In a larger bowl, cream the butter, sugar and vanilla. Beat in the eggs, and then the flour mixture, until well blended. With floured hands, spread the batter over the bottom and sides of the prepared pan to ½" (1.3 cm) from the top rim. Refrigerate while you prepare the remaining ingredients. There is no need to wash the beaters before continuing with the next 2 steps.

Final Temptations

Cream Cheese Custard Cake (continued)

4. **To make the filling,** combine all ingredients in a small bowl and beat until smooth.
5. **To make the custard**, combine all ingredients in a small bowl and beat until well blended.
6. Remove the pan from the refrigerator and spread the filling over the bottom. Arrange the apples over the filling. Pour the custard over the apples and sprinkle with pecans.
7. Bake at 350°F (180°C) for 1 hour on the rack below the center of the oven. Cover the top with foil and continue to bake for another hour, or until a cake tester inserted in the center comes out clean.
8. Place the pan on a cooling rack and allow to cool completely. Remove the foil. Loosen the pan sides with a knife and remove the band. Serve at room temperature.

Serves 12-16.

Egg whites may be frozen for up to 1 year.

You can replace a missing egg with 1 tsp. (5 mL) of white vinegar.

Final Temptations

Regal Chocolate Cheesecake with Raspberry Crown

A cheesecake fit for royalty, this has been a favorite with us since day one. Allow time for the cheesecake to bake and chill.

Chocolate Crust:
1¼ cups	chocolate wafer cookie crumbs	300 mL
⅓ cup	butter, melted	75 mL

Chocolate Filling:
8 oz.	semisweet chocolate, coarsely chopped	250 g
2 x 8 oz.	cream cheese, softened	2 x 250 g
1 cup	sugar	250 mL
3	eggs, warmed to room temperature*	3
1 tsp.	vanilla	5 mL

Raspberry Topping:
10 oz.	pkg. frozen raspberries, thawed	300 g
2 tsp.	gelatin	10 mL
½ cup	sugar	125 mL

1. Assemble a 9" (23 cm) springform pan with base lip-side down. Preheat oven to 325°F (160°C).
2. **To make the crust**, stir cookie crumbs with butter until moistened. Press evenly onto the bottom of the springform pan. Center the pan on a square of foil; press foil up to cover pan sides. Bake for 5 minutes. Set aside.
3. **To make the filling**, melt the chocolate in a medium bowl in a microwave**– 2 minutes on medium high. Stir until remaining chocolate is melted.
4. In a separate bowl, using an electric mixer beat the cream cheese with sugar for 2 minutes, until smooth and light. Beat in the eggs, 1 at a time, scraping down the sides of the bowl often. Beat in the vanilla.
5. Stir half of the cream cheese mixture into the melted chocolate. Spread evenly over the baked crust. Gently pour the remaining cream cheese mixture evenly over the chocolate layer.

Chocolate Cheesecake (continued)

6. Set the springform pan in a larger pan; pour in hot water to come 1" (2.5 cm) up the side of the pan. Bake at 325°F (160°C) for 1 hour. It should no longer be shiny and the top shouldn't jiggle. Turn the oven off and let the cheesecake cool in the oven for 1 hour.
7. Remove the cake from the oven and from the water bath. Let cool to room temperature. Refrigerate, uncovered, until chilled. At this point, the cheesecake may be covered and refrigerated for 1-2 days before adding the topping.
8. **To make the topping**, pour ¼ cup (60 mL) raspberry juice into a small bowl. Sprinkle gelatin over the liquid. (Do not be tempted to use the whole package, which is 3 tsp. [15 mL].) In a saucepan, combine the sugar and remaining juice with the berries. Bring to a boil, then pour gradually into the gelatin. Refrigerate, stirring often, until it is about the consistency of liquid honey. Pour the topping over the chilled cake while it is still in the springform pan. Refrigerate until the glaze is set – 1 hour or longer.
9. This cheesecake keeps well in the refrigerator for 2 or 3 days.

Serves 16-20.

*   Bring eggs to room temperature by covering them with hot water while they are still in the shells.

** Chocolate may also be melted over low heat or over hot water on the stovetop; stir constantly.

Final Temptations

Cinnamon Torte

(HELEN) Picture 16 layers of buttery cinnamon crisps, layered with chocolate whipped cream. "THE GIRLS" were going by snowmobile to Bonnie's cabin on Warkworth Lake. It was going to be a rugged weekend – no showers, melting ice and snow for dishwater, a chemical toilet. We can handle all of that BUT we have to have our gourmet food. This was one of the desserts we took with us – 15 miles by snowmobile. It arrived in perfect condition.

Cinnamon Cookie Layers:

2	eggs	2
2 cups	sugar	500 mL
1½ cups	butter, softened	375 mL
2 tbsp.	ground cinnamon	30 mL
2⅔ cups	flour	650 mL

Chocolate Filling:

4 cups	whipping cream	1 L
⅔ cup	cocoa powder	150 mL
	semisweet chocolate	

1. Tear 16 sheets of waxed paper, large enough to cover the bottom of a 9" (23 cm) round pan. Stack the paper and draw a circle on the top sheet, using the 9" (23 cm) round pan as a pattern. Cut out 16 circles.
2. **To make the cookies**, in a large bowl, break the eggs. Add the sugar, butter, cinnamon, and **2 cups (500 mL)** of flour. Beat well with an electric mixer at low speed until well mixed. Scrape down the sides of the bowl with a rubber spatula. Increase speed to medium and beat for 3 minutes, or until light and fluffy. Add the remaining flour to make a soft dough.
3. With a damp cloth, moisten 2 large cookie sheets. Place 2 waxed paper rounds on each sheet. With a metal spatula, spread ¼ cup (60 mL) of dough evenly over each circle. It should be a very thin layer. Bake at 375°F (190°C) for 8 minutes, or until lightly browned around the edges.
4. Remove the cookie sheets to a wire rack, cool for 5 minutes. With a pancake turner, carefully remove the cookies to a wire rack and let cool for another 5 minutes, then remove the waxed paper and stack the cookies. Let the cookie sheets cool completely before spreading more waxed paper sheets with dough. Repeat until all of the dough is used.

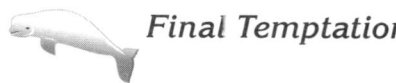

Cinnamon Torte (continued)

5. Stack the cooled cookies on a flat plate. Cover with plastic wrap and store in a cool dry place until ready to fill. This can be done up to 3 days ahead.
6. **To make the filling**, early in the day, in a large bowl, beat the whipping cream and cocoa until soft peaks form.
7. **To assemble the torte**, place 1 cookie on a flat plate. Spread the cookie with a scant ½ cup (125 mL) of the chocolate whipped cream. Repeat layering until all cookies are used, ending with the whipped cream.
8. Refrigerate for at least 3 hours, to soften the cookie layers slightly for easier cutting.
9. Just before serving, coarsely grate chocolate over the cake.

Serves 20.

See photograph on page 87.

The hostess must be like the duck – calm and unruffled on the surface, and paddling madly underneath.

Final Temptations

Apple Bread Pudding with Rum Sauce

Succulent and moist, this bread pudding has a wonderful flavor.

4 cups	cubed, firm, white bread, crusts removed	1 L
2 tsp.	butter	10 mL
2	medium apples, peeled, cored, sliced	2
8 tbsp.	sugar, divided	120 mL
1 tbsp.	dried currants OR raisins	15 mL
2 cups	milk	500 mL
2	eggs	2
1 tsp.	vanilla	5 mL
¼ tsp.	ground cinnamon	1 mL

1. Lightly butter or spray an 8" (20 cm) square glass pan. Arrange 2 cups (500 mL) bread cubes in the pan.
2. Melt the butter in a saucepan over medium heat. Add the apples and sauté for 5 minutes. Sprinkle with **2 tbsp. (30 mL) sugar** and sauté until the apples are golden, about 6 minutes. Arrange the apples on top of the bread.
3. Sprinkle currants over apples. Top with remaining bread cubes.
4. In a small saucepan, bring the milk to a simmer.
5. Whisk together the eggs and remaining **6 tbsp. (90 mL) sugar**. Blend well. Add gradually to the hot milk, whisking to combine. Add the vanilla and cinnamon. Pour over the bread.
6. Let the bread stand until the liquid is almost absorbed, about 30 minutes. You could press down on the bread to help it along at first.
7. Place the baking dish in a larger pan. Add water to come halfway up the sides of the dish. Bake at 350°F (175°C) until the top is golden and the custard is set, about 40 minutes. Remove from the water. Serve warm with Rum Sauce or Grand Marnier Creamy Caramel Sauce, page 191.

Serves 9.

Rum Sauce

½ cup	butter	125 mL
1 cup	brown sugar	250 mL
2 tbsp.	lemon juice	30 mL
¼-½ cup	rum OR bourbon OR brandy	60-125 mL
⅓ cup	water	75 mL

Melt the butter in a small saucepan. Whisk in the sugar, lemon juice, rum and water. Bring to a boil and simmer, whisking occasionally, for 5 minutes.

Chocolate Bread Pudding

(MARIE) Helen and I use homemade French bread, which has a softer crust, so we don't remove the crust. You might be tempted to increase the amount of bread. This will affect the wonderful creamy texture of the pudding – definitely not something to trifle with. In this version a smooth and creamy chocolate custard surrounds a lesser proportion of French bread, giving a whole new meaning to "bread pudding". Serve with spiked whipped cream.

6 cups	1" (2.5 cm) cubes, crustless French bread*	1.5 L
¼ cup	butter, melted	60 mL
1¾ cups	whole milk	425 mL
1 cup	whipping cream OR evaporated milk	250 mL
4 oz.	semisweet chocolate, chopped	115 g
1 cup	sugar	250 mL
4	egg yolks	4

1. Butter or spray an 8" (20 cm) square glass baking dish. Spread the bread cubes evenly in the baking dish. Drizzle the butter over the bread.
2. In a heavy saucepan, bring the milk and cream just to a simmer. Remove from the heat and add the chocolate. Whisk until melted and smooth.
3. In a medium bowl, using an electric mixer, beat the sugar and egg yolks. Whisk the chocolate mixture into the egg mixture.
4. Pour the chocolate custard over the bread. Cover and let stand for at least 1 hour in the refrigerator.
5. Bake, uncovered, at 350°F (175°C) for 35 minutes, or until the center moves only slightly when the dish is shaken. Longer baking gives a firmer pudding, if that is your preference.

Serve warm or at room temperature with whipped cream. (We like to spike our whipped cream with Kahlúa or Tia Maria or amaretto.)

Serves 9.

NOTE: We often prepare this pudding early in the day and bake it later, so that it comes out of the oven at dinner time. Double this recipe for a 9 x 13" (23 x 33 cm) pan. Increase the baking time by about 15 minutes.

Final Temptations

Half-Hour Pudding

(HELEN) Comfort food from our childhood – this is one of Doug's. It is one of the dishes I have never made quite as well as his mother, but he still enjoys it. Warm pudding with caramel sauce and a scoop of vanilla ice cream – there won't be any left. It derives its name from the fact that if you mix it up quickly it is ready to eat in about half an hour.

Raisin Pudding:

1 cup	flour	250 mL
2 tsp.	baking powder	10 mL
2 tsp.	sugar	10 mL
1/8 tsp.	salt	0.5 mL
2 tbsp.	butter	30 mL
1 cup	raisins	250 mL
1/2 cup	milk	125 mL

Caramel Sauce:

1 cup	brown sugar	250 mL
1 tbsp.	butter	15 mL
1 3/4 cups	boiling water	425 mL
1 tsp.	vanilla	5 mL
1/8 tsp.	salt	0.5 mL

1. In a medium-sized bowl, combine the flour, baking powder, sugar and salt.
2. Cut the butter into the flour mixture with a pastry blender until quite fine.
3. Add the raisins and milk and stir until blended
4. Turn the batter into a greased 2-quart (2 L) casserole.
5. **To make the sauce**, in a small bowl, combine the brown sugar, butter, water, vanilla and salt. Pour carefully over the batter.
6. Bake at 350°F (160°C) for 25-30 minutes.

Serves 4.

Grand Marnier Creamy Caramel Sauce

Creamy caramel with just a hint of orange – this is good enough to eat by the spoonful, as long as the kids don't catch you. It is wonderful over Bread Pudding or Christmas Pudding, or transform gingerbread into a gourmet dessert by floating it in a pool of sauce and garnishing with a dollop of whipped cream. Try it on ice cream too!

3 cups	brown sugar	750 mL
¾ cup	water	175 mL
⅔ cup	corn syrup	150 mL
½ cup	butter	125 mL
1 tbsp.	vanilla	15 mL
2 tbsp.	Grand Marnier	30 mL
2 cups	whipping cream	500 mL

1. Place the sugar, water and corn syrup in a heavy saucepan and bring to a boil. Continue to cook at a fast simmer for 8-10 minutes, until somewhat thickened. Reduce the heat to low and add the butter, vanilla and Grand Marnier. Simmer for 5 minutes.
2. Remove the sauce from the heat and slowly whisk in the cream.

Makes 5 cups (1.25 L).

Caramel Sauce

Delicious over gingerbread, bread pudding, ice cream or – use your imagination!

1 cup	corn syrup	250 mL
1 cup	brown sugar	250 mL
¼ tsp.	salt	1 mL
½ cup	milk	125 mL
¼ cup	flour	60 mL
3 tbsp.	butter	45 mL

1. Blend the corn syrup, brown sugar, salt, milk and flour in a saucepan, whisking to keep smooth. Slowly bring to a boil and cook five minutes over low, stirring occasionally.
2. Remove from the heat and add the butter.

Makes 1¼ cups (300 mL).

Final Temptations

Vanilla Sauce

(HELEN) *This is the sauce I remember Mom making for our Christmas Pudding. It evokes memories of wonderful big Christmas dinners with, at times, more than 40 family members and friends gathered around.*

¼ cup	sugar	60 mL
1 tbsp.	flour	15 mL
⅛ tsp.	salt	0.5 mL
1 cup	boiling water	250 mL
2 tbsp.	butter	30 mL
1 tsp.	vanilla	5 mL
⅛ tsp.	nutmeg	0.5 mL

1. Combine the sugar, flour and salt in a saucepan. Add the boiling water gradually, stirring constantly. Cook and stir over low heat until the sauce is clear and thickened, about 5 minutes
2. Remove from the heat and add the butter, vanilla and nutmeg.

Makes 1 cup (250 mL).

VARIATIONS: Brandy, rum or sherry may replace the vanilla.

Hard Sauce

Serve with Christmas pudding, bread pudding or mince pies.

½ cup	butter	125 mL
¾ cup	brown sugar	175 mL
¾ cup	icing (confectioner's) sugar	175 mL
⅓ cup	whipping cream	75 mL
1 tsp.	vanilla	5 mL
2 tsp.	brandy (optional)	10 mL

1. In a small bowl, cream the butter, gradually add the brown sugar and icing sugar, whisking thoroughly.
2. Slowly add the cream and vanilla, continuing to whisk.
3. Pile the sauce into a smaller dish and make a well in the center.
4. Pour the brandy into the well and let sit until the brandy is absorbed.
5. Chill and serve.

Makes 2 cups (500 mL).

VARIATIONS: **Lemon Hard Sauce**: *Add 1 tsp. (5 mL) fresh lemon juice and 1 tbsp. (15 mL) grated lemon rind.*
Spicy Hard Sauce: *Add ½ tsp. (2 mL) lemon juice, ½ tsp. (2 mL) cinnamon and ¼ tsp. (1 mL) cloves.*

Buttercream Meringue

(HELEN) We are always on a quest for the perfect cake frosting. We usually use our old favorite – Jeanne's Bakery Icing from Blueberries and Polar Bears *– as it lends itself to the shaped cakes our grandchildren love. We have made airplanes, rocket ships, dogs, dinosaurs and Barney, but the one they won't let me forget is the Barbie princess. I used a bundt cake for the skirt and the torso of a Barbie doll. I decorated the skirt and the torso with frosting – a nice off-the-shoulder dress – but my frosting was not quite stiff enough and it began to slide!! The grandchildren now refer to the cake as the Barbie with her boobs hanging out!*

This recipe is nice and buttery. It is great for decorated cakes and it stays on!

10 tbsp.	sugar	150 mL
3	egg whites, room temperature	3
1 tsp.	vanilla	5 mL
1 cup	butter, room temperature	250 mL
4 cups	icing (confectioner's) sugar	1 L

1. Combine the sugar, egg whites and vanilla in a heatproof bowl. Set the bowl over a pan of simmering water. Whisk constantly until the sugar has dissolved and whites are hot to the touch, 5-7 minutes.
2. Remove the pan from the heat and, using an electric mixer, beat on low speed, gradually increasing to high speed, beat until stiff glossy peaks form, about 10 minutes.
3. In a separate bowl, beat the butter until creamy and fluffy.
4. At low speed, add the butter to egg whites, mixing until smooth.
5. Gradually beat in the icing sugar.

Makes about 4 cups (1 L).

NOTE: *This icing lends itself very well to coloring and is enough to decorate a large shaped cake.*

2 tbsp. (30 mL) of egg white equals the white of 1 egg.

Mrs. Herrett's Chocolate Frosting

(HELEN) *Mrs. Herrett was a close friend of Doug's mother and she became a good friend to me also. She was well into her 70s when I first met her and her husband, Angus. No trip to Stettler was complete without partaking of one of her delicious meals. I knew there was something a little different about her chocolate frosting and she was kind enough to share the secret – a whole egg, which seems to cut the sweetness.*

2 cups	icing (confectioner's) sugar	500 mL
2 tbsp.	cocoa powder	30 mL
⅛ tsp.	salt	0.5 mL
1 tsp.	vanilla	5 mL
1 cup	butter, softened	250 mL
1	egg	1

1. Combine all of the ingredients in a medium-sized mixing bowl. Using an electric mixer, beat until creamy.
2. Use to frost your favorite cake.

Makes about 2 cups (500 mL).

Hot Milk Sponge Cake

This old standby is perfect for trifle. It is a nice light cake that lends itself well to Blueberry Trifle, see page 173, and Nan's Trifle, page 161, Black Currants & Caribou.

4	eggs	4
1½ cups	sugar	375 mL
2 tsp.	vanilla	10 mL
2 cups	flour	500 mL
2 tsp.	baking powder	10 mL
¼ tsp.	salt	1 mL
6 tbsp.	butter	90 mL
1 cup	boiling milk	250 mL

Hot Milk Sponge Cake (continued)

1. In a large bowl, using an electric mixer, beat the eggs, sugar and vanilla until light and fluffy, about 5 minutes.
2. In a separate bowl, combine the flour, baking powder and salt and stir it into the egg mixture.
3. In a small saucepan, bring the butter and milk to boiling, add to the egg mixture and mix by hand just until combined.
4. Pour into a greased 9 x 13" (23 x 33 cm) pan. Bake at 350°F (180°C) for 30 minutes, or until a toothpick comes out clean when inserted in the center.
5. Serve topped with fruit and custard, whipped cream or ice cream.

Serves 15.

Chocolate Soufflé Cups

Jeff, our chef in residence, is always delighting our guests with his creations. Not only does he whip up a great soufflé, he also presents it so that it is a delight to behold.

3 tbsp.	butter	45 mL
¼ cup	flour	60 mL
2 cups	milk	500 mL
8	eggs, separated	8
¼ tsp.	salt	1 mL
½ tsp.	vanilla	2 mL
½ cup	cocoa powder	125 mL
3 tbsp.	corn syrup	45 mL
3 tbsp.	water	45 mL
⅓ cup	cornstarch	75 mL
½ cup	sugar	125 mL

1. In a medium saucepan, melt the butter and add the flour to make a roux. Add the milk and heat to scalding.
2. Add 4 egg yolks and heat to bubbling. Remove from the heat and add the rest of the egg yolks, salt and vanilla. Remove to a mixing bowl.
3. In a small bowl, combine the cocoa, corn syrup and water; add to the batter.
4. Mix the cornstarch with ¼ cup (60 mL) sugar; add to the batter.
5. Beat the egg whites to soft peaks; slowly add ¼ cup (60 mL) sugar and beat until stiff peaks form. Fold into the batter.
6. Grease 12, ¾ cup (175 mL) ramekins and sprinkle lightly with sugar. Spoon the soufflé batter into ramekins. Place the ramekins on a baking tray and bake at 375°F (190°C) for 25-30 minutes.

Serves 12.

Chocolate Volcanoes with Warm Cinnamon Cherry Sauce

Molten chocolate centers with a cinnamon twist! Individual ramekins allow you to prepare what you need – pure lust will urge you to make more!

Cinnamon Cherry Sauce:

2 x 14 oz.	cans sweet dark cherries, pitted if you are lucky enough to find them*	2 x 398 mL
¼ cup	sugar	60 mL
¼ - ½ cup	kirsch OR cherry brandy	60-125 mL
½ tsp.	ground cinnamon	2 mL

Chocolate Volcano Cake:

¼ cup	cocoa powder	60 mL
½ cup	sugar	125 mL
4 oz.	semisweet chocolate, chopped	115 g
½ cup	butter	125 mL
4	egg yolks	4
2	eggs	2
4 tsp.	flour	20 mL
	icing (confectioner's) sugar	
	fresh mint	

1. Combine the undrained cherries, sugar, kirsch and cinnamon in a heavy, medium-sized saucepan. Bring to a simmer and cook until the sauce thickens and is slightly reduced, about 20 minutes. Remove from the heat. Using a slotted spoon, remove ½ cup (125 mL) of the cherries from the sauce and drain well. Remove pits if necessary, chop coarsely and reserve for the cakes. Set the cherry sauce aside.
2. Butter 4, ¾ cup (175 mL) ramekins or custard cups.
3. Combine the cocoa and ½ cup (125 mL) sugar in a small bowl.
4. Melt the chocolate and butter in a heavy saucepan. Remove from the heat and whisk in the cocoa mixture. Whisk in the egg yolks, then the whole eggs and flour. Fold in reserved chopped cherries. Divide the batter among the prepared ramekins.

Chocolate Volcanoes (continued)

5. Bake at 350°F (180°C) until the edges are set but the center is still shiny, about 22 minutes**. A tester inserted into the center should come out with some wet batter attached.
6. Warm the sauce over low heat. Cut around the edges of the cakes to loosen, turn the cakes out onto plates and spoon the warm sauce alongside.
7. Sprinkle with icing sugar and garnish with mint if desired.

Serves 4.

NOTE: Sauce and cake batter can be made 1 day ahead. Cover separately and chill until ready to bake.

VARIATION: For a flavor variation, substitute the Grand Marnier Creamy Caramel Sauce on page 205, or a Raspberry Coulis, for the Cherry Sauce.

* If the cherries are not pitted, we just let our guests discreetly remove the pits.
** Narrow-bottomed ramekins take longer to bake than straight-sided ramekins.

See photograph on page 175.

Window cleaner:
½ cup (125 mL) ammonia, ½ cup (125 mL) vinegar,
2 tbsp. (30 mL) cornstarch in a bucket of warm water.
Wipe on, allow to dry, then wipe off.

Wash windows on a cloudy day. On a sunny day, they dry too fast and leave streaks.

Len's window washing mixture:
2 capfuls Sunlight dishwashing liquid
1 cup (250 mL) vinegar
2 gallons (4 L) hot water

Final Temptations

Chocolate Fudge Cake with Sour Cream Ganache

When Marie has two servings of dessert you know you have a winner. The Tia Maria adds an extra kick to this fudgy icing. Don't let the length of instructions for the ganache deter you from trying this recipe. It is actually very simple, with outstanding results.

2 cups	flour	500 mL
½ cup	cocoa powder	125 mL
½ tsp.	baking soda	2 mL
1 tsp.	baking powder	5 mL
¼ tsp.	salt	1 mL
1 cup	butter, softened	250 mL
1 ½ cups	brown sugar	375 mL
2	eggs*	2
⅔ cup	sour cream	150 mL
1 tsp.	vanilla	5 mL
1 cup	boiling water	250 mL

1. In a medium bowl, combine the flour, cocoa, baking soda, baking powder and salt.
2. In a large bowl, using an electric mixer, beat the butter on low until light and fluffy. Add the brown sugar and beat for 2-3 minutes, until fluffy. Still beating, add the eggs 1 at a time. Add the sour cream and vanilla in 3 additions, scraping down the sides of the bowl after each addition. Continue to beat just until the mixture is combined.
3. With the mixer running, pour in the water. Scrape down the sides of the bowl and continue to beat just until the mixture is combined. The batter will be runny.
4. Pour the batter into a greased 10-cup (2.5 L) bundt pan or a greased 9 x 13" (23 x 33 cm) pan. Bake at 375°F (190°C) for 40-45 minutes, or until a toothpick inserted in the center comes out clean. Remove from oven and place the pan on a wire rack. Allow to cool 10 minutes; turn out of the pan onto a wire rack and allow to cool completely.

Chocolate Fudge Cake (continued)

Sour Cream Ganache:

1¼ cups	chocolate chips OR 12 oz. (340 g) good-quality semisweet chocolate**	300 mL
⅔ cup	sour cream	150 mL
2 tsp.	Tia Maria OR Kahlúa	10 mL

1. Melt the chocolate chips in a glass bowl in a microwave or in a saucepan over very low heat. If using a saucepan, stir constantly until the chips are melted and smooth. If using a microwave, use medium-high heat for 2 minutes, remove from the oven and stir.** Repeat for thirty seconds until the chocolate is melted and smooth.
2. Stir in the sour cream and Tia Maria or Kahlúa. Using an electric mixer, beat until smooth. The ganache should be the consistency of smooth peanut butter. If it is too thin, refrigerate for a short time, checking the consistency every 5 minutes. Spread over the cooled cake.

Serves 12-16.

NOTE: This is a very moist fudge cake. It doesn't rise as high as you might expect.

* *A large egg should weigh about 2 ounces (60 mL). Unless otherwise noted, all eggs used throughout this book are large eggs. You get better volume if eggs are room temperature before using. If you do not have time for this, just cover them with hot water for a couple of minutes.*

** *Be sure to stir the chocolate – it tends to hold its shape so that it doesn't look like it is melting until it is stirred.*

Final Temptations

Chocolate Caramel Nut Upside-Down Cake

There is no need to frost this scrumptious cake, although a scoop of creamy French vanilla ice cream is a nice complement.

Caramel:

½ cup	packed golden brown sugar	125 mL
3 tbsp.	butter	45 mL
2 tbsp.	water	30 mL
1½ cups	coarsely chopped assorted unsalted nuts, toasted* (almonds, pecans, walnuts, hazelnuts)	375 mL
1¼ cups	flour	300 mL
¼ cup	cocoa powder	60 mL
½ tsp.	baking powder	5 mL
⅛ tsp.	baking soda	0.5 mL
⅛ tsp.	salt	0.5 mL
½ cup	butter, room temperature	125 mL
¾ cup	sugar	175 mL
1 tsp.	vanilla	5 mL
2	eggs	2
⅓ cup	buttermilk	75 mL

1. Grease the sides of a 9" (23 cm) round cake pan.
2. In a small saucepan, combine the brown sugar, butter and water. Cook over medium heat, stirring often, until the butter is melted and the sugar is dissolved. Bring to a boil and pour into the cake pan.
3. Sprinkle the nuts evenly over the caramel sauce, pressing them into the sauce.
4. In a small bowl, combine the flour, cocoa, baking powder, baking soda and salt. Set aside.
5. In a large bowl, cream the butter and sugar with an electric mixer until light and fluffy. Beat in the vanilla and then add the eggs, 1 at a time, beating briefly after each addition.

Final Temptations

Upside-Down Cake (continued)

6. Sprinkle half of the flour over the butter mixture and beat on low just until the flour disappears. Add the buttermilk and mix until blended. Add the remaining flour and mix on low until just mixed.
7. Scoop spoonfuls of batter onto the nuts and spread evenly.
8. Bake at 350°F (180°C) for 35-40, or until a toothpick inserted in the center comes out clean.
9. Run a knife around the edge of the pan, place a flat serving plate over the cake and turn the cake over. Leave the pan over the cake for 5 minutes to let the topping settle. Remove the pan.
10. Serve warm or at room temperature.

Serves 8-10.

NOTE: This recipe doubles well – bake in 2, 9" (23 cm) pans.

*God put me on earth to accomplish
a certain number of things.
Right now, I'm so far behind,
I'm going to live forever.*

White Chocolate Brownie Dessert

***(HELEN)** This is my daughter, Toni's favorite dessert. She first sampled it at Moxie's and set us to the task of duplicating it. After several attempts – all of which were edible, we are very happy with this one!*

White Chocolate Brownie:

½ cup	butter	125 mL
3 oz.	white chocolate, chunks or chips	85 g
1 tsp.	baking powder	5 mL
½ cup	sugar	125 mL
1¼ cups	flour	300 mL
½ tsp.	baking powder	2 mL
¼ tsp.	salt	1 mL
4	eggs	4
2 tsp.	vanilla	10 mL
1½ cups	milk OR semisweet chocolate, chunked*	375 mL

Chocolate Ganache Sauce:

¾ cup	semisweet chocolate	175 mL
¼ cup	half and half OR whipping cream (approximately)	60 mL
2 tbsp.	Tia Maria OR Kahlúa	30 mL

1. Melt the butter and white chocolate in a large heavy saucepan over low heat, stirring constantly OR in a glass bowl in a microwave. If you use a microwave, check after 1 minute, being sure to stir, as the chocolate holds its shape even when melting. Check every 30 seconds until melted and smooth. A whisk works well for this job.
2. Whisk the sugar, flour, baking powder and salt into the melted chocolate.
3. Whisk the eggs and vanilla into the chocolate mixture until well blended. Fold in the chocolate chunks.
4. Pour into a greased 9" (23 cm) square pan and bake at 325°F (160°C) for 30 minutes. The center should still be moist.
5. **To make the sauce**, place the chocolate and whipping cream in a small saucepan and heat over low heat until smooth. Remove from the heat and add the liqueur and a little more cream, if necessary, to make the sauce of drizzling consistency. This is also great over ice cream or use it as dip for fresh fruit!
6. Serve the brownie warm with a scoop of ice cream and drizzle with Chocolate Ganache and a large dollop of whipped cream. (The whipped cream is optional.)

Serves 6.

* We use a chopping knife and just coarsely chop the chocolate.

Final Temptations

Chocolate Banana Cake

Rich, moist, with a subtle banana flavour. This could quickly become a family favorite.

⅔ cup	milk	150 mL
1 tbsp.	vinegar	15 mL
¾ cup	butter OR margarine	175 mL
1⅔ cups	sugar	400 mL
2	eggs	2
1¼ cups	puréed bananas	300 mL
1 tsp.	vanilla	5 mL
2 cups	flour	500 mL
¾ cup	cocoa powder	175 mL
1½ tsp.	baking powder	7 mL
1 tsp.	baking soda	5 mL
¾ tsp.	salt	3 mL

1. In a small bowl, combine the milk and vinegar and set aside.
2. In a large separate bowl, cream together the butter, sugar and eggs. Stir in the banana and vanilla.
3. Sift together the dry ingredients and add to the creamed mixture alternately with the milk and vinegar.
4. Spread the batter in a greased or sprayed 9 x 13" (23 x 33 cm) pan. Bake at 350°F (180°C) for 40-45 minutes.

Serves 16.

Cocoa Banana Frosting

¼ cup	melted butter	60 mL
½ cup	cocoa powder	125 mL
¼ cup	puréed banana	60 mL
2 tbsp.	milk	30 mL
½ tsp.	vanilla	2 mL
3 cups	icing (confectioner's) sugar	750 mL

1. Combine the butter and cocoa. Blend in the banana, milk, vanilla and icing sugar until smooth.
2. Spread the frosting over the cooled cake.

Final Temptations

Caribbean Fruit Cake

(MARIE) I have coveted this recipe for several years, but always got the same answer – "I don't measure anything." So, I created the opportunity to be there while the cake was being made – and we measured everything – though it still helps to know exactly what the batter is supposed to look like! Thanks to Eileen Williams from St Kits for her patience and her recipe!

Step One:*

3 cups	raisins	750 mL
2 cups	currants	500 mL
1 cup	chopped prunes	250 mL
½ cup	mixed peel	125 mL
1½ cups	quartered glacé cherries	375 mL
3 cups	dark rum (approx.)	750 mL
3 cups	sweet red wine (approx.)	750 mL

Step Two:

1 cup	butter OR margarine	250 mL
½ cup	shortening	125 mL
1 cup	brown sugar	250 mL
4	eggs	4
2 tbsp.	vanilla	30 mL
3 cups	flour	750 mL
2 tsp.	baking powder	10 mL
3 tbsp.	browning**	45 mL

Step one – Plan ahead – at least a month!

1. Combine all fruit and place in a large glass jar. Cover with the rum and wine. Actually, Eileen uses more wine than rum, but you can do whatever pleases you. Let soak for at least a month, preferably 5 or 6 months. As the fruit soaks up the liquid, you might want to top it up with rum or wine. To hasten the process, gently simmer the fruit in the liquid to plump it up.

Step Two – When you are ready to bake!

2. Place a pan of water on the lowest rack of an electric oven OR on the floor of a gas oven.
3. Prepare 3, 9" (23 cm) round or square cake pans. Either grease and flour them, or spray them and line bottoms with parchment, brown or waxed paper for easy removal. Pans with removable bottoms work best.

Final Temptations

Caribbean Fruit Cake (continued)

4. In a very large mixing bowl, beat the butter, shortening and brown sugar with an electric mixer until VERY light and fluffy – don't skimp on time.
5. Add the eggs to the butter mixture 1 at a time, beating well after each addition. Add vanilla and beat well.
6. Add the fruit and liquid to the batter and mix by hand. (It should be about 8 cups (2 L) of fruit.)
7. Mix together the flour and baking powder. Gradually fold into the fruit mixture by hand.
8. Add 3 tbsp. (45 mL) browning**, or more if you want a darker color. Browning just adds color, not flavor.
9. Pour the batter into prepared pans. Bake at 350°F (180°C) for 50-55 minutes, or until a toothpick inserted in the center comes out clean. Remove the cakes from the oven onto a cooling rack.
10. While still hot, pour ½ cup (125 mL) wine (or rum) over each cake. Allow the cakes to cool before turning them out of the pans – HIDE at least 1 cake!

Makes 3 cakes.

NOTE: The cakes may be wrapped in foil and frozen in an airtight container for longer storage.

* Dates may also be used as part of the fruit mixture. It just needs to add up to 8 cups (2 L).
** Traditionally, burnt sugar was used for color. Browning is found in a bottle in the Specialty Foods department of your grocery store. It makes your job a lot easier.

Families are like fudge – mostly sweet with a few nuts!

Final Temptations

Tipsy Cake

Many of our best recipes are "discovered" at social events. We rarely miss the opportunity to ask for a copy. Our thanks to Sheila Leigh who passed on this South African favorite.

Date Cake:

½ lb.	dates, chopped	250 g
1 tsp.	baking soda	5 mL
1 cup	boiling water	250 mL
2 tbsp.	butter, melted	30 mL
1	egg, room temperature	1
1½ cups	flour	375 mL
4 tsp.	baking powder	20 mL
⅛ tsp.	salt	0.5 mL

Brandy Syrup:

¾ cup	water	175 mL
1½ cups	sugar	375 mL
1 tsp.	butter	5 mL
½ cup	brandy	125 mL

1. In a small bowl, combine the dates with the baking soda and boiling water. Let stand.
2. In a large bowl, whisk together the butter and egg, it won't be a smooth mixture.
3. In a small bowl, combine the flour, baking powder and salt.
4. Stir the date mixture into the butter mixture, then fold in the flour mixture. Mix just until combined.
5. Pour into a greased or sprayed 8" (20 cm) square pan. Bake at 350°F (180°C) for 30 minutes.
6. **To make the syrup**, combine the water, sugar and butter in a small saucepan. Bring to a boil and simmer for 20-25 minutes.
7. As soon as the cake is out of the oven, add the brandy to the syrup. Poke a few holes in the cake with a skewer, then pour the syrup over the hot cake. (It will seem like a lot of syrup – but it's a thirsty cake!) Allow the cake to cool in the pan. Serve with whipped cream.

Serves 9.

NOTE: This recipe may be doubled for a 9 x 13" (33 x 23 cm) pan.

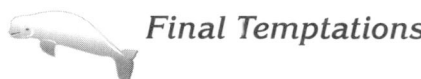

Icebergs & Belugas Index

A
Almond-Crusted Char with Leek, Lemon
  Cream 20
Any Port in a Storm Blue Cheese Spread 94
Appetizers
  Any Port in a Storm Blue Cheese Spread 94
  Artichoke-Heart Dip 95
  Baked Brie with Cranberry Ginger Chutney . 98
  Blue Cheese Soufflé 96
  Hummus 92
  Kahlúa Barbecued Wings 101
  Parmesan Mustard Chicken Wings 102
  Smoked Char or Salmon Torte 94
  Snowball Dip 96
  Soused Salmon or Trout Barbecue 21
  Spinach and Mushroom Melts 67
  Tomato Cheese Tart 99
  Tortillas with Hummus 92
  Tortillas 92
  Tundra Tapenade 93
  Veggie Strudels 100
  Zucchini Cheese Bites 97
Apple Bread Pudding with Rum Sauce 188
Apple Streusel Muffins 44
Apple Walnut Pancakes 48
Apricot Biscotti 72
Apricot Ginger Sauce 14
Artichoke-Heart Dip 95

B
Baked Brie with Cranberry Ginger Chutney 98
Baked Creamed Fish 27
Baked Fish Fillets with Lemon Mustard Sauce . 23
Baked Potato Cakes 133
Baking With Yeast 30
Balsamic Reduction Sauce 24
Balsamic Vinaigrette 112
Banana Oatmeal Cake 89
Béchamel Sauce 130
Béchamel Turnip 130
Best-Ever Cookies 75
Black Bean Soup 63
Blue Cheese Soufflé 96
Blueberry Chiffon Pie 171
Blueberry Topping 170
Blueberry Trifle 173
Bobotie 144
Braised Caribou Meatballs in Red Wine Sauce . 12
Brandy Syrup 206
Bread & Breakfast
  Breads & Muffins
    Apple Streusel Muffins 44
    Baking With Yeast 30
    Butterhorns 36
    Cornmeal Jambuster Muffins 45
    Cornmeal Rolls 37
    Cranberry Citrus Cream Cheese Pull-Apart
      Buns 34
    Cranberry Walnut Muffins 42
    Date Nut Loaf 39
    Jeff's Banana Nut Muffins 42
    Kalamata Olive Bread 33
    Light Rye Bread 31
    Rhubarb Muffins 43
    Russian Black Bread 32
    Sunshine Muffins 41
    Whole-Wheat Soda Bread 38
  Breakfast
    Apple Walnut Pancakes 48
    Breakfast Bites 53
    Cranberry Orange Coffee Cake 46
    Feather-Crisp Waffles 47
    Fruit Sauces 50
    Grunt Cake 49
    Hash Brown Breakfast Casserole 55
    Maple Pumpkin Brunch Cake 40
    Peach Blueberry Compote 50
    Vanilla Waffle Topping 49
    Weekender Special 54
Breaded Eggplant with Cheese 126
Breaded Pork Fillet 146
Breakfast Bites 53
Broccoli Soufflé 125
Broiled Lamb Chops with Lemon Caper
  Sauce 147
Brown Sugar Topping 89, 128
Brownies for a Bunch 84
Buttercream Meringue 193
Butterhorns 36
Buttermilk 84

C
Cappuccino Nanaimo Bars 81
Cappuccino Flats 74
Caramel Sauce 190, 191
Caramel 200
Caribbean Fruit Cake 204
Caribou Salad 14
Cedar Planked Trout with Balsamic Sauce 24
Cheddar Sauce 145
Cheddar Wild Rice Meat Loaf 145
Cheesy Broccoli Salad 114
Cherry Blueberry Sauce 50
Chewy Chocolate Chip Skor-Bit Cookies 76
Chicken in Mushroom Wine Sauce 151
Chicken Lasagne 161
Chilled Cucumber Soup 58
Chocolate Banana Cake 203
Chocolate Banana Filling 181
Chocolate Bread Pudding 189
Chocolate Butter Frosting 84
Chocolate Caramel Nut Upside-Down Cake .. 200
Chocolate Crust 181, 184
Chocolate Dip 73
Chocolate Dream Pudding 177
Chocolate Filling 181, 184, 186
Chocolate Fudge Cake with Sour Cream
  Ganache 198
Chocolate Ganache Sauce 202
Chocolate Soufflé Cups 195
Chocolate Volcano Cake 195

Chocolate Volcanoes with Warm Cinnamon
  Cherry Sauce 196
Cider Dijon Dressing... 109
Cinnamon Cherry Sauce 196
Cinnamon Cookie Layers................................. 186
Cinnamon Topping 43, 172
Cinnamon Torte.. 186
Citrus Salad with Raspberry Wine Vinaigrette. 108
Classic Nanaimo Bars 80
Cloudberry Jelly... 167
Cloudberry Meringue Pie 168
Cocoa Banana Frosting.................................... 203
Cornmeal Rolls 37
Cornmeal Jambuster Muffins 45
Corny Mexicali Vegetable Mix 120
Cranberry Blondies 86
Cranberry Citrus Cream Cheese Pull-Apart
  Buns 34
Cranberry Ginger Chutney 98
Cranberry-Glazed Chicken 154
Cranberry Orange Chicken 155
Cranberry Orange Coffee Cake.........................46
Cranberry Orange Sauce.................................. 155
Cranberry Walnut Muffins 42
Cream Cheese Apple Custard Cake 182
Cream Cheese Filling 182
Cream of Carrot Soup 60
Cream of Spinach Soup 60
Creamy Chocolate Banana Dessert................ 181
Creamy Hollandaise Sauce 161
Creamy Tomato Macaroni and Cheese 65
Crème Fraîche 177
Crisped Brined Roast Turkey 148
Crisped Brined Wild Goose............................... 15
Crumb Topping 46
Crusted Caribou Tenderloin with Mushroom
  and Red Wine Reduction 10
Crusty Baked Potatoes 132
Curried Caribou.. 13
Curried Squash Soup... 61
Custard Topping.. 182

D
Dad's Raisin Spice Cookies............................... 76
Dancing Chickens 152
Dark Chocolate Filling....................................... 82
Date Cake.. 206
Date Nut Loaf 39

Desserts
Cakes
Banana Oatmeal Cake...................................... 89
Caribbean Fruit Cake 204
Chocolate Banana Cake 203
Chocolate Caramel Nut Upside-Down
  Cake 200
Chocolate Fudge Cake with Ganache 198
Chocolate Volcano Cake................................. 196
Cranberry Orange Coffee Cake........................ 46
Date Cake.. 206
Hot Milk Sponge Cake 194
Maple Pumpkin Brunch Cake 40
Tipsy Cake... 206

Cheesecakes
Chocolate Crust... 184
Coconut Crumb Crust 180
Piña Colada Cheesecake................................ 180
Regal Chocolate Cheesecake......................... 184

Cookies
Apricot Biscotti 72
Best-Ever Cookies 75
Cappuccino Flats... 74
Chewy Chocolate Chip Skor-Bit Cookies 76
Cinnamon Cookie Layers................................ 186
Dad's Raisin Spice Cookies.............................. 76
Double Chocolate Nut Cookies 77
Honey Crisps 78
Pecan Bites 75
Pecan Espresso Biscotti 73
Sand Art Cookies.. 76
Scottish Oat Cakes 78

Desserts
Apple Bread Pudding with Rum Sauce......... 188
Blueberry Trifle 173
Chocolate Bread Pudding............................... 189
Chocolate Crust... 181
Chocolate Dream Pudding 177
Chocolate Soufflé Cups 195
Chocolate Volcanoes with Warm Cherry
  Sauce.. 196
Cinnamon Torte... 186
Cream Cheese Apple Custard Cake 182
Creamy Chocolate Banana Dessert............... 181
Crème Fraîche 177
Custard Topping.. 182
Final Act Raspberry Tiramisu 178
Half-Hour Pudding 190
Lynne's Fruit and Cheese Compote............... 166
Mascarpone Substitutes 179
No Ordinary Custard 174
Raisin Pudding 190
Strawberry Shortbread Dessert 172
White Chocolate Brownie Dessert................. 202

Icings, Fillings, Glazes, Sauces & Toppings
Blueberry Topping... 170
Brandy Syrup... 206
Brown Sugar Topping............................. 89, 128
Buttercream Meringue.................................... 193
Caramel Sauce.. 190, 191
Caramel 200
Cherry Blueberry Sauce 50
Chocolate Banana Filling 181
Chocolate Butter Frosting................................. 84
Chocolate Dip.. 73
Chocolate Filling....................... 181, 184, 186
Chocolate Ganache Sauce............................. 202
Chocolate Topping.. 80
Cinnamon Cherry Sauce 196
Cinnamon Topping 43, 172
Cloudberry Jelly... 167
Cocoa Banana Frosting.................................. 203
Coconut Pineapple Filing 180
Cream Cheese Filling 182
Crumb Topping 46
Custard Topping.. 182
Grand Marnier Creamy Caramel Sauce........ 191
Dark Chocolate Filling...................................... 82

 208 Index

Icings, Fillings, Glazes, etc. (continued)
Hard Sauce 192
Lemon Filling 170
Lemon Hard Sauce 192
Lemon Icing 34
Mango Nectarine Sauce 50
Maple Pecan Topping 40
Mascarpone 179
Mrs. Herrett's Chocolate Frosting 194
Raspberry Topping 184
Rum Sauce 188
Sour Cream Ganache 199
Spicy Hard Sauce 192
Streusel Topping 44
Vanilla Sauce 192
Vanilla Waffle Topping 49
White Chocolate Topping 82

Pies
Blueberry Chiffon Pie 171
Cloudberry Meringue Pie 168
Coconut Crumb Crust 180
Fresh Cloudberry Pie 167
Lemon Pie with Blueberry Topping 170
Peach Praline Pie 169
Sour Cream Apple Pie 172

Squares
Brownies for a Bunch 84
Cappuccino Nanaimo Bars 81
Classic Nanaimo Bars 80
Cranberry Blondies 86
Grand Marnier Nanaimo Bars 81
Lemon Walnut Squares 79
Nanaimo Bar Filling Variations 81
Outrageous Brownies 85
Peanut Butter Nanaimo Bars 81
Sweet Marie Bars 83
White Chocolate Brownies 202
White Chocolate Nanaimo Bars 82

Dijon Marinade 132
Dilled Potato Topping 133
Double Chocolate Nut Cookies 77

F
Feather-Crisp Waffles 47
Fennel Roast Pork 146
Final Act Raspberry Tiramisu 178

Fish
Almond-Crusted Char with Leek and
  Lemon 20
Baked Creamed Fish 27
Baked Fish Fillets with Lemon Mustard
  Sauce 23
Cedar Planked Trout 24
Honey-Glazed Salmon 19
Lemon Thyme Fish 24
Pan-Seared Salmon 22
Rainbow Trout & Wild Rice Wine Sauce 25
Soused Salmon OR Trout Barbecue 21
Tarragon-Tomato Pike and Eggplant ... 26

Fresh Cloudberry Pie 167
Fruit Sauces 50

G
Garbanzo and Green Bean Salad 115
Garlic Ginger and Soy Marinade 9
Garlic Roasted Veggies 120
Ginger Caribou Salad 14
Ginger Cranberry Chutney 98
Ginger Garlic Marinade 8
Ginger Peanut Stir-Fry 159
Ginger Pear Braised Cabbage 126
Ginger Soy Marinade 142
Ginger Soy Sherry Flank Steak 142
Grand Marnier Creamy Caramel Sauce 191
Grand Marnier Nanaimo Bars 81
Gravy Making 149
Greek Lemon Soup 59
Green Curry Paste: 143
Grilled Dijon Potatoes 132
Grilled Tomato Vinaigrette 110
Grunt Cake 49

H
Half-Hour Pudding 190
Hard Sauce 192
Hash Brown Breakfast Casserole 55
Honey Crisps 78
Honey Dijon Dressing 110
Honey-Glazed Salmon 19
Hot Milk Sponge Cake 194
Hummus 92

J
Jalapeño Dressing 115
Jeff's Green Curry Beef 143
Jeff's Banana Nut Muffins 42

K
Kahlúa Barbecued Wings 101
Kalamata Olive Bread 33

L
Leek and Lemon Cream Sauce 20
Lemon Greek Chicken 156
Lemon Hard Sauce 192
Lemon Icing 34
Lemon Mustard Sauce 23
Lemon Pie with Blueberry Topping 170
Lemon Thyme Fish 24
Lemon Thyme Marinade 24
Lemon Walnut Squares 79
Len's Coconut Rice 137
Light Rye Bread 31

Lunches
Creamy Tomato Macaroni and Cheese 65
Pizza Dough 66
Spinach and Mushroom Melts 67
Stuffed Pizza 66
Tomato Mushroom Pasta Sauce 64

Lynne's Fruit and Cheese Compote 166

M
Main Dishes
Beef
Bobotie 144
Cheddar Wild Rice Meat Loaf 145
Ginger Soy Sherry Flank Steak 142
Jeff's Green Curry Beef 143
Wild Rice Meat Loaf 145

Index  209

Lamb
Broiled Lamb Chops with Lemon Caper Sauce 147

Pork
Breaded Pork Fillet 146
Fennel Roast Pork 146
New Orleans Jambalaya 150

Poultry
Chicken in Mushroom Wine Sauce 151
Chicken Lasagne 161
Cranberry-Glazed Chicken 154
Cranberry Orange Chicken 155
Crisped Brined Roast Turkey 148
Dancing Chickens 152
Ginger Peanut Stir-Fry 159
Kahlúa Barbecued Wings 101
Lemon Greek Chicken 156
New Orleans Jambalaya 150
Parmesan Mustard Chicken Wings 102
Peachy Picante Chicken 160
Roast Chicken and Potatoes 153

Seafood
New Orleans Jambalaya 150

Mango and Red Pepper Salsa 160
Mango Nectarine Sauce 50
Maple Pecan Topping 40
Maple Pumpkin Brunch Cake 40
Marinated BBQ Moose Roast 8
Marinated Five-Bean* Salad 116
Mascarpone Substitutes 179
Mashed Potatoes with Spinach and Cheese ... 136
Mayonnaise Dressing 115
Minty Beet Salad and Mint Dressing 113
Mozzarella Mashed Potatoes 136
Mrs. Herrett's Chocolate Frosting 194
Mushroom and Red Wine Reduction 10
Mushroom Soup, Simply Delicious 62
Mushrooms and Onion Gratin 121
Mushroom Wine Sauce 16

N
Nanaimo Bar Filling Variations 81
New Orleans Jambalaya 150
No Ordinary Custard 174
Not Just Any Spinach Salad" 109

O
Onion Soup 59
Orange Vegetable and Apple Casserole 128
Oriental Coleslaw and Dressing 114
Outrageous Brownies 85
Oven-Roasted Carrots, Parsnips and Celery ... 129

P
Pan-Seared Salmon with Capers and Peppercorns 22
Parmesan Mustard Chicken Wings 102

Pasta
Chicken Lasagne 161
Creamy Tomato Macaroni and Cheese 65
Tomato Mushroom Pasta Sauce 64

Peach Blueberry Compote 50
Peach Praline Pie 169
Peachy Picante Chicken 160
Peanut Butter Nanaimo Bars 81
Pecan Bites 75
Pecan Espresso Biscotti 73
Piña Colada Cheesecake 180
Pizza Dough 66
Pizza Stuffing 66

Preserves
Cloudberry Jelly 167
Ginger Cranberry Chutney 98

R
Rainbow Trout & Wild Rice Wine Sauce 25
Raisin Pudding 190
Raspberry Topping 184
Raspberry Wine Vinaigrette 108
Red Wine Sauce 12
Regal Chocolate Cheesecake/Raspberry Crown 184
Rhubarb Muffins 43
Roast Chicken and Potatoes 153
Roasted Red Pepper Salad 111
Roasting peppers 159
Rosemary, Pepper and Potato Medley 134
Rum Sauce 188
Russian Black Bread 32
Rye, Garlic and Soy Marinade 21

S

Salads
Cheesy Broccoli Salad 114
Citrus Salad with Raspberry Wine Vinaigrette 108
Garbanzo and Green Bean Salad 115
Grilled Tomato Vinaigrette 110
Marinated Five-Bean* Salad 116
Minty Beet Salad 113
Not Just Any Spinach Salad" 109
Oriental Coleslaw 114
Roasted Red Pepper Salad 111
Spinach, Apple & Pecan Salad 110
Zucchini, Red Onion & Tomato Salad 112

Salad Dressings
Balsamic Vinaigrette 112
Cider Dijon Dressing 109
Honey Dijon Dressing 110
Jalapeño Dressing 115
Mayonnaise Dressing 115
Mint Dressing 113
Oriental Dressing 114
Raspberry Wine Vinaigrette 108
Sun-Dried Tomato Dressing 111

Sand Art Cookies 76

Savory Sauces, Marinades
Apricot Ginger Sauce 14
Balsamic Reduction Sauce 24
Béchamel Sauce 130
Cheddar Sauce 145
Cranberry Ginger Chutney 98
Cranberry Orange Sauce 155
Creamy Hollandaise Sauce 161
Créme Fraîche 177
Dijon Marinade 132
Dilled Potato Topping 133
Garlic Ginger and Soy Marinade 9
Ginger Garlic Marinade 8

Savory Sauces, Marinades *(continued)*
- Ginger Soy Marinade 142
- Gravy 149
- Green Curry Paste 143
- Honey Glaze 19
- Leek and Lemon Cream Sauce 20
- Lemon Mustard Sauce 23
- Lemon Thyme Marinade 24
- Mango and Red Pepper Salsa 160
- Mushroom and Red Wine Reduction 10
- Mushroom Wine Sauce 16
- Red Wine Sauce 12
- Rye, Garlic and Soy Marinade 21
- Seasoned Rub 152
- Sweet and Sour Cranberry Sauce 154
- Wild Rice Wine Sauce 25

Schmock Lake Caribou Liver 9
Scottish Oat Cakes 78
Seasoned Rub 152
Shredded Beets and Red Cabbage with
 Cranberries 127
Simply Delicious Mushroom Soup 62
Smoked Char or Salmon Torte 94
Snowball Dip 96
Tomato Paste 63

Soups
- Black Bean Soup 63
- Chilled Cucumber Soup 58
- Cream of Carrot Soup 60
- Cream of Spinach Soup 60
- Curried Squash Soup 61
- Greek Lemon Soup 59
- Onion Soup 59
- Simply Delicious Mushroom Soup 62

Sour Cream Apple Pie 172
Sour Cream Ganache 199
Sour milk 45
Soused Salmon OR Trout Barbecue 21
Speedy, Creamy Scalloped Potatoes 135
Spiced, Roasted Sweet Potatoes 131
Spicy Hard Sauce 192
Spinach and Mushroom Melts 67
Spinach, Apple & Pecan Salad 110
Strawberry Shortbread Dessert 172
Streusel Topping 44
Stuffed Pizza 66
Sun-Dried Tomato Dressing 111
Sunshine Muffins 41
Sweet and Sour Cranberry Sauce 154
Sweet Marie Bars 83
Sweet Potatoes and Carrots with Honey
 Glaze 131

T
Tarragon-Tomato Pike and Eggplant 26
Tipsy Cake 206
Toasting coconut 181
Toasting pecans 108
Tomato Cheese Tart 99
Tomato Mushroom Pasta Sauce 64
Tomato Paste 63
Tortillas with Hummus 92
Tundra Tapenade 93

V
Vanilla Sauce 192
Vanilla Waffle Topping 49

Vegetables
- Baked Potato Cakes 133
- Béchamel Turnip 130
- Breaded Eggplant with Cheese 126
- Broccoli Soufflé 125
- Corny Mexicali Vegetable Mix 120
- Crusty Baked Potatoes 132
- Dilled Potato Topping 133
- Garlic Roasted Veggies 120
- Ginger Pear Braised Cabbage 126
- Grilled Dijon Potatoes 132
- Len's Coconut Rice 137
- Mashed Potatoes with Spinach and Cheese 136
- Mozzarella Mashed Potatoes 136
- Mushrooms and Onion Gratin 121
- Orange Vegetable and Apple Casserole 128
- Oven-Roasted Carrots, Parsnips and
   Celery 129
- Rosemary, Pepper and Potato Medley 134
- Shredded Beets and Red Cabbage with
   Cranberries 127
- Speedy, Creamy Scalloped Potatoes 135
- Spiced, Roasted Sweet Potatoes 131
- Sweet Potatoes and Carrots with Honey
   Glaze 131
- Vegetarian Chili 122
- Wild Rice Poultry Stuffing 138
- Wild Rice 138

Vegetarian Chili 122
Veggie Strudels 100

W
Weekender Special 54
White Chocolate Brownie Dessert 202
White Chocolate Nanaimo Bars 82
Whole-Wheat Soda Bread 38

Wild Game
- Braised Caribou Meatballs in Red Wine
   Sauce 12
- Caribou Salad 14
- Crisped Brined Wild Goose 15
- Crusted Caribou Tenderloin 10
- Curried Caribou 13
- Ginger Caribou Salad 14
- Marinated BBQ Moose Roast 8
- Schmock Lake Caribou Liver 9
- Wild Rice and Goose Casserole in Sauce 16

Wild Rice 138
Wild Rice and Goose Casserole in Mushroom
 Wine Sauce 16
Wild Rice Meat Loaf 145
Wild Rice Poultry Stuffing 138
Wild Rice Wine Sauce 25

Z
Zucchini Cheese Bites 97
Zucchini, Red Onion & Tomato Salad with
 Balsamic Vinaigrette 112

Comprehensive Index

(Black) – Black Currants & Caribou
(Blue) – Blueberries & Polar Bears
(Cran) – Cranberries & Canada Geese
(Ice) – Icebergs & Belugas

Appetizers

Antipasto	111	(Cran)
Any Port in a Storm Blue Cheese Spread	94	(Ice)
Artichoke-Heart Dip	95	(Ice)
Baked Brie with Cranberry Ginger Chutney	98	(Ice)
Basket of Warm Fry Breads	107	(Black)
Blue Cheese Country Buns	103	(Black)
Blue Cheese Soufflé	96	(Ice)
Brie with Basil and Sun-Dried Tomatoes	104	(Black)
Chicken Strips with Honey Dill Sauce	109	(Blue)
Chili Cheese Log	100	(Blue)
Cold-Smoked Lake Trout Hors d'Oeuvres	27	(Cran)
Crab Cheese Puffs	114	(Cran)
Crab-Stuffed Mushroom Caps	115	(Cran)
Doug's Smoked Fish	26	(Blue)
Duck Liver Pâté	16	(Cran)
Duck Taste Teaser With Bacon & Water Chestnuts	19	(Blue)
Fish Balls	25	(Blue)
Fisherman's Surprise Spread	102	(Blue)
Fry Breads	107	(Black)
Gavin's Caribou Strips	9	(Blue)
Golden Caviar Hors d'Oeuvres	28	(Cran)
Goose Liver Mousse	15	(Cran)
Goose Tidbits	16	(Blue)
Guacamole ¡Estupendo!	150	(Cran)
Honey-Mustard Chicken Bites	115	(Cran)
Hot Jalapeño Cheese Dip	102	(Black)
Hummus	92	(Ice)
Jeanne's Magic Disappearing Chicken Wings	110	(Blue)
Kahlúa Barbecued Wings	101	(Ice)
Kahlúa or Amaretto Fruit Dip	110	(Cran)
Landlocked Lobster	30	(Cran)
Louisiana Hot Wings – Screamin' or Whimperin'	116	(Cran)
Mexican Antipasto	114	(Cran)
Mexican Bean Dip	105	(Blue)
Mushroom Turnovers	111	(Blue)
Nachos Suprême	106	(Blue)
Olive Lover's Cheese Ball	113	(Cran)
Our Own Spinach Dip	101	(Blue)
Parmesan Mustard Chicken Wings	102	(Ice)
Peanut Sauce	108	(Black)
Pizza Roll-Ups	108	(Blue)
Polynesian Mushrooms	106	(Blue)
Quesadillas, #1, #2 & #3	112	(Cran)
Salsa	200	(Cran)
Seviche	29	(Cran)
Shari's Shrimp Spread	111	(Cran)
Shrimp Puffs	107	(Blue)
Smoked Char or Salmon Torte	94	(Ice)
Smoked Trout Pâté	100	(Blue)
Snowball Dip	96	(Ice)
Soused Salmon or Trout Barbecue	21	(Ice)
Spinach and Mushroom Melts	67	(Ice)
Sweet Brie with Pecans	103	(Black)
Tangy Orange Fruit Dip	110	(Cran)
Texas Caviar	102	(Black)
Toast Cups	102	(Blue)
Tomato Cheese Tart	99	(Ice)
Tortillas with Hummus	92	(Ice)
Tundra Tapenade	93	(Ice)
Veggie Strudels	100	(Ice)
Venison Hot Shots	8	(Cran)
Warm Artichoke and Tomato Mousse – Basket of Warm Fry Breads	107	(Black)
Warm Brie with Basil and Sun-Dried Tomatoes	104	(Black)
Warm Brie with Red Peppers	104	(Black)
Wild Meatball Taste Teasers	8	(Blue)
Zucchini Cheese Bites	97	(Ice)

Beverages

Banana Slush	44	(Cran)
Crab Apple Liqueur	46	(Cran)
Eggnog	48	(Cran)
Frozen Fruit Shake	44	(Cran)
Moose Milk	48	(Cran)
Orange Julius	45	(Cran)
Pineapple Fruit/Wine Punch	45	(Cran)
Pink Pastel Punch	46	(Cran)
Tea Essence	46	(Cran)

Bread & Breakfast

Breads & Muffins

Apple Streusel Muffins	44	(Ice)
Bagels	52	(Cran)
Baking Powder Cinnamon Rolls	47	(Blue)
Baking with Yeast	36	(Blue)
Baking with Yeast	40	(Black)
Baking With Yeast	50	(Cran)
Baking With Yeast	30	(Ice)
Bannock	50	(Blue)
Bannock On A Stick	53	(Blue)
Blueberry Bagels	52	(Cran)
Blueberry Muffins	54	(Blue)
Bran Muffin Mix	54	(Blue)
Bran Muffins	58	(Black)
Brown Bread	43	(Blue)
Butterhorns	36	(Ice)
Camping Bannock	53	(Blue)
Cheddar Biscuit Crust	148	(Black)
Cheese Biscuits	49	(Blue)
Cheese-Filled Buns	42	(Black)
Christmas Bread	64	(Cran)
Christmas Danish	62	(Cran)
Cinnamon and Raisin Bagels	53	(Cran)
Cinnamon Balls	43	(Black)
Cinnamon Buns	39	(Blue)
Cornmeal Jambuster Muffins	45	(Ice)
Cornmeal Rolls	37	(Ice)
Cranberry Citrus Cream Cheese Pull-Apart Buns	34	(Ice)
Cranberry Go Round	65	(Cran)
Cranberry Muffins	54	(Blue)
Cranberry Orange Bubble Bread	46	(Black)
Cranberry Orange Muffins	68	(Cran)
Cranberry Sauce Muffins	54	(Blue)
Cranberry Walnut Muffins	42	(Ice)

Breads & Muffins (continued)

Crazy Buns	42	(Black)
Crunchy Brown Buns	60	(Cran)
Crunchy Onion Loaf	48	(Black)
Crusty Rolls	40	(Blue)
Date Nut Loaf	39	(Ice)
Dilly Ham and Cheese Loaf	80	(Black)
English Muffin Loaves	50	(Black)
English Muffins	37	(Blue)
French Bread	44	(Blue)
French Breakfast Muffins	56	(Blue)
Fried Bread	62	(Blue)
Galette	41	(Black)
Garlic Bubble Bread	47	(Black)
Giant Peaches and Cream Muffins	67	(Cran)
Golden Corn Bread	46	(Blue)
Harvest Bread	52	(Black)
Herbed Focaccia	58	(Cran)
Hot Cross Buns	61	(Cran)
Jalapeño Cheese Muffins	67	(Cran)
Jeanne's Croûtons	72	(Blue)
Jeff's Banana Nut Muffins	42	(Ice)
Kalamata Olive Bread	33	(Ice)
Lemon Loaf	99	(Black)
Light Rye Bread	31	(Ice)
Marie's Mom's Yorkshire Pudding	55	(Blue)
Oatmeal Molasses Bread	59	(Cran)
Parmesan Rye Bread	55	(Black)
Pilgrim's Bread	55	(Black)
Pizza Bread & Sticks	56	(Cran)
Pizza Bread with Cheese	57	(Cran)
Pretzels	190	(Black)
Red River Bread	41	(Blue)
Red River Muffins – Moist and Hearty	57	(Black)
Red River Muffins – Sweet and Crunchy	56	(Black)
Rosemary Rye Bread	55	(Black)
Rhubarb Muffins	43	(Ice)
Russian Black Bread	32	(Ice)
Sesame Buns	38	(Blue)
Sheepherder's Bread	49	(Black)
Sour Cream Jam Buns	44	(Black)
Sourdough Biscuits	54	(Cran)
Sourdough Bread/Pancakes	55	(Cran)
Sourdough Starter or Sponge	54	(Cran)
Sunshine Muffins	41	(Ice)
Sweet and Spicy Raisin Bread	43	(Black)
Sweet Biscuits or Scones	43	(Blue)
Sweet Fried Bannock	65	(Black)
Traditional Steamed French Bread	51	(Black)
Traditional Tea Biscuits	48	(Blue)
Trail Bread	46	(Blue)
White Bread	42	(Blue)
White Buns	38	(Blue)
Whole-Wheat Bagels	53	(Cran)
Whole-Wheat Soda Bread	38	(Ice)
Yeast Scones	51	(Cran)

Breakfast

Apple Pancakes	57	(Blue)
Apple Walnut Pancakes	43	(Ice)
Bacon and Eggs Casserole	75	(Cran)
Baked Eggs and Tomato Casserole	74	(Cran)
Banana-Stuffed French Toast	64	(Black)
Black Currant Crêpe Filling	63	(Black)
Blender Waffles	56	(Blue)
Blueberry Sausage Breakfast Cake	61	(Black)
Breakfast Bites	53	(Ice)
Buttermilk Oat Waffles	53	(Black)
Cornmeal Jambuster Muffins	45	(Ice)
Cranberry Crunch Cake	59	(Black)
Cranberry Orange Coffee Cake	46	(Ice)
Cranberry Streusel Coffee Cake	66	(Cran)
Crêpes	62	(Black)
Crunchy Granola	76	(Cran)
Danish Puff Pastry	172	(Black)
Easy Blender Hollandaise Sauce	60	(Blue)
Eggs Benedict	60	(Blue)
Eggs Scramble	66	(Black)
Fabulous French Toast	71	(Cran)
Feather-Crisp Waffles	47	(Ice)
Finnish Oven Pancake	72	(Cran)
French Toast	45	(Blue)
Fruit Sauces	50	(Ice)
Galette	41	(Black)
Grunt Cake	49	(Ice)
Hash Brown Breakfast Casserole	55	(Ice)
Maple Pumpkin Brunch Cake	40	(Ice)
Miniature Oven Omelets	73	(Cran)
Overnight Cheese Strata	59	(Blue)
Peach Blueberry Compote	50	(Ice)
Sour Cream Coffee Cake	60	(Black)
Sour Cream Pancakes	58	(Blue)
Vanilla Waffle Topping	49	(Ice)
Wake-Up Eggs	72	(Cran)
Weekender Special	54	(Ice)
Yeast Pancakes	43	(Black)

Dumplings

Herb Dumplings	15	(Black)
Parsley Dumplings	22	(Black)

Desserts

Cakes

Banana Cake	170	(Cran)
Banana Oatmeal Cake	89	(Ice)
Blintz Torte	164	(Black)
Blueberry Pudding Cake	177	(Black)
Caribbean Fruit Cake	204	(Ice)
Chiffon Cake	168	(Black)
Chocolate Banana Cake	203	(Ice)
Chocolate Cake	170	(Black)
Chocolate Cake	176	(Cran)
Chocolate Cake Roll	167	(Blue)
Chocolate Caramel Nut Upside-Down Cake	200	(Ice)
Chocolate Fudge Cake with Sour Cream Ganache	198	(Ice)
Chocolate Volcano Cake	196	(Ice)
Christmas Fruitcake	200	(Black)
Cinnamon Pecan Apple Cake	177	(Cran)
Cranberry Cake with Butter Sauce	168	(Blue)
Cranberry Crunch Cake	59	(Black)
Cranberry Orange Coffee Cake	46	(Ice)
Cranberry Streusel Coffee Cake	66	(Cran)
Crazy Cake	176	(Cran)
Cream Cheese Apple Custard Cake	182	(Ice)
Date Cake	206	(Ice)
Dutch Cake	98	(Black)
Fourteen Carat Cake	176	(Blue)
Fruit Cocktail Cake	177	(Blue)
Gingerbread Cake & Lemon Sauce	171	(Cran)
Grand Marnier Bundt Cake	169	(Cran)
Helen's Heavenly Cake	169	(Blue)
Hot Milk Sponge Cake	194	(Ice)
Kirschenobertorte	170	(Black)
Lemon Loaf	99	(Black)
Maple Pumpkin Brunch Cake	40	(Ice)
Miami Beach Birthday Cake	172	(Cran)
Oatmeal Chocolate Chip Cake	97	(Black)
Old-Fashioned Apple Cake with Rum Sauce	174	(Black)

Comprehensive Index

Desserts, Cakes (continued)

Orange Alaska Chiffon Cake .... 168 (Black)
Orange Lard Cake .... 108 (Cran)
Peach Kuchen .... 167 (Black)
Peach or Nectarine Roll .... 166 (Blue)
Rhubarb Cake .... 98 (Blue)
Rhubarb Custard Cake .... 107 (Cran)
Sour Cream Coffee Cake .... 60 (Black)
Sour Cream Pound Cake .... 166 (Black)
Strawberry Cream Angel Cake .... 166 (Black)
Tipsy Cake .... 206 (Ice)
Tomato Soup Cake .... 97 (Blue)
Triple Chocolate Cake .... 172 (Blue)
Triple Chocolate Cake (Scratch Model) ... 175 (Blue)
Vinarterta .... 198 (Black)
White Chocolate Cranberry Cake .... 168 (Cran)
White Chocolate-Filled Banana Cake ... 170 (Cran)
Zucchini Chocolate Cake .... 96 (Blue)

Cheesecakes

Amaretto Mousse Cheesecake .... 189 (Cran)
Chocoholic Cheesecake .... 186 (Cran)
Chocolate Black Currant Cheesecake ... 158 (Black)
Cranberry Orange Cheesecake .... 188 (Cran)
Cream Cheese Apple Custard Cake .... 182 (Ice)
Frozen Blueberry Swirl Cheesecake ... 190 (Cran)
Mocha Marble Cheesecake .... 182 (Blue)
Orange Chocolate Swirl Cheesecake ... 187 (Cran)
Piña Colada Cheesecake .... 180 (Ice)
Regal Chocolate Cheesecake .... 184 (Ice)
White Chocolate Cheesecake Wrapped
  in Phyllo .... 162 (Black)

Confections

Almond Crunch .... 193 (Black)
Caramel .... 200 (Ice)
Chocolate Fudge .... 194 (Black)
Chocolate Marble Bark .... 189 (Black)
Christmas Rum Balls .... 195 (Black)
Dried Cranberries .... 202 (Cran)
Hiker's Snack .... 88 (Black)
Jelly Jigglers .... 187 (Black)
Microwave Butterscotch Fudge .... 194 (Black)

Cookies

Almond Ice-Box Cookies .... 92 (Cran)
Apricot Biscotti .... 72 (Ice)
Best-Ever Cookies .... 75 (Ice)
Boiled Raisin Spice Cookies .... 85 (Black)
Cappuccino Flats .... 74 (Ice)
Caramel Aggression Cookies .... 86 (Black)
Caramel Surprise Cookies .... 185 (Black)
Chewy Chocolate Chip Cookies .... 92 (Cran)
Chewy Chocolate Chip Skor-Bit Cookies ... 76 (Ice)
Chinese Noodle Cookies .... 186 (Black)
Chocolate Chip Crispy Cookies .... 82 (Blue)
Chocolate Nut Chip Cookies .... 94 (Cran)
Cinnamon Cookie Layers .... 186 (Ice)
Cookie Pizza .... 183 (Black)
Crispy Coconut Cookies .... 95 (Cran)
Dad's Cookies .... 84 (Blue)
Dad's Raisin Spice Cookies .... 76 (Ice)
Deep-Fried Krispies .... 82 (Black)
Double Chocolate Nut Cookies .... 77 (Ice)
Double Whammy Cookies .... 93 (Cran)
Gingersnaps .... 83 (Blue)
Gourmet Chocolate Cookies .... 81 (Blue)
Hamburger Cookies .... 184 (Black)
Hammer and Chisel Cookies .... 94 (Cran)
Honey Crisps .... 78 (Ice)

Melt-In-Your-Mouth Chocolate Chip
  Cookies .... 80 (Blue)
New Year's Cookies .... 96 (Cran)
Oatmeal and Dried-Fruit Cookies .... 87 (Black)
Oatmeal Jam Sandwich Cookies .... 84 (Black)
Oreo Cookies .... 184 (Black)
Peanut Butter Bran Cookies .... 84 (Black)
Peanut Butter Cookies .... 84 (Blue)
Peanut Butter Cups .... 187 (Black)
Peanut Butter White Chocolate Pecan
  Cookies .... 83 (Black)
Pecan Bites .... 75 (Ice)
Pecan Espresso Biscotti .... 73 (Ice)
Sand Art Cookies .... 76 (Ice)
Scottish Oat Cakes .... 78 (Ice)
Shari's Delicious Nut Cookies .... 86 (Black)
Smartie Nut Crispy Cookies .... 82 (Blue)
Soft Chocolate Cookies .... 80 (Blue)
Sour Cream Cookies .... 186 (Black)
Stained Glass Cookies .... 182 (Black)
Whipped Shortbread .... 196 (Black)
White Chocolate Crisps .... 82 (Black)

Desserts

Apple Bread Pudding with Rum Sauce ... 188 (Ice)
Bavarian Apple Torte .... 188 (Blue)
Blintz Torte .... 164 (Black)
Blueberry Cream Cheese Tart .... 183 (Blue)
Blueberry Pudding Cake .... 177 (Black)
Blueberry Trifle .... 173 (Ice)
Boreal Bread Pudding with Brandy
  Sauce .... 179 (Blue)
Brandied Bananas Flambé .... 153 (Black)
Brandy Snap Fruit Baskets .... 184 (Cran)
Caramel Apple Crisp .... 178 (Cran)
Chocolate Bread Pudding .... 189 (Ice)
Chocolate Dream Pudding .... 177 (Ice)
Chocolate Fondue .... 185 (Cran)
Chocolate Mousse Flan .... 181 (Blue)
Chocolate Soufflé Cups .... 195 (Ice)
Chocolate Volcanoes with Warm
  Cinnamon Cherry Sauce .... 196 (Ice)
Cinnamon Torte .... 186 (Ice)
Cream Puffs or Profiteroles .... 193 (Blue)
Creamy Caramel Flan .... 183 (Cran)
Creamy Chocolate Banana Dessert ... 181 (Ice)
Créme De Cassis .... 175 (Black)
Créme Fraîche .... 177 (Ice)
Danish Puff Pastry .... 172 (Black)
Dessert Crêpes .... 62 (Black)
Drumstick Cake .... 193 (Cran)
Final Act Raspberry Tiramisu .... 178 (Ice)
Fruit Pizza .... 190 (Blue)
Half-Hour Pudding .... 190 (Ice)
Lemon Pudding Cake .... 178 (Blue)
Lynne's Fruit and Cheese Compote ... 166 (Ice)
Mascarpone Substitutes .... 179 (Ice)
Meringue Nests .... 189 (Blue)
No Ordinary Custard .... 174 (Ice)
Nan's Trifle .... 161 (Black)
Oreo Cookie Dessert .... 188 (Black)
Pavlova Nests from "Up Over" .... 189 (Blue)
Peach Cobbler with Spiced Cream ... 180 (Blue)
Peaches in Black Currant Sauce .... 152 (Black)
Pumpkin Pie Squares .... 181 (Cran)
Raisin Pudding .... 190 (Ice)
Raspberry Walnut Torte .... 175 (Cran)
Rhubarb Crunch .... 180 (Cran)
Rhubarb Custard Dessert .... 156 (Black)
Rice Pudding Suprême .... 182 (Cran)

Comprehensive Index

Desserts (continued)

Sticky Date Pudding with Toffee Sauce ... 176 *(Black)*
Strawberries and Peppercorns .... 152 *(Black)*
Strawberry Cream Meringues .... 157 *(Black)*
Strawberry Shortbread Dessert .... 172 *(Ice)*
Strawberry Temptation Puffs .... 193 *(Blue)*
Tia Maria Torte .... 185 *(Cran)*
Victorian Summer and Winter Puddings... 154 *(Black)*
Whipped Rhubarb Fantasy .... 155 *(Black)*
White Chocolate Brownie Dessert .... 202 *(Ice)*
Wild Berry Cobbler .... 179 *(Cran)*

Icings, Fillings, Glazes, Sauces & Toppings

Almond Icing .... 172 *(Black)*
Amaretto Filling .... 190 *(Blue)*
Apricot Glaze .... 190 *(Blue)*
Brandy Sauce .... 179 *(Blue)*
Brandy Syrup .... 206 *(Ice)*
Blueberry Sauce .... 61 *(Black)*
Blueberry Sauce .... 198 *(Blue)*
Blueberry Topping .... 183 *(Blue)*
Blueberry Topping .... 170 *(Ice)*
Brandy Syrup .... 206 *(Ice)*
Brown Sugar Raisin Topping .... 98 *(Black)*
Brown Sugar Topping .... 89, 128 *(Ice)*
Buttercream Meringue .... 193 *(Ice)*
Butter Icing .... 197, 198 *(Black)*
Butter Icing .... 97 *(Blue)*
Butter Sauce .... 168 *(Blue)*
Caramel Sauce .... 104 *(Cran)*
Caramel Sauce .... 190, 191 *(Ice)*
Caramel Topping .... 177 *(Cran)*
Cherry Blueberry Sauce .... 50 *(Ice)*
Chocolate Banana Filling .... 181 *(Ice)*
Chocolate Buttercream Filling .... 170 *(Black)*
Chocolate Butter Frosting .... 84 *(Ice)*
Chocolate Cranberry Icing .... 100 *(Cran)*
Chocolate Dip .... 73 *(Ice)*
Chocolate Filling .... 184, 185 *(Ice)*
Chocolate Frosting, Mrs. Herrett's .... 194 *(Ice)*
Chocolate Ganache Sauce .... 202 *(Ice)*
Chocolate Glaze .... 98 *(Black)*
Chocolate Icing .... 170 *(Blue)*
Chocolate Topping .... 167 *(Blue)*
Chocolate Topping .... 80 *(Ice)*
Cinnamon Cherry Sauce .... 196 *(Ice)*
Cinnamon Topping .... 43, 172 *(Ice)*
Cloudberry Jelly .... 167 *(Ice)*
Cocoa Banana Frosting .... 203 *(Ice)*
Coconut Pineapple Filing .... 180 *(Ice)*
Cranberry Orange Relish .... 199 *(Cran)*
Cranberry Orange Topping .... 183 *(Cran)*
Cream Cheese Filling .... 182 *(Ice)*
Cream Cheese Icing .... 175 *(Blue)*
Cream Filling .... 173 *(Black)*
Creamy Filling .... 184 *(Black)*
Créme De Cassis .... 175 *(Black)*
Créme Fraîche .... 177 *(Ice)*
Crumb Topping .... 46 *(Ice)*
Crumb Topping .... 178 *(Cran)*
Crunchy Buttercream Icing .... 176 *(Cran)*
Custard Sauce .... 150 *(Black)*
Custard Sauce .... 179 *(Black)*
Custard Topping .... 182 *(Ice)*
Dark Chocolate Filling .... 82 *(Ice)*
Fruit Sauces .... 50 *(Ice)*
Gooey Topping .... 177 *(Blue)*
Grand Marnier Creamy Caramel Sauce ... 191 *(Ice)*
Grand Marnier Sauce .... 198 *(Blue)*
Grand Marnier Syrup .... 169 *(Cran)*

Hard Sauce .... 192 *(Ice)*
Heavenly Rum Sauce .... 175 *(Black)*
Hot Butter Rum Sauce .... 174 *(Black)*
Jeanne's Bakery Icing .... 170 *(Blue)*
Jeanne's Quick Icing .... 169 *(Blue)*
Lemon Butter Icing .... 99 *(Cran)*
Lemon Filling .... 189 *(Blue)*
Lemon Filling .... 170 *(Ice)*
Lemon Glaze .... 98 *(Cran)*
Lemon Glaze .... 99 *(Black)*
Lemon Hard Sauce .... 192 *(Ice)*
Lemon Icing .... 34 *(Ice)*
Lemon Sauce .... 171 *(Cran)*
Mango Nectarine Sauce .... 50 *(Ice)*
Maple Pecan Topping .... 40 *(Ice)*
Mascarpone .... 179 *(Ice)*
Meringue .... 156, 168, 180 *(Black)*
Mocha Icing .... 94 *(Blue)*
Mocha Icing .... 95 *(Black)*
Orange Butter .... 71 *(Cran)*
Orange Buttercream Frosting .... 108 *(Cran)*
Orange Cream Filling .... 170 *(Blue)*
Orange Filling .... 168 *(Black)*
Orange Glaze .... 105 *(Cran)*
Pancake Syrup .... 201 *(Cran)*
Peach or Nectarine Filling .... 166 *(Blue)*
Peach Topping .... 167 *(Blue)*
Peanut Butter Icing .... 86 *(Blue)*
Praline Topping .... 176 *(Cran)*
Prune Filling .... 198 *(Black)*
Raspberry Coulis .... 162 *(Black)*
Raspberry Sauce .... 175 *(Cran)*
Raspberry Topping .... 184 *(Ice)*
Rhubarb Custard Filling .... 156 *(Black)*
Rum Sauce .... 188 *(Ice)*
Sour Cream Ganache .... 199 *(Ice)*
Spiced Cream .... 180 *(Blue)*
Spicy Hard Sauce .... 192 *(Ice)*
Strawberry Filling .... 157 *(Black)*
Strawberry Filling .... 193 *(Blue)*
Strawberry Orange Sauce .... 194 *(Blue)*
Streusel Topping .... 44 *(Ice)*
Toffee Sauce .... 176 *(Black)*
Vanilla Almond Custard .... 164 *(Black)*
Vanilla Frosting .... 65 *(Cran)*
Vanilla Icing .... 63 *(Cran)*
Vanilla Sauce .... 192 *(Ice)*
Vanilla Waffle Topping .... 49 *(Ice)*
White Chocolate and Orange Glaze ...... 168 *(Cran)*
White Chocolate Topping .... 82 *(Ice)*

Loaves

Cherry Loaf .... 106 *(Cran)*
Cranberry Orange Loaf .... 105 *(Cran)*
Date Nut Loaf .... 39 *(Ice)*
Lemon Loaf .... 99 *(Black)*
Spicy Pumpkin Loaf .... 106 *(Cran)*

Pies & Tarts

Almond Crust .... 190 *(Blue)*
Apple Krumtorte .... 173 *(Black)*
Apple Pie .... 185 *(Blue)*
Banana Cream Pie .... 178 *(Black)*
Bavarian Apple Torte .... 188 *(Blue)*
Blueberry Chiffon Pie .... 171 *(Ice)*
Blueberry or Saskatoon Pie Filling .... 185 *(Blue)*
Butter Tarts .... 89 *(Black)*
Chocolate Cream Pie .... 179 *(Black)*
Cinnamon Pastry Rolls .... 184 *(Blue)*
Cloudberry Meringue Pie .... 168 *(Ice)*
Coconut Cream Pie .... 178 *(Black)*

Comprehensive Index  **215**

Desserts, Pies & Tarts (continued)

Coconut Crumb Crust	180	(Ice)
Coconut Jam Tarts	90	(Black)
Cranberry Pecan Pie	180	(Cran)
Cream Cheese Pastry	111	(Blue)
Cream Pies	178	(Black)
Flaky Pastry	90	(Black)
Flapper Pie	180	(Black)
Fresh Cloudberry Pie	167	(Ice)
Fresh Strawberry Pie Glacé	155	(Black)
Fruit Turnovers	187	(Blue)
Graham Wafer Crust	180	(Black)
Helen's Pastry	184	(Blue)
Irresistible Pecan Pie	187	(Blue)
Lemon Pie with Blueberry Topping	170	(Ice)
Marie's Pastry	185	(Blue)
Meringue	180	(Black)
Peach Praline Pie	169	(Ice)
Puff Pastry	186	(Blue)
Rhubarb Pie with Custard Sauce	179	(Black)
Sour Cream Apple Pie	172	(Ice)
Sour Cream Raisin Pie	177	(Black)

Squares

Almond Coconut Bars	91	(Black)
Almond Macaroon Brownies	93	(Black)
Barb's Chocolate Toffee Squares	85	(Blue)
Boreal Forest Cranberry Brownies	100	(Cran)
Brownies for a Bunch	84	(Ice)
Butter Tart Squares	88	(Blue)
Cappuccino Nanaimo Bar Filling	81	(Ice)
Cherry Chews	197	(Black)
Chocolate Coffee Swirl Brownies	95	(Black)
Chocolate Cream Cheese Brownies	92	(Blue)
Chocolate Truffle Brownies	96	(Black)
Classic Nanaimo Bars	80	(Ice)
Couldn't-Be-Easier Almond Squares	96	(Cran)
Cranberry Blondies	86	(Ice)
Cranberry Squares	99	(Cran)
Grand Marnier Nanaimo Bar Filling	81	(Ice)
Creamy Lemon Squares	188	(Black)
Crispy Crunch Bars	86	(Blue)
Date Squares	89	(Blue)
Fudge Nut Bars	101	(Cran)
Golden Fruit and Nut Bars	88	(Black)
Hiker's Snack	88	(Black)
Jam Snacks	90	(Blue)
Lemon Love Notes	97	(Cran)
Lemon Raspberry Squares	98	(Cran)
Lemon Walnut Squares	79	(Ice)
Marie's Ski Cake	95	(Blue)
Mocha-Iced Brownies	94	(Blue)
Old-Fashioned Raisin Bars	102	(Cran)
Outrageous Brownies	85	(Ice)
Peanut Butter Nanaimo Bar Filling	81	(Ice)
Pecan Pie Squares	102	(Cran)
Raspberry Nut Meringue Squares	92	(Black)
Saucepan Brownies — No Icing	91	(Blue)
Sour Cream Raisin Bars	87	(Blue)
Sweet Marie Bars	83	(Ice)
Turtle Brownies	93	(Blue)
White Chocolate Chunk Javies	94	(Black)
White Chocolate Brownies	202	(Ice)
White Chocolate Nanaimo Bars	82	(Ice)

Fish

Almond-Crusted Char with Leek and Lemon Cream	20	(Ice)
Arctic Char or Trout Fillets au Gratin	41	(Cran)
Baked Arctic Char Steaks	40	(Cran)
Baked Creamed Fish	27	(Ice)
Baked Fish Fillets with Lemon Mustard Sauce	23	(Ice)
Baked Lake Trout	33	(Blue)
Barbecued Lake Trout with Dill or A Bite	31	(Cran)
Broiled Char with Dijon Cream	40	(Cran)
Cajun Brook Trout	33	(Cran)
Canadian Walleye Medley	26	(Black)
Canned Fish	33	(Black)
Cedar Planked Trout with Balsamic Reduction Sauce	24	(Ice)
Cheddar-Baked Fish Fillets	27	(Blue)
Cold Smoked Lake Trout Hors d'Oeuvres	27	(Cran)
Cold Smoking	25	(Black)
Cold Smoking	27	(Cran)
Corn-Crusted Roast Trout or Salmon	32	(Black)
Creamy Lemon Baked Fish	30	(Black)
Crispy Fish with Lemon Caper Sauce	34	(Cran)
Crispy Fried Fish	28	(Blue)
Curried Fish Kedgeree	27	(Black)
Doug's Smoked Fish	26	(Blue)
Extra-Ordinary Fish Soup	69	(Black)
Fish Balls	25	(Blue)
Fish Balls	68	(Black)
Fish Cakes Suprême	42	(Cran)
Fish Fillets in Fresh Lemon Sauce	29	(Black)
Gail's Maple-Marinated Fish Fillets	29	(Blue)
Golden Caviar Hors d'Oeuvres	28	(Cran)
Herbed Baked Whole Fish	39	(Cran)
Honey-Glazed Salmon	19	(Ice)
Honey Pickerel	30	(Cran)
Landlocked Lobster	30	(Cran)
Lemon Butter Arctic Char	37	(Cran)
Lemon Thyme Fish	24	(Ice)
Maple-Marinated Cold-Smoked Trout	25	(Black)
Marie's Fish Chowder	28	(Blue)
Marinated Cold-Smoked Lake Trout	26	(Cran)
Marinated Lake Trout with Spruce Needles	38	(Cran)
Mike's Beer Batter Fish	30	(Blue)
Mushroom and Dill-Stuffed Lake Trout	32	(Cran)
Pan-Seared Salmon with Capers and Peppercorns	22	(Ice)
Poached Lake Trout with Peppery Egg Sauce	28	(Black)
Rainbow Trout & Wild Rice Wine Sauce	25	(Ice)
Soused Salmon OR Trout Barbecue	21	(Ice)
Seviche	29	(Cran)
Sloppy Joes — Something's Fishy Here!	68	(Blue)
Smoking — A Dissertation by Doug	27	(Blue)
Stuffed Baked Lake Trout	32	(Blue)
Tarragon-Tomato Pike and Eggplant	26	(Ice)
White Clam Linguine	166	(Cran)
Wine and Dill Poached Salmon	31	(Black)
Winnie's Sweet 'N' Sour Fish	31	(Blue)

Jams, Jellies & Juice

Apple Butter	196	(Cran)
Black Currant Jam	199	(Blue)
Chili Sauce	200	(Cran)
Cloudberry Jelly	167	(Ice)
Crab Apple Butter	196	(Cran)
Crab Apple Jelly	202	(Blue)
Crab Apple Juice	202	(Blue)
Cranapple Butter	198	(Cran)
Cranapple Jelly	197	(Cran)
Cranberry Chutney	198	(Cran)
Cranberry Ketchup	199	(Cran)
Cranberry Orange Relish	199	(Cran)
Doug's Peach Honey	201	(Blue)
Elma's Rhubarb Jam	200	(Blue)

Jams, Jellies & Juice (continued)

Ginger Cranberry Chutney	98	(Ice)
Jelly Jigglers	187	(Black)
Lime Marmalade	202	(Cran)
Pancake Syrup	201	(Cran)
Raspberry Jelly	201	(Blue)
Ripe Gooseberry Jam	200	(Blue)
Salsa	200	(Cran)
Sterilizing Jars	196	(Blue)
Vinegars – Flavored	201	(Cran)

Lunches

Caesar Chicken Pasta Salad	77	(Black)
Creamy Tomato Macaroni and Cheese	65	(Ice)
Croque	80	(Cran)
Dilly Ham and Cheese Loaf	80	(Black)
Fried Bread	62	(Blue)
Greek Pizza with Herbed Crust	78	(Cran)
Grilled Pizza	79	(Black)
Hamburger Noodle Bake	66	(Blue)
Hot Chicken Salad with Lemon Dressing	79	(Cran)
Incredible Bread and Cheese Surprise	81	(Cran)
"Jerzy's Special Pizza Topping"	64	(Blue)
Pizza Bread	62	(Blue)
Pizza Buns	62	(Blue)
Pizza Dough	79	(Black)
Pizza Dough	66	(Ice)
Pizza Pizza Pizza	63	(Blue)
Pizza Sauce & Toppings	64	(Blue)
Quesadillas	112	(Cran)
Sausage Combo	67	(Blue)
Savory Poached Chicken	80	(Cran)
Sloppy Joes — Something's Fishy Here!	68	(Blue)
Spinach and Mushroom Melts	67	(Ice)
Stuffed Pizza	66	(Ice)
Sweet and Sour Pasta Salad	78	(Black)
Taco Salad	65	(Cran)
Tomato Basil Sauce	122	(Black)
Tomato Mushroom Pasta Sauce	65	(Ice)

Main Dishes

Beef

Bobotie	144	(Ice)
Beef Burgundy	143	(Blue)
Beef Tostadas	152	(Cran)
Best Oven-Barbecued Meatballs	136	(Black)
Braised Short Ribs	148	(Cran)
Cheddar Cheese Tourtière	153	(Cran)
Cheddar Wild Rice Meat Loaf	145	(Ice)
Cornish Pasties	154	(Cran)
Dymond Lake Spaghetti Sauce	144	(Blue)
Dynamite Lasagne	145	(Blue)
Enchiladas	149	(Cran)
French Steak	142	(Blue)
Ginger Soy Sherry Flank Steak	142	(Ice)
Goulash with Sauerkraut	132	(Black)
Hamburger Noodle Bake	66	(Blue)
Jeff's Green Curry Beef	143	(Ice)
Len's Steak with Seasoned Butter	141	(Blue)
Macho Barbecued Sirloin Steak	145	(Cran)
Marie's Meat Loaf	151	(Cran)
Meatballs	135	(Black)
Mexican Lasagne	153	(Cran)
Miner's Steak	140	(Blue)
Pizza Casserole	135	(Black)
Prime Rib with Mushrooms Au Jus	140	(Blue)
Sombreros	134	(Black)
Steak and Kidney Pie	147	(Cran)
Sweet and Sour Beef	133	(Black)
Wild Rice Meat Loaf	145	(Ice)

Lamb

Broiled Lamb Chops with Lemon Caper Sauce	146	(Ice)
Roast Lamb with Mint Jelly or Sauce	147	(Blue)

Pasta

Chicken Lasagne	161	(Ice)
Creamy Tomato Macaroni and Cheese	65	(Ice)
Dymond Lake Spaghetti Sauce	144	(Blue)
Dynamite Lasagne	145	(Blue)
Dymond Lake Spaghetti Sauce	144	(Blue)
Hamburger Noodle Bake	66	(Blue)
Pasta Carbonara with Chicken and Fresh Vegetables	147	(Black)
Peppers and Pasta Alfredo	137	(Blue)
Very Vegetarian Lasagne	144	(Cran)
White Clam Linguine	166	(Cran)
Tomato Mushroom Pasta Sauce	64	(Ice)

Pork

Barbecued Mandarin Pork Chops	138	(Black)
Breaded Pork Fillet	146	(Ice)
Crispy Breaded Pork Chops	139	(Black)
Fennel Roast Pork	146	(Ice)
Golden Glazed Ham	149	(Blue)
Herbed Lemon Pork Chops	158	(Cran)
Honey Garlic Ribs	159	(Cran)
Hot 'N' Spicy Spareribs	150	(Blue)
Len's Delicious Honey-Ginger Ribs	151	(Blue)
New Orleans Jambalaya	150	(Ice)
Roast Pork with Black Currant Sauce	148	(Blue)
Saucy Lemon Pork Chops	157	(Cran)
Sausage Combo	67	(Blue)
Sombreros	134	(Black)
Sour Cream Pork Chops	154	(Blue)
Spiced Cranberry Pork Roast	137	(Black)
Sweet 'N' Sour Beans and Ribs	152	(Blue)
Sweet and Pungent Pork	158	(Cran)
Traditional Tourtière	140	(Black)

Poultry

Baked Chicken and Spicy Rice	121	(Black)
Chicken Cacciatore	157	(Blue)
Chicken in Mushroom Wine Sauce	151	(Ice)
Chicken Lasagne	161	(Ice)
Chicken Stir-Fry with Ginger Soy Sauce	164	(Cran)
Chicken Vegetable Cobbler	148	(Black)
Coriander Chicken	144	(Black)
Cranberry-Glazed Chicken	154	(Ice)
Cranberry Orange Chicken	155	(Ice)
Crisped Brined Roast Turkey	148	(Ice)
Crispy Oven-Fried Chicken	160	(Blue)
Dancing Chickens	152	(Ice)
Elegant Mushroom Chicken	165	(Cran)
Feta-Stuffed Chicken Breasts	161	(Cran)
Ginger Curry Chicken	146	(Black)
Ginger Peanut Stir-Fry	159	(Ice)
Herb-Roasted Chicken	163	(Cran)
Honey Garlic Cornish Game Hens	153	(Blue)
Jeanne's Magic Disappearing Chicken Wings	110	(Blue)
Kahlúa Barbecued Wings	101	(Ice)
Lemon Greek Chicken	156	(Ice)
Liz's Peach-Glazed Chicken	159	(Blue)
New Orleans Jambalaya	150	(Ice)
Orange Chicken Chow Mein	146	(Black)
Orange-Thyme Roasted Chicken with Honey Glaze	143	(Black)
Parmesan Mustard Chicken Wings	102	(Ice)
Pasta Carbonara with Chicken and Fresh Vegetables	147	(Black)

Comprehensive Index  **217**

Poultry (continued)
Peachy Picante Chicken	160	(Ice)
Roast Chicken and Potatoes	153	(Ice)
Roast Turkey with Stuffing & Gravy	161-163	(Blue)
Saucy Sweet 'N' Sour Chicken Legs	158	(Blue)
Savory Poached Chicken	80	(Cran)
Sombreros	134	(Black)
Sour Cream Chicken	154	(Blue)
Tarragon Mushroom Chicken	162	(Cran)
Tex-Mex Chicken	145	(Black)

Seafood
New Orleans Jambalaya	150	(Ice)

Veal
Len's Veal with Marsala Sauce	146	(Blue)
Veal Parmesan	160	(Cran)

Salads & Salad Dressings
Salads
Broccoli Salad	115	(Blue)
Caesar Chicken Pasta Salad	77	(Black)
Cheesy Broccoli Salad	114	(Ice)
Citrus Salad with Raspberry Wine Vinaigrette	108	(Ice)
Creamy Green Coleslaw with Elaine's Dressing	124	(Blue)
Creamy Spinach Caesar	110	(Black)
Cucumber Sour Cream Salad	119	(Blue)
Egyptian Salad	119	(Cran)
Exotic Spinach Salad	110	(Black)
Festive Cranberry Mold	128	(Cran)
Four-Bean Greek Salad	113	(Black)
Garbanzo and Green Bean Salad	115	(Ice)
Greek Pasta Salad	123	(Cran)
Greek Salad	114	(Blue)
Hot Chicken Salad with Lemon Dressing	79	(Cran)
Len's Caesar Salad	118	(Blue)
Mandarin Orange Salad	120	(Blue)
Mandarin Rice Salad	124	(Cran)
Marinated Five-Bean* Salad	116	(Ice)
Marie's Caesar Salad Par Excellence!!!	117	(Blue)
Minted Green Bean Salad	120	(Cran)
Minty Beet Salad	113	(Ice)
Mushroom Bacon Spinach Salad	116	(Blue)
Neptune Pasta Salad	124	(Cran)
Not Just Any Spinach Salad"	109	(Ice)
Onion Salad	123	(Blue)
Oriental Coleslaw	114	(Ice)
Pepper and Sugar Pea Salad	119	(Blue)
Pineapple Cheese Mold	127	(Cran)
Ribbon Salad	192	(Black)
Roasted Red Pepper Salad	111	(Ice)
Simply Delicious Apple Coleslaw	125	(Cran)
Spinach, Apple & Pecan Salad	110	(Ice)
Stilton Berry Salad	111	(Black)
Strawberries, Greens and Feta with Black Currant Vinaigrette	112	(Black)
Strawberry Salad	120	(Blue)
Sweet and Sour Pasta Salad	78	(Black)
Tabbouleh	114	(Black)
Taco Salad	65	(Blue)
Tender-Crisp Cauliflower and Caper Salad	115	(Black)
Tomato & Cucumber Salad with Feta Cheese	119	(Cran)
Tomatoes Vinaigrette	118	(Cran)
Triple Orange Salad	126	(Cran)
24-Hour Fruit Salad	126	(Cran)
Waldorf Salad	125	(Cran)
Wheat Berry Salad with Dried Cranberries	114	(Black)
White Bean Salad	112	(Black)
Wild Rice and Chicken Salad	113	(Black)
Zucchini, Red Onion & Tomato Salad	112	(Ice)

Salad Dressings & Vinegars
Balsamic Vinaigrette	112	(Ice)
Black Currant Vinaigrette	112	(Black)
Blue Cheese Dressing/Dip – In the Pink	127	(Cran)
Cider Dijon Dressing	109	(Ice)
Creamy Caesar Dressing	77	(Black)
Creamy Cider Dressing	115	(Blue)
Creamy DLS* Dressing	128	(Cran)
Creamy Stilton Dressing	111	(Black)
Elaine's Dressing	124	(Blue)
Greek Dressing	114	(Blue)
Greek Dressing	123	(Cran)
Grilled Tomato Vinaigrette	110	(Ice)
Herb and Garlic Dressing	119	(Blue)
Herb Dressing	113	(Black)
Herbed Mustard Vinaigrette	115	(Black)
Herbed Wine Vinegar Marinade	118	(Cran)
Honey Dijon Dressing	110	(Ice)
Jalapeño Dressing	115	(Ice)
Lemon Dressing	79, 119	(Cran)
Len's Caesar Salad Dressing	118	(Blue)
Marie's Caesar Salad Dressing	117	(Blue)
Mayonnaise Dressing	115	(Ice)
Mint Dressing	113	(Ice)
Mint Dressing/Vinegar	120	(Cran)
Mustard Wine Dressing	116	(Blue)
Old-Fashioned Salad Dressing	124	(Blue)
Oriental Dressing	114	(Ice)
Raspberry or Cranberry Vinaigrette	114	(Black)
Raspberry Wine Vinaigrette	108	(Ice)
Sesame and Poppy Seed Dressing	110	(Black)
Sun-Dried Tomato Dressing	111	(Ice)
Sweet and Sour Dressing	78	(Black)
Sweet Mustard Dressing	120	(Blue)

Savory Sauces, Batters, Marinades & Toppings
Apple Basting Sauce	138	(Black)
Apple Mandarin Marinade	138	(Black)
Apricot Ginger Sauce	14	(Ice)
Balsamic Reduction Sauce	24	(Ice)
Béchamel Sauce	130	(Ice)
Black Currant Sauce	148, 199	(Blue)
Caramel Sauce	145, 190	(Ice)
Cheddar Sauce	66	(Black)
Cheddar Sauce	145	(Ice)
Chunky Barbecue Sauce	136	(Black)
Cranberry Ginger Chutney	98	(Ice)
Cranberry Orange Sauce	155	(Ice)
Cranberry Chutney	198	(Cran)
Cranberry Ketchup	199	(Cran)
Cranberry Sauce	198	(Blue)
Creamy Dill Sauce	14	(Black)
Creamy Hollandaise Sauce	161	(Ice)
Creamy Mustard Sauce	30	(Black)
Creamy Mustard Sauce	42	(Cran)
Crème Fraîche	177	(Ice)
Dijon Marinade	132	(Ice)
Dill Sauce	31	(Black)
Dill Sauce	33	(Cran)
Dilled Potato Topping	133	(Ice)
Easy Blender Hollandaise Sauce	60	(Blue)
Fresh Lemon Sauce	29	(Black)
Fruit Sauce	8, 199	(Blue)
Garlic Butter Dip	47	(Black)

Comprehensive Index

Savory Sauces, Batters, etc. (continued)

Garlic Ginger and Soy Marinade	9	(Ice)
Garlic Mint Marinade	147	(Blue)
Garlicky Wine Marinade	9	(Blue)
Ginger Garlic Marinade	8	(Ice)
Ginger Soy Marinade	142	(Ice)
Ginger Soy Sauce	164	(Cran)
Gravy	149	(Ice)
Green Curry Paste:	143	(Ice)
Guacamole ¡Estupendo!	150	(Cran)
Herb and Spice Infused Oil Mixture	38	(Cran)
Herbed Tomato Sauce	78	(Cran)
Honey Dill Sauce	109, 197	(Blue)
Honey Glaze	19	(Ice)
Honey-Mustard Marinade or Sauce	115	(Cran)
Leek and Lemon Cream Sauce	20	(Ice)
Lemon Mustard Sauce	23	(Ice)
Lemon Thyme Marinade	24	(Ice)
Madeira Game Sauce à la Rebhun	14	(Cran)
Mango and Red Pepper Salsa	160	(Ice)
Mushroom and Red Wine Reduction	10	(Ice)
Mushroom Sauce	137	(Cran)
Mushroom Sauce	16	(Black)
Mushrooms Au Jus	140	(Blue)
Mushroom Wine Sauce	16	(Ice)
Mustard Dill Sauce	34, 197	(Blue)
Peanut Sauce	108	(Black)
Peppery Egg Sauce	28	(Black)
Pesto Sauce	142	(Cran)
Pizza Sauce	64	(Blue)
Pizza Sauce	79	(Black)
Predator Batter	8	(Cran)
Provençale Sauce	34, 197	(Blue)
Red Wine Sauce	12	(Ice)
Rye, Garlic and Soy Marinade	21	(Ice)
Seasoned Butter	141	(Blue)
Seasoned Rub	152	(Ice)
Spiced Cranberry Marinade	137	(Black)
Spicy Pear Sauce	23	(Black)
Sweet and Sour Cranberry Sauce	154	(Ice)
Sweet 'N' Sour Sauce	31	(Blue)
Sweet and Sour Sauce	21	(Black)
Tangy Sauce	110	(Blue)
Tangy Soy Marinade	146	(Cran)
Tomato Basil Sauce	122	(Black)
Turkey Gravy	163	(Blue)
Wild Rice Wine Sauce	25	(Ice)
Vermouth Marinade	23	(Black)

Soups

Albóndigas Soup	68	(Black)
All Vegetable Beet Borscht	82	(Cran)
Black Bean Soup	63	(Ice)
Chilled Cucumber Soup	58	(Ice)
Chunky Corn Chowder	85	(Cran)
Cream of Broccoli Soup	77	(Blue)
Cream of Carrot Soup	60	(Ice)
Cream of Cauliflower Soup	77	(Blue)
Cream of Potato Soup	78	(Blue)
Cream of Spinach Soup	60	(Ice)
Cream of Tomato Soup	70	(Black)
Cream of Wild Rice Soup	71	(Blue)
Creamy Zucchini (Or Squash) Soup	86	(Cran)
Curried Squash Soup	61	(Ice)
Extra-Ordinary Fish Soup	69	(Black)
Fish Stock	69	(Black)
Gazpacho	90	(Cran)
Greek Lemon Soup	59	(Ice)
Hamburger Soup	75	(Blue)
Jeanne's Croûtons	72	(Blue)
Jeanne's Turkey Chowder	84	(Cran)
Leek and Potato Soup	74	(Black)
Marie's Fish Chowder	28	(Blue)
Minestrone	76	(Blue)
Mushroom Soup, Simply Delicious	62	(Ice)
Northwoods Wild Rice Soup	76	(Black)
Onion Soup	59	(Ice)
Orchard Soup	90	(Cran)
Peasant Soup	75	(Black)
Potato Sausage Soup	74	(Black)
Sopa De Cilantro	73	(Black)
Soup Après Ski	84	(Cran)
Tomato Chicken Rice Soup	73	(Blue)
Turkey Carcass Soup	74	(Blue)
Viennese Potato Cream Soup	82	(Cran)
Wild Rice Lemon Soup	89	(Cran)

Vegetable Dishes

Béchamel Turnip	130	(Ice)
Breaded Eggplant with Cheese	126	(Ice)
Cheddar Spinach Squares	118	(Black)
Cheesy Squash Casserole	135	(Cran)
Garlic Roasted Veggies	120	(Ice)
Ginger Pear Braised Cabbage	126	(Ice)
Lazy Perogie Casserole	127	(Black)
Mushrooms and Onion Gratin	121	(Ice)
Mushrooms Au Jus	140	(Blue)
Orange Vegetable and Apple Casserole	128	(Ice)
Pasta Carbonara with Chicken and Fresh Vegetables	147	(Black)
Pepper Side Dish	141	(Cran)
Peppers and Pasta Alfredo	137	(Blue)
Ratatouille	143	(Cran)
Roasted Winter Vegetables	125	(Black)
Shredded Beets and Red Cabbage with Cranberries	127	(Ice)
Vegetables	147	(Black)
Vegetarian Chili	122	(Ice)
Very Vegetarian Lasagne	144	(Cran)

Vegetables

Beans

Aphrodisiac Green Beans	133	(Blue)
Garlicky Fried Rice 'N' Peas or Beans	130	(Cran)
Saucy Green Beans	118	(Black)
Sudden Valley Green Beans	137	(Cran)
Sweet and Sour Baked Beans	136	(Cran)

Broccoli

Broccoli and Onion Au Gratin	139	(Cran)
Broccoli Au Gratin	135	(Blue)
Broccoli or Zucchini Scallop	141	(Cran)
Broccoli Soufflé	125	(Ice)

Carrots

Carrots in Dilled Wine Sauce	126	(Black)
Carrots Provençale	134	(Blue)
Dilled Carrots	134	(Blue)
Glazed Carrots	134	(Blue)
Julienned Carrots with Sun-Dried Tomatoes	126	(Black)
Nifty Carrots	136	(Cran)
Oven-Roasted Carrots, Parsnips and Celery	129	(Ice)

Cauliflower

Cauliflower Au Gratin	135	(Blue)
Cauliflower Tomato Scallop	140	(Cran)
Elegant Parmesan Cauliflower	136	(Blue)

Comprehensive Index

Corn
Corn with Creamed Cheese .... 125 *(Black)*
Corny Mexicali Vegetable Mix .... 120 *(Ice)*
Creamed or Curried Corn .... 138 *(Cran)*

Onions
Baked Garlic and Onion .... 133 *(Cran)*
Baked Onions .... 120 *(Black)*
Onion Pie .... 120 *(Black)*

Potatoes
Baked Potato Cakes .... 133 *(Ice)*
Baked Potato – What a Slice! .... 132 *(Cran)*
Creamy Cheesy Scalloped Potatoes .... 128 *(Black)*
Creamy Oven-Mashed Potatoes .... 131 *(Blue)*
Crispy Round Oven Fries .... 131 *(Cran)*
Crusty Baked Potatoes .... 132 *(Ice)*
Dilled Potato Topping .... 133 *(Ice)*
Garlicky Mashed Potatoes .... 133 *(Cran)*
Grilled Dijon Potatoes .... 132 *(Ice)*
Heavenly Hash Browns .... 130 *(Blue)*
Len's Herbed & Spiced Oven-Roasted
   Potatoes .... 128 *(Blue)*
Mashed Potatoes with Spinach and
   Cheese .... 136 *(Ice)*
Mozzarella Mashed Potatoes .... 136 *(Ice)*
Paprika Potatoes .... 132 *(Cran)*
Parmesan Potatoes .... 129 *(Blue)*
Rosemary, Pepper and Potato Medley .... 134 *(Ice)*
Speedy, Creamy Scalloped Potatoes .... 135 *(Ice)*
Sweet 'N' Sassy Potatoes .... 132 *(Blue)*

Rice
Garlicky Fried Rice 'N' Peas or Beans .... 130 *(Cran)*
Len's Coconut Rice .... 137 *(Ice)*
Oven-Fried Rice .... 127 *(Blue)*
Rice with Dried Cranberries and
   Pine Nuts .... 128 *(Black)*
Saffron Rice .... 131 *(Cran)*
Spicy Rice .... 121 *(Black)*

Sweet Potatoes
Spiced, Roasted Sweet Potatoes .... 131 *(Ice)*
Sweet 'N' Sassy Potatoes .... 132 *(Blue)*
Sweet Potato/Squash .... 134 *(Cran)*
Sweet Potatoes and Carrots with
   Honey Glaze .... 131 *(Ice)*

Tomatoes
Creamy Tomato and Onion Surprise .... 140 *(Cran)*
Julienned Carrots with Sun-Dried
   Tomatoes .... 126 *(Black)*
Tomato Basil Sauce .... 122 *(Black)*

Wild Rice
Marie's Wild Rice Casserole Suprême .... 126 *(Blue)*
Wild Rice, cooking .... 138 *(Ice)*
Wild Rice and Goose Casserole in
   Mushroom Wine Sauce .... 16 *(Ice)*
Wild Rice Pilaf .... 129 *(Black)*
Wild Rice Poultry Stuffing .... 138 *(Ice)*

Zucchini
Pesto Zucchini .... 142 *(Cran)*
Zucchini Casserole .... 132 *(Blue)*
Zucchini-Tomato Spanish Casserole .... 119 *(Black)*

Wild Game

Caribou, Deer & Moose
Aging Wild Game .... 9 *(Cran)*
Barbecued Caribou Steak .... 8 *(Cran)*
Black Currant and Caribou Stew .... 15 *(Black)*
Braised Caribou Meatballs in Red
   Wine Sauce .... 12 *(Ice)*
Caribou Salad .... 14 *(Ice)*
Crusted Caribou Tenderloin with Mushroom
   and Red Wine Reduction .... 10 *(Ice)*
Curried Caribou .... 13 *(Ice)*

Caribou, Deer & Moose (continued)
Deer Sausage .... 12 *(Cran)*
Gavin's Caribou Strips .... 9 *(Blue)*
Ginger Caribou Salad .... 14 *(Ice)*
Hip of Caribou .... 12 *(Black)*
Marinated BBQ Moose Roast .... 8 *(Ice)*
Meatballs with Creamy Dill Sauce .... 14 *(Black)*
Miner's Steak .... 10 *(Blue)*
Moose Meat Loaf .... 19 *(Black)*
Moose or Caribou Wellington .... 12 *(Blue)*
Moose Pot Roast — 2 Ways! .... 11 *(Blue)*
Moose Stroganoff .... 14 *(Cran)*
Mushroom Onion Pot Roast .... 11 *(Blue)*
Onion-Smothered Deer Steak .... 11 *(Cran)*
Rack of Caribou .... 10 *(Cran)*
Red Wine and Garlic Moose Roast .... 13 *(Cran)*
Schmock Lake Caribou Liver .... 9 *(Ice)*
Schnitzel with Mushroom Sauce .... 16 *(Black)*
Spicy Game Chili .... 13 *(Black)*
Sweet 'N' Sour Caribou Steaks .... 11 *(Cran)*
Venison Hot Shots .... 8 *(Cran)*
Wild Meatball Taste Teasers .... 8 *(Blue)*

Duck & Goose
Barbecued Goose with Spicy Pear Sauce ... 23 *(Black)*
Crisped Brined Wild Goose .... 15 *(Ice)*
Drambuie Goose .... 25 *(Cran)*
Duck à l'Orange .... 20 *(Cran)*
Duck Liver Pâté .... 16 *(Cran)*
Duck Taste Teaser With Bacon & Water
   Chestnuts .... 19 *(Blue)*
Dymond Lake Goose Gumbo .... 14 *(Blue)*
Ernie and Derek's Rabbits and
   Ptarmigan – Rocky Style .... 20 *(Black)*
Goose à la Cherry Sauce .... 24 *(Cran)*
Goose Burritos .... 24 *(Black)*
Goose Fajitas .... 21 *(Blue)*
Goose Liver Mousse .... 15 *(Cran)*
Goose Pie .... 23 *(Blue)*
Goose Pot Roast .... 11 *(Blue)*
Goose Stew with Parsley Dumplings .... 22 *(Black)*
Goose Stir-Fry .... 22 *(Cran)*
Goose Tidbits .... 16 *(Blue)*
Jalapeño Goose Breasts Suprême .... 20 *(Blue)*
Mandarin Goose .... 23 *(Cran)*
Mushroom Goose .... 22 *(Blue)*
Mushroom, Wild Rice and Goose Casserole 21 *(Cran)*
Oven-Roasted Goose .... 24 *(Blue)*
Sweet and Sour Duck .... 21 *(Black)*
Wild Duck Casserole .... 19 *(Cran)*
Wild Rice and Goose Casserole in Mushroom
   Wine Sauce .... 16 *(Ice)*

Comprehensive Index

Story Index

Black Currants & Caribou

Boozy Foot 116
A Dangerous Mission? 130
A Duke and Duchess for
  Dinner 169
Ernie Welburn – Chef of
  Churchill River....................... 20
A Fish Tale of Two Sisters......... 33
Helen Loves Surprises............. 108
How Was the Shoot? 8
Left Behind 57
Lost in the Barrens.................. 193
Maguse River Trading Post
  – 1941 to 1947....................... 34
Raising Catitanic – a Northern
  Thriller 100
River Rescue 150

Cranberries & Canada Geese

All Bush Pilots Must be Crazy.. 103
Calm, Cool and Collected 74
CCCofffee PPlleease! (Bear
  vs Helicopter) 6
Double Trouble 138
Icebound 194
I Didn't Know Anyone Was
  In Here.................................. 83
"I'm Not a Bear!"....................... 47
"Maggie Goes to Expo"........... 110
Rock Star in the Bush 97
Snowmobiling Fun? 85
Vanity, Thy Name is Helen 118
Wait for Me – I'm the Pilot! 63

Blueberries & Polar Bears

By Hook or by Crook 34
Cards, Anyone? 19
The Chilly Awakening 196
Dymond Lake Leftovers Soup ... 72
Grin and Bare It 112
A Little "Seasoned" Humor 145
"North Knife Lake, Where
  Are Youuuu?" 138
Old McWebber had a Farm 127
Polar Bear Alert 115
She "Don't" Do Mornings 6
Sheep Hunting, Anyone?......... 147
Trapper Don "Bear Guide
  of the North" 164

Icebergs & Belugas

"Air Born" 68
A Bear in the Woodpile 11
Barrow Bay 117
Beluga Whales 56
Double Trouble 67
Fire at North Knife Lake...........139
Great White Bear......................90
Jacob Hooks A Big One!...........22
My Churchill River Swim/
  Tragically Wet......................162
Show Bear 164
"That's Not Funny, Shari!"........15
This Bears Repeating – Part 1 ..103
This Bears Repeating – Part II 104
  (We've Seen the Light)
Two Fires and a Flood and I
  have only been here a Week!...28

BLUEBERRIES & POLAR BEARS – The FIRST batch of our most requested recipes. Recipes for Moose, Goose and Things that Swim introduce this comprehensive collection of outrageously good recipes for breakfasts, lunches and dinners. Splendid food photos are backed up with northern landscape photos.

CRANBERRIES & CANADA GEESE – The SECOND batch of our most requested recipes. Imaginative wild game and fish recipes, plus a new array of tempting recipes for appetizers to desserts, developed for easy preparation, using good basic ingredients. Superb on-site food and northern landscape photos.

BLACK CURRANTS & CARIBOU – The THIRD batch of our most requested recipes. The glorious scenery and superb hunting and fishing at Webber's Lodges are surpassed only by the array of succulent breakfast, lunch and dinner dishes. The splendid food and landscape photos were shot on site at Dymond Lake Lodge north of Churchill.

ICEBERGS & BELUGAS – The FOURTH batch of our most requested recipes. Pristine northern wilderness and the Belugas and icebergs of Hudson Bay are the setting and inspiration for this extraordinary collection of delicious recipes enjoyed by the fortunate guests at Webber's Lodges. Stunning on-site photos from Seal River on Hudson Bay. **Comprehensive index included.**

The above books are 7" x 10", 208 pages, 18-24 colour photos, lay-flat coil binding.

WILD & WONDERFUL:
        BLUEBERRIES
        CRANBERRIES
        FISH
        GOOSE & GAME
        WILD RICE

The *Wild & Wonderful* books provide the best possible range of Cranberry, Blueberry, Fish, Goose & Game, and Wild Rice recipes in small affordable books designed for easy preparation, using good basic ingredients. Ideal for gift giving or your personal pleasure, *Goose & Game* and *Fish* recipes include appetizers, soups, roasts, stews, sausages and more. *Blueberries* and *Cranberries* recipes include muffins, loaves, cookies, brownies, cheesecakes, pies, jellies, vinegars and making your own dried berries. *Wild Rice* recipes include baking, appetizers, soups, salads, side and main dishes, even desserts.

The above books are 5¼" x 8¼", 48 pages, saddle stitched binding.

Other Books Available

SHARE WITH A FRIEND
$4.00 (TOTAL ORDER) FOR SHIPPING AND HANDLING

Blueberries & Polar Bears _____ x $21.95 = $_____

Cranberries & Canada Geese _____ x $19.95 = $_____

Black Currants & Caribou _____ x $19.95 = $_____

Icebergs & Belugas *(comprehensive index)* _____ x $21.95 = $_____

Wild & Wonderful – Blueberries _____ x $5.95 = $_____

Wild & Wonderful – Cranberries _____ x $5.95 = $_____

Wild & Wonderful – Fish _____ x $5.95 = $_____

Wild & Wonderful – Goose & Game _____ x $5.95 = $_____

Wild & Wonderful – Wild Rice _____ x $5.95 = $_____

Postage and handling (total order) _____ = $_____

Subtotal _____ = $_____

In Canada add 7% GST_____(Subtotal x .07) = $_____

Book Total _____ = $_____

DLS – 4 oz. (113 g), see page 3 _____ x $4.00 = $_____

DLS – 12 oz. (340 g), see page 3 _____ x $9.00 = $_____

Total enclosed _____ = $_____

U.S and international orders payable in U.S. funds./Price is subject to change.

Name:_____

Street: _____

City: _____ Prov./State: _____

Country: _____ Postal Code/ZIP: _____

Please make cheque or money order payable to:

Blueberries & Polar Bears Publishing
Box 6104 Calgary South P.O.   OR   P.O. Box 304
Calgary, Alberta   Churchill, Manitoba
Canada T2H 2L4   Canada R0B 0E0
Fax/Phone: (403) 251-9569/1-800-490-2228
            E-mail: mwoolsey@bbpbcookbooks.com

For volume purchases, contact
Blueberries & Polar Bears Publishing for volume rates.
Please allow 2-3 weeks for delivery.

www.bbpbcookbooks.com

Order form